Mafia
Secrets

Mafia
Secrets

Untold Tales from the
Hollywood Godfather

Gianni Russo

with **Michael Benson**

Foreword by **Steve Schirripa,**
actor, *The Sopranos*

CITADEL PRESS
Kensington Publishing Corp.
kensingtonbooks.com

CITADEL PRESS BOOKS are published by

Kensington Publishing Corp.
900 Third Avenue
New York, NY 10022

All Kensington titles, imprints, and distributed lines are available at special quantity discounts for bulk purchases for sales promotions, premiums, fund-raising, educational, or institutional use. Special book excerpts or customized printings can also be created to fit specific needs. For details, write or phone the office of the Kensington sales manager: Kensington Publishing Corp., 900 Third Avenue, New York, NY 10022, attn Sales Department; phone 1-800-221-2647.

10 9 8 7 6 5 4 3 2 1

First Citadel hardcover printing: December 2025

Printed in the United States of America

ISBN: 978-0-8065-4475-5

ISBN: 978-0-8065-4477-9 (e-book)

Library of Congress Control Number: 2025939611

The authorized representative in the EU for product safety and compliance
is eucomply OU, Parnu mnt 139b-14, Apt 123,
Tallinn, Berlin 11317; hello@eucompliancepartner.com

For Mr. Costello, who saved me

CONTENTS

FOREWORD
by Steve Schirripa

When I met my friend Gianni Russo forty-three years ago, I was working as a bouncer at Paul Anka's club on Harmon Avenue in Las Vegas between Koval Lane and the Strip. The place was called Jubilation, and at 10,000 square feet, it was billed as the largest disco in the world. I'd gotten my bachelor's degree at Brooklyn College and was taking courses at the University of Nevada at Las Vegas (UNLV) at the time.

Gianni loves to dance and had a couple of booths in Jubilation near the staircase that led to the dance floor. He later hired me to watch the door at his place, Gianni Russo's State Street. His club's gimmick, which never ceased to delight the masses, was that it looked like the wrong side of the tracks, a dark and grubby alley on the outside, but once you got past the speakeasy-style entrance, everything was luxurious. Just when you thought you couldn't be dazzled any more, there was Gianni, greeting you with his million-dollar smile.

At a time when everything in Vegas was going big, bigger, biggest, the State Street club was an intimate place, and Gianni was the very visible owner—his charm and sense of humor gave his place a comfortable but sophisticated feel, just how Mr. and Mrs. America liked their Vegas. I'll never forget the night

Frank Sinatra came into Gianni's club with a party of six or eight people and handed out hundred-dollar bills.

Gianni and I had things in common. We were both New Yorkers who'd gone west. And we both had the show-biz bug. Not only was he a movie and TV star, but he'd get up on his own stage now and then and sing a few numbers, totally charming the crowd.

From the start, Gianni was more than just a boss to me. He taught me the ropes. After I left the State Street, I continued to work in Vegas clubs, using the lessons Gianni had taught me every day. I was the entertainment director at the Riviera when I was cast as Bobby Baccalieri for Season Two of *The Sopranos* and things for me changed forever.

These days, Gianni is working for many causes. He loves working for his charity, Yes, You Can, that gives scholarships to kids in need. His other cause is his all-out effort to reclaim Marilyn Monroe's legacy, and to open in Burbank a Marilyn Monroe Museum. I'll let him tell you more about that.

As some of you may know, I have a beloved dachshund named Willie Boy. Sometimes he helps me throw out the first pitch at ball games. Willie Boy is an excellent judge of character, and Gianni Russo is one of his favorite humans. So, that's a very good sign.

Gianni has been a friend of mine for forty-three years. There is no one funnier, more charming, or more entertaining than my pal Gianni. Also, there is no better storyteller. You will love this book, I promise. *Salute,* my friend!

INTRODUCTION
Making Bones

When I was little, five or six, I used to see my father on the street, but he wouldn't acknowledge me. He pretended he had no idea who I was. I was always afraid to talk to my father, but one day I plucked up the courage: "How come you won't talk to me on the street?" I asked, looking almost straight up.

"Because I don't want anyone to know I'm married," he said. "Now beat it."

My mom's name was Inez. She was very beautiful but always seemed tired, weary of life, and when I asked her why my father wouldn't talk to me in public, she just rolled her eyes. She was probably clinically depressed. She'd stare into space, but I had no idea what that meant back then.

I was attending church school, catechism class, and one spring I received a slip from the Police Athletic League (PAL) that said I could go to PAL summer camp for free for the whole summer. I showed it to my mother.

"You better talk to your father," she said.

I hadn't talked to him since he told me he was too busy pretending to be a bachelor to acknowledge me. The only time I heard his voice was when he was giving my mother a beating. Once my dad heard that my mom had received a male visitor while he was away, so he had the guy beat up, and it turned out to be her brother. He was a serial cheater, and when I was little, he had my mom committed as being mentally unfit. She lost two years of her life before she got out of the asylum. In the meantime, my dad moved one of his girlfriends into our apartment.

We lived in a two-bedroom flat on Mulberry Street. I had two older sisters, Theresa and Joanne. My parents had one bedroom, my sisters the other. I lived in the pantry with the kerosene can. My "room" was so small that there was just enough room for me to lie down. And all night I heard *glug glug, glug glug,* the kerosene-burning stove that provided our heat.

My job, again I'm five or six years old, was to take the five-pound kerosene can and fill it up. (Later in life, when I thought I was going crazy, because I wanted to be an assassin and had already taken a couple of people out without feeling bad about it, I used to think that, should I ever get caught, I could use that kerosene stove as my defense. I probably have brain damage from breathing those fumes every night. Before he died, my physician Dr. Blumquist told me that, with me breathing those fumes for years, I "had to be nuts.")

My grandfather, my dad's dad, was Vito Russo. He and his brother John came over on the boat. Since they couldn't get to America from Sicily, they went to Naples, and emigrated from there. Their brother, Angelo Russo, was mafioso, and made sure the Russos had a "living" in America, usually in the form of a no-show job.

His wife, my paternal grandmother, oversaw saving my soul. She and I went to mass every day when I was little, and I remain a good Catholic—which wasn't always easy considering my lifestyle and the fact I knew things about the Vatican that will burn off your ears, secrets I will reveal in this book.

My dad wasn't just pretending to be a bachelor, he was impersonating a Jewish bachelor, a Jewish bachelor *musician.* He was a mediocre saxophone player, and wore a yarmulke to get more jobs, but his real income came from a no-show job he had on the Brooklyn docks. That job was provided by Albert Anastasia and his brother, my future confirmation sponsor, Anthony "Tough Tony" Anastasio, who ran the docks and who were closely associated with my great-uncle.

When I was little, my grandfather, who I liked, lived in the Rosebank section of Staten Island and had a no-show job with the sanitation department. He had a club in Rosebank. My grandmother's patron saint was Our Lady of Mount Carmel, whose feast falls on July 16, and my grandfather hosted a two-week celebration that funded the club. We used to take the ferry to go see him.

My people come from Sicily, which is a tough island with poor soil and a harsh climate. Throughout its history, it's been repeatedly overrun by the conquering armies of other countries. The universally poor natives felt helpless. From that was born the Mafia, a fraternal *secret* society that offered a structure of power and protection outside the usually corrupt Italian government—thus the name "La Cosa Nostra," which means "Our Thing."

Between 1880 and 1914, millions of Italians and Sicilians entered the U.S., legally and illegally. These were poor people who almost always settled in large cities. Jobs were hard to come by and usually involved backbreaking work, like working the docks. Many of those ill-treated immigrants had come to distrust all governments, all authority, U.S., Italy, Timbuktu, whatever. It was Us vs. Them.

Some of the immigrants were mafiosi, sent to America to straighten out things in the New World. Gangs organized themselves along the lines of the Sicilian Mafia. Carlo Gambino was one of those guys. Joseph Bonanno was another. And thus, the gangs in America tended to identify with one city or another in Sicily. Those from Palermo usually didn't get along with those from Castellamare, and vice versa.

Although anyone could be an associate of a mafioso, all sworn members—known as made men, button men, soldiers—had to trace their roots to Sicily, and take the pledge of *omertà*: "Those who call the police are fools or cowards. Those who need police protection are both. If you are attacked, do not give the name of your attacker. Once you recover, you will want to avenge the attack yourself. A wounded man shall say to his assailant, 'If I live, I will kill you. If I die you are forgiven.'"

The Mafia name tag didn't make it across the Atlantic at first. Sicilian hoods were called the Black Hand, which was also the name of their top racket: extortion. In exchange for money, a person's place of business would be "protected" from harm. Those who didn't pay had bad things happen. A fire might break out in the store during the middle of the night. The owner might fall down a flight of stairs and break a leg. You couldn't tell.

The biggest favor the U.S. government ever did for the American Mob was outlaw the production and consumption of alcoholic beverages in 1920 with the passing of the Eighteenth Amendment. The number of Americans who quit drinking because of Prohibition was zero. A multimillion-dollar industry, once taxed by the federal government, was now entirely in the hands of organized crime.

Two of the most successful bootleggers were Meyer Lansky—who I would meet and spend much time with, soaking up his wisdom—and Lansky's childhood friend Benjamin "Bugsy" Siegel, who died young. It was in the papers. Lansky and Siegel were Jewish, but worked side by side with the Sicilian gangsters because Meyer Lansky had another childhood friend named Charles "Lucky" Luciano.

Later, when Lansky and Luciano worked together in the casino biz, they were like an old married couple, finishing each other's sentences, sometimes understanding without speaking at all. It was funny. Other than running the rackets, the two men had nothing in common.

* * *

As teenagers, Lansky and Siegel ran a juvenile delinquent gang, the Meyers and Bugs Gang, and moved seamlessly into the big time with Prohibition, working for the number-one Jewish gangster of that era, Arnold Rothstein.

The pair put together a tremendous bootlegging operation. Unlike other bootleggers who concentrated on establishing turf, Bugs and Meyer went about it a different way. They imported massive quantities of high-quality liquor, much of it from a Canadian distillery run by Samuel Bronfman, who later went legit and merged his company with Seagram & Sons, ultimately becoming Seagram's.

Though younger than their competitors, they became rich and developed a liquor empire that made them the envy of many rumrunners, most of them grown men who would repeatedly underestimate them.

The Bugs and Meyer gang ran their bootlegging operation out of a garage on Cannon Street, which was south of Delancey in a deep tenement-lined portion of the Lower East Side that is long gone today, replaced by behemoth projects. When men came around trying to take away a piece of their turf, their booze, or their money, they fended off the attack with violence, even murder. Working for Mr. Rothstein also involved violence. If a guy couldn't pay his loan, the young'ns would be sent out to collect.

There was more marinating than killing, though, as dead men never paid their bills.

On November 4, 1928—around the time that the word "racketeer" was first coined by a British newspaper meaning a criminal who operates like a corporate CEO—Arnold Rothstein was holding court in Lindy's, his restaurant headquarters in Manhattan.

While there, Rothstein received a phone call. After hanging up, he excused himself and went to the Park Central Hotel in New York. What happened there is unknown. Some said he partook in a poker game that went bad. What we do know is that he was found in a heap beside the hotel's servant entrance, shot in the stomach. He was taken to a hospital and died two days later.

The investigation into Rothstein's death was distracted by politics. Revealed in the hunt was a network of corruption that emanated from Rothstein, through Tammany Hall, right up to the mayor of New York City, Jimmy Walker (Bob Hope would play him in the movie *Beau James*), who wrote the popular 1906 song "Will You Love Me in December as You Do in May?", and was forced to resign from office due to the scandal in 1932.

From a criminal standpoint, Rothstein left nothing in writing that would help uncover a crime. When he died, he took his secrets with him. Not a single prosecution stemmed from Rothstein's death.

With their boss dead, creating a tremendous power vacuum, Lansky, Siegel, and Luciano did their best to fill it and went into business for themselves.

Another pair of bootleggers who simultaneously built an empire was Joseph Kennedy of Boston and Frank Costello of New York, who teamed up to make a fortune. Costello—the man who would become more of a father to me than my real father, and it wasn't close—was born Francesco Castiglia on January 26, 1891, in Calabria. He came over on the boat when he was four with his mom and brother and they joined Dad, who ran a corner store in East Harlem, which was Little Italy back then. He was probably in a gang from the time he could walk, first got in trouble at thirteen, and by the time he was a young man had a string of robbery and assault arrests under his belt. At age twenty-seven, he married a Jewish woman and promptly went to prison for ten months on a bullshit gun charge.

Costello, too, was friends with Lucky Luciano, whose hardcore Mafia friends told him to stay away from Costello because he was Calabrian. Those Sicilian guys, the made guys, were still fighting over turf, but it wasn't the turf under their feet, but some metaphorical turf in their heritage. It was all part of the same craziness that made Italian men for generations shoot one another for reasons that made the rest of the world scratch their heads.

And why I never wanted a button. It's insanity.

But don't feel bad for Mr. Costello. There were plenty of guys, smart guys, who didn't care where he came from. Costello aligned himself with a Hall of Fame of gangsters: Lansky, Siegel, Vito Genovese, Tommy "Three-Finger Brown" Lucchese, the Outfit in Chicago, and all the satellite cities.

After prohibition, the biggest gangsters were forced to re-invent themselves. Many went into gambling—with shylocking and extortion part of the mix. Costello at one time had 25,000 slot machines in illegal parlors. I don't know who counted. There were a lot of them. Many of them were in Louisiana, which is how he developed a close allegiance to the New Orleans boss, Carlos "Little Man" Marcello. He's going to be important to our story, as well.

By the time Luciano put a stop to the Castellammarese War and set up the Five Families system—with himself as godfather of one of the families—Costello was Luciano's consigliere. His top advisor.

One of Costello's prime skills was exerting his influence over the legitimate world, purchasing judges, cops, and politi-cians by the dozens. By 1937, Costello rose to underboss when Genovese fled the country to evade a murder charge. Luciano himself promoted Costello to "acting boss."

While Costello came out of Prohibition, a well-known hood, Joseph P. Kennedy, a master at bullying his way into respecta-bility, emerged with his reputation well scrubbed. His official biography would list the source of his wealth as "stock and commodity investments."

That might've been how he laundered his money, but it wasn't how he made it.

Kennedy was born, perhaps without a soul, in 1888 in East Boston. From the start, it would seem, he courted political power. He met future president Franklin Delano Roosevelt during World War I when he was general manager of a Boston shipyard. At the same time he was raking in cash by making and selling rotgut.

Kennedy made a bundle in Hollywood becoming an early owner of RKO studios. Silent film legend Gloria Swanson was his sideline girlfriend. He also became the owner of what was then the world's largest privately owned building, the Merchandise Mart in Chicago.

FDR became president and named Kennedy the first chairman of the Securities and Exchange Commission, then as the U.S. Ambassador to the United Kingdom. The reputation, already scrubbed clean, now sparkled like Joe Kennedy's teeth.

Befriending FDR was one of two major moves Kennedy made to legitimize his reputation and attach himself to power. The other was to marry Rose Fitzgerald, daughter of John F. "Honey Fitz" Fitzgerald, the beloved Boston mayor and political powerhouse. Joe and Rose's sons were crooks on their dad's side, and savvy political players on their mom's. Three of Joe and Rose's sons would die violently.

This is important to our story because Joseph Kennedy eventually became the father of the president and attorney general, and Frank Costello became a sort of stepfather to me.

Joe cared little for his daughters, but from the moment Rose started popping out boys, he saw them as tools with which to conquer the world. There was a pecking order. Joe, Jr. was first, destined perhaps to be president one day. Then Jack, Bobby, and Teddy.

Naturally Joe's sons went to Ivy League schools, then into public service. World War II put a serious dent in Joe's plans. Joe, Jr. became a Naval bomber pilot and was killed in action in

August 1944, shot down over the English Channel while on his way to execute Operation Anvil, the obliteration of Germany. Joe, Jr. had so many bombs aboard his plane that when it exploded it was estimated to be the largest-ever man-made explosion until the first atom bomb test the following year. Look up "smithereens" in the dictionary and there's a picture of Joe, Jr.

Like a battlefield promotion, Joe's remaining sons all moved up a notch. Jack was now The One. Joe would make any deal, pull any strings, and cash in all favors, to get Jack into the White House. And that was what he did. Promises were made that the Kennedys didn't plan on keeping, and this would be their downfall.

And, of course, Jack did become leader of the free world. For a thousand days.

Joe, in a classic instance of instant karma, didn't get to enjoy the reign of President Kennedy. He was invalided by a stroke soon after Jack's inauguration and sat after that, expressionless, in a wheelchair. His mental state deteriorated, and he was eventually institutionalized. By the time Joe passed in 1969, three of his sons were dead and buried.

During the summer of 1951, when I was seven, I woke up one morning with no feeling on my left side. Men came and carried me down the stairs and into a car. I was taken to Bellevue Hospital, First Avenue and Thirty-First Street in Manhattan. They gave me a few quick tests and, proclaimed contagious, I was immediately quarantined in the ward for polio-stricken children.

For a long time, my left side remained paralyzed. During the five years I spent in that room, five thousand kids died around me. And I lived. I prayed a *novena* to St. Anthony that I should not die, and I never have.

On one side of the quarantine ward was a big window where the other kids' parents would come to visit. They'd wave and press their hands against the glass—and cry a little. My parents never came to see me. I didn't expect to see my dad. But my mom didn't come either. I didn't see them for five years.

Watching the other parents banging on the glass, I felt bitter, and they looked ugly to me, as if they were banging on the glass of a fishbowl. The parents were all in a hallway, and we were pathetic animals in the saddest of all zoos.

My mom probably was under orders not to come. My dad never acknowledged me to begin with, so I'm sure he did his best to forget me once I was a sick kid. He had probably taken steps to ensure that he wasn't going to have to foot the bill for my care. Cripples weren't in his budget.

My floor nurse was an angelic woman and easy on the eyes. Even as a little kid I could tell there was a lot going on in those starched whites. Her name was Dolores Barone, and she, like me, came from Little Italy, which by the middle of the twentieth century had moved downtown from East Harlem and was a neighborhood on Manhattan's Lower East Side.

Without Dolores, I would have died. Just from loneliness. Because they figured all of us polio kids were going to die anyway, no education was offered. No entertainment. No social workers. No anything. All we had to do was listen to each other cry.

When Dolores first came to work in the quarantine ward, she was just a teenager and a volunteer candy striper. By the time I left she was a full-fledged nurse and in charge of the floor.

She became my whole family.

I quickly learned not to make friends. I remember Robert Martuciak. During my first year, he was the kid I knew the best. The feet of our cribs faced each other. And Robert was my friend, then one morning he wasn't there, and some guy was sterilizing his crib.

"Where's Robert?" I asked, a little panicky.

"Went to Heaven," the guy muttered.

After they sanitized Robert's crib, many others came and went, but I kept to myself.

Nights were the worst. Trying to screen out the sounds, the crying, the screaming, and gaspy muffled noises from those on their way to Heaven. It came from all sides.

For years my crib was in the middle of the room, but eventually, with attrition, I was moved to a window that faced west. What a day that was. I was on the seventh floor. That window opened up the world for me.

I could see the Empire State Building. I had never seen a building that big before. All of my experiences were downtown where the tallest buildings were five or six stories. Along with being able to see out the window, I also felt safer by the fresh air. I felt far less likely to be contaminated than I did when I was in the middle.

Other than Dolores, the only person who gave me hope—that one day I'd leave and have a life—was Dr. Blumquist, who explained to me what had happened to my body and how I could work to get better. As I grew, infected with infantile paralysis, my left-side elastic muscles didn't develop. He brought me a bicycle tire with no wheel. I was to loop it around a leg of my crib and use my left side muscles, arm and leg, to stretch the rubber tire. I did get stronger, and I felt less lonely. Here was a man who was interested in making me get better.

I didn't find out until much later that Dolores was also the niece of Carlo Gambino, the future Boss of the family that would bear his name. One day he would be the acknowledged Boss of Bosses.

There was a lot I didn't know, being a kid in a sick room, and one of those things was that my family in Sicily had had a long relationship with the Gambinos, and their cousins the Castellanos.

I would one day learn that my great-uncle Angelo, the mafioso boss in Palermo, Sicily, was also the guy who made Carlo Gambino as a teenager and sent him to America to set up shop and build an army.

In 1948, when the government tried to purge the Mafia from Sicily, my uncle, who was a mass murderer, was convicted of a slew of crimes that took fifteen minutes to read. Then they hanged him in public. His body was left in public view for three days, getting picked at by the buzzards like so much carrion, before someone cut him down.

They did that—hanged him and left him—to send a message, that they were closing in on La Cosa Nostra. That would happen about once every six years, usually during election time.

It was my last few months in Bellevue that changed my life forever and set my course toward a life that included knowledge of the crimes of the century, the Saudi family, the Shah of Iran, shadow governments, movie goddesses, the finest entertainers, the glory days and downfall of Las Vegas, several popes—and, of course, a role in the greatest movie ever made, *The Godfather.*

Dolores usually tried to keep it light, but one day she came to me with a heavy tone. I thought she was going to read me a death sentence, but it turned out to be just a warning. I should beware of a massage therapist named Harold at the hospital. There had been complaints that he was abusing sick kids. She warned me never to allow myself to be alone with him.

I took the warning seriously. For years I used a bedpan, but by this time I could get to the bathroom on my own. It was hard work, and it wasn't pretty, but I'd had it with the bedpan.

During late-night hours, Bellevue was scary and dark. I could get to the john but it took a while. I practically dragged myself along. I was most vulnerable to the pervert when I went to the bathroom, so I took measures to protect myself.

I found a broom in a janitor's closet and broke off the bristles. I snapped it off using a pipe that ran along the wall. I threw the bristles in the garbage and wrapped the broom handle in paper towel.

When I went to the bathroom I brought my weapon with me, just in case. I always used the same stall, stall number four, in the middle. It had the best light. As I sat on the toilet, I held the stick under my arm because one hand still wouldn't grip.

With my good hand I sharpened one end of the broom handle—whittled it to a point. When I wasn't in the bathroom, I stashed the pointy stick behind a radiator. Every time I went to the bathroom, I retrieved the stick from behind the radiator. Nobody ever found it.

Weeks went by. One night, I was just relaxing on the toilet, when I heard the door open. Soft footsteps. I had a visitor. I felt beads of cold sweat pop out along my forehead.

It was *him*, and the only thing between him and me was a canvas curtain for privacy. Then he spoke.

"You need any help?" he asked.

"No!" I said emphatically.

He tried pulling the curtain open. I grabbed the curtain and tried to hold it shut—but he won the tug-of-war. Now he was standing in front of me unbuttoning his pants, and out popped his dick.

"It's a Tootsie Roll, put it in your mouth," he said.

My weapon was right by my right (strong) arm. As he grabbed my head and pulled me toward him, I picked up the stick, and laid the pointy end on my left arm. I turned the point toward him and lunged forward with all my strength. I stuck him underneath his rib cage on his left side and kept pushing until—as I later learned—the stick punctured his heart.

All hell broke loose. He didn't fall dead. He began to run around the bathroom screaming and bleeding. Blood was spattered onto the walls. It was like my whole life had been in black and white, mostly industrial gray, until that moment. The blood splattering the walls was the most red I'd ever seen.

Hearing the commotion, Dolores ran into the bathroom. She threw a blanket over my head so I wouldn't see the blood.

She took me back to my crib. After that, I was moved into the psych ward for "observation."

In other words, there must have been somebody other than Dolores at the hospital who knew a guy got killed and I was the one who did it. But there were no police that I know of, and no press. It was like it didn't happen.

The last thing Bellevue wanted was for New York State to know about the pedophile who worked in the pediatric ward. Nobody told me the guy had died. Only years later did I learn his full name, which was Harold Stanton.

While I was in the psych ward, Dolores went to visit her uncle, Uncle Carlo, at the Ravenite Social Club on Mulberry Street in Little Italy. She told him that there was a kid she liked who'd pretty much grown up in quarantine, no parental interest in him.

She told him, "You're not going to believe what this kid did last night. He killed a pedophile."

When I was released from the psych ward, I wasn't returned to quarantine. They decided, I guess, that after five years I wasn't contagious anymore, and they discharged me.

I will never forget being outside for the first time in five years. I didn't remember the feel of sun on my face, so I felt like I was experiencing it for the first time. The sky. The trees. All those buildings and people. I was twelve and a half years old. What an amazing feeling. No more black and white. Now *everything* was in color.

Dolores told the hospital that my parents were picking me up at curbside, which wasn't true. I don't even know if they knew I was being released. But this gave Dolores the opportunity to leave the hospital with me. She gave me clothes to put on and handed me a small suitcase with a couple changes of clothes. I'd been living in a nightgown for five years.

Dolores put me in a cab.

"Two-forty-seven Mulberry," she said to the cabdriver. I didn't know specifically what that address was but I recognized the

street name and knew I was heading back to my old neighborhood.

During the ride downtown I remember the magical feeling
of being in motion. I don't think I blinked once. I was busy trying to remember everything I saw out the cab's windows. When
I got to 247 Mulberry, Carlo Gambino was standing outside at
the curb, ready to greet me with open arms.

He kissed me on both cheeks and said to me, in English,
"I'm proud of what you did! You killed a bad man."

That stunned me a little. It was the first I'd heard that the
guy died. I didn't know who this old man was, but he looked
nice. The guys with him were clearly tough guys, but Gambino
seemed like a loving uncle or something. I wasn't quick to grasp
what was going on. I'd killed a man, it apparently earned me
my freedom, and now I was being treated as a little hero. I
must've just looked stunned. I was still reeling with the fact
that I was outside and moving from place to place after five
years in a room.

With time, I've realized how important that moment was.
With Mr. Gambino saying those words, it meant I would be accepted. And he said it in front of underboss Aniello "Neil" Dellacroce, who ran Gambino's blue-collar rackets, and Joe "The
Cat" LaForte, who was a great earner, moved well in the legit
business world, and ended up buying the building that the
Ravenite was in. They also kissed me and told me how proud
they were of me. That solidified my acceptance. In a Sicilian
ceremony, I could've been made right then and there. I had
made my bones. Now, there was the matter of my bloodline.

Gambino pinched my cheeks and said, "Russo. You have rel-
atives in Sicily?"

"Yes."

"Do you know of a man named Angelo Russo?"

"My great-uncle."

"He is your grandfather's brother?"

"Yes."

"Do you know what happened to him?"

I shook my head. He patted my cheek and smiled. He looked to be the kindest and nicest man I'd ever met. It would be years before I learned what he was talking about, the noose and the buzzards.

"The apple does not fall far from the tree," Carlo Gambino said. He was letting everyone know: I was a kid with a future in the Life. They knew far more about who I was than I knew about them.

And that was how it began. I'd made my bones and was qualified to be made (which never happened, by the way). Being made would have limited me. I went on to work with every crime family there was, around the world, always at the top levels. But that moment—my mind swimming from the events of the day, cheeks being kissed and pinched outside the Ravenite—was the beginning of a life in which I received a tremendous amount of respect.

I was given a head start by a very rich man, but I worked my money well. I accrued much wealth and power, without ever being greedy or misusing it. And during that time of working with the world's power brokers, I learned many secrets.

Some of the lessons I learned may shock readers. Power works without a conscience. The hundred richest people in America all know one another. Most have U.S. intelligence or organized-crime connections. The only eulogy at Howard Hughes's funeral was delivered by the CIA's top counterintelligence officer, James Angleton. Joe Kennedy had points in the Cal-Neva Lodge, which was owned by Chicago boss Sam Giancana. That fact, perhaps not that shocking in itself, will give you the willies when you learn what went on in the Cal-Neva cabins.

Some of the biggest banks in the world make most of their profits laundering money for cartels of all sorts. For centuries, deep within Italy at the Vatican, from which Roman Catholicism radiates globally, there has been until recently an ongoing operation as crooked as a Tijuana dice game.

The power that comes with being independently wealthy quickly turns psychopathic. Disruptions of the money flow, threats to the power, can result in brutal retaliations. There even came a time when a pope failed to do the right thing and had to die.

At a tender age, I found myself in the middle of all of it.

This book, so aptly entitled *Mafia Secrets*, will reflect upon how I came to know what I know, knowledge that includes many of the twentieth century's most notorious crimes: the murders of Marilyn Monroe, Jack Kennedy, Bobby Kennedy, Jimmy Hoffa, and Pope John Paul I.

CHAPTER 1

Mr. Costello's Good Luck— and Mine

Magnatti's bakery was on Mott Street. I'd gone there with my mom from the days before I got sick, and now that I was out of the hospital, the owner, Funzi Magnatti, was nice enough to give me a job—plus I was allowed to sleep in the basement with the sacks of flour.

I worked at night, prepping the dough by hand, which over time made me very strong. For as long as I could remember my right arm had been bigger than my left. I dreamed of a day when they were the same, and kneading dough helped.

In addition to working at Magnatti's, I had a typical job for handicapped boys back then: I sold pens on the street corner. Ballpoint pens were still relatively new. Before that, fountain pens were the norm. Ballpoints came out after World War II and at first were expensive. Now, for the first time, they were being made of plastic and were relatively cheap. So, I sold ballpoints for a buck apiece on the street, hustling and bustling corner of Fifty-Ninth Street and Fifth Avenue.

And because I had one side of my body that still didn't work that well—my left leg still dragged and my left arm was smaller than my right—some people gave me money and didn't take a pen.

On one spring afternoon, a well-dressed older man—fedora, suit, and tie—came out of the Sherry-Netherland Hotel and walked to my corner. He rubbed my left shoulder and gave me a five-dollar bill. He didn't want a pen.

I didn't know who he was, but I could tell by the way he carried himself he was somebody big. As it turned out he was Frank Costello, the Boss, then sixty-five years old. Most Americans knew his name but not his face, which was the way he liked it. Six years earlier, he'd been called to testify before the Kefauver Committee on organized crime, a proceeding that was televised live to a shocked America. He told them he'd show up only if the cameras didn't show his face, so TV viewers saw only his hands as he repeatedly pleaded the Fifth.

As it happened, only a few hours after Mr. Costello gave me the fin and touched me, there was an attempt on his life. It was eleven p.m. on Thursday night, May 2, 1957. He was coming home from a party at a plush East Side eatery—a joint called Monsignore, at 61 East 55th Street. In the cab with Costello was a good friend named Philip Kennedy, a theatrical agent.

Costello got out of the cab and chatted with Kennedy for a moment before saying his goodbyes. He then turned to enter his apartment building, the Majestic Apartments, at tony 115 Central Park West near Seventy-First Street. He got as far as the foyer, which contained three steps down to the lobby.

He was followed in by a large, heavyset gunman: Vincent "The Chin" Gigante, who would one day be Boss of the Genovese crime family. Chin got just inside the front door and went down two steps into the sunken foyer before aiming at Costello's head and pulling the trigger.

The bullet hit Costello above the left ear and burrowed along his scalp partway around to the back of his head. X-rays showed that the bullet never pierced the skull and managed only to give him a new permanent part in his hair.

Chin waved his .38 around menacingly after firing that single shot, then turned and fled. He jumped into the passenger side of a double-parked getaway car, a black Cadillac sedan driven by an accomplice.

"Never saw it before," Costello said.

Doorman Norvel Keith was grilled at length and recalled that the shooter had been in the lobby of the apartment building earlier in the evening, casing the joint. This was corroborated by the elevator operator, who saw the man earlier but missed the shooting.

The NYPD put sixty detectives on the case, working under the assumption that they were not alone in their hunt, that at least two crime families were interested in getting to the shooter before the police did—one family out for revenge, and another out to punish the gunman for missing his target.

This was a miscalculation. Chin was just fine, although it must've been annoying to read the eyewitness descriptions of him, saying things like "waddled like a duck" and "pot-bellied." Witnesses said the shooter gave off the aura of an ex-con.

The day after the shooting, wearing a fresh shirt and jacket, Mr. Costello again came to my corner. I didn't know he'd been shot, but I couldn't miss the bandage on his head. He gave me a five, rubbed my shrunken shoulder, and gave me a wink.

He was thrilled to be alive, but his problems with the Law didn't improve just because he'd been shot. Only a few days after the shooting, he was called before a grand jury and asked about the suspicious note in his pocket. He refused to answer, was charged with contempt. Talk about punishing the victim!

As this was going on, Costello's lawyer, Edward B. Williams, was having a fit because the note in question had been taken from Costello when he was neither under arrest nor suspected of any crime. He may have given police verbal permission to search but he was in no condition to make such a decision. He'd just taken a .38 to the head. He was suffering from a slight concussion at the very least. Who could think clearly under those circumstances?

After living a blessed life for a gangster, the Life was starting to catch up with Mr. Costello. He'd been convicted of tax evasion and served eleven months of a five-year jail sentence before he was released on bail pending his appeal. He was still being investigated for possible deportation proceedings. He was a guy with a lot on his mind, and a guy who could use all the luck he could get.

But I knew none of that. Standing on my street corner selling ballpoints, all I knew was that this guy kept giving me money and rubbing my shoulder. I'd already killed a guy for trying to sexually abuse me. I wanted to know more about this touchy-feely guy with all the money.

There was a doorman who worked near my corner who'd seen the man in the suit with the bandage on his head. I asked him what the rubbing was all about.

"That's because you're, you know, handicapped. Rubbing your gimpy part. It's good luck."

To hell with that, I thought. I bought a rabbit's foot and put it in my pocket. The next time the guy came by, bandage on his head, gave me the money and went for my shoulder, I pulled myself away.

"Hey, kid, what's up?"

"I ain't your gimp," I said. "Here's a rabbit's foot. Keep your hands off me."

I almost cried when I said it because I was sure he was going to take the money back. They say don't bite the hand that feeds, and that was exactly what I was doing.

"What the fuck?" he said, tilting his head a little to one side. He reached in his pocket, pulled a wad, and peeled off two hundred-dollar bills.

"Give me all those pens. No more pens. From now on, you work for me."

I gave him the pens.

Mr. Costello was longtime married to one woman but childless. From that moment on, he would take care of me, and he didn't stop until he died. I take it back. He is still taking care of me.

"What do I do?" I asked the man with the bandage.

"I give you envelopes and you deliver them to who I say. Sometimes they give you an envelope and you deliver it to me. Never hand me an envelope. My packages are to be delivered to my assistant Carmine, even if I'm in the room."

"Got it," I said.

"I give you money for clothes. You got to look good. You represent me, now. And another thing . . ."

"What?"

"Never be late!"

"Okay."

"You start tomorrow morning. Meet my man Blackie here"—Blackie was standing behind his right shoulder—"at the Waldorf Astoria."

As soon as he was gone, I asked my friend the doorman, "Who was that guy?"

"That's the Ambassador, son, Frank Costello," the doorman said in a reverent voice.

I had a feeling that after a lifetime of bad luck, things had just taken a major turn for the better. Maybe I was his good luck, but he was definitely mine.

Early on, Mr. Costello asked me where I lived. I lied and told him I lived with my parents. I didn't want him to know I was sleeping in a bakery cellar. I was embarrassed. The lesson I learned in the hospital was that I was the kid whose parents didn't care. I was as emotionally hurt as physically hurt by my ordeal. I told Mr. Costello I slept at home and worked at Magnatti's.

I still saw Mr. Gambino now and again, when I was walking on Mulberry Street; sometimes he'd be in a chair out in front of the Ravenite. He'd give me a little wave. I thought of him as Dolores's uncle.

One day, Mr. Costello called Gambino and the men got together to "walk and talk" from the Ravenite to Ferrara's Bakery, on Grand Street. The subject, believe it or not, was me.

Two Bosses talking about a twelve-year-old kid. Gambino filled Costello in on who I was, a longtime patient of his niece, why I walked with a limp, how working at the bakery was excellent for my rehabilitation, and how and why I'd killed a bad man while in quarantine. Then he told him about my great-uncle in Sicily.

"I know him," Costello said. "He sent my mom and dad over."

Gambino said I was a good Catholic boy, intensely loyal, and viciously violent when threatened. It was just the combination Costello was looking for. The waves of good luck just kept coming.

I really was a good Catholic boy. During the evenings, when Mr. Costello went home for the night, I went to St. Patrick's where I continued to pray a *novena* to St. Anthony. My faith was so strong. I believed if I didn't pray to St. Anthony every night, I might fall down a cripple again. It wasn't just fear. St. Anthony gave me strength and the confidence to do the things I needed to do.

When I wasn't praying I would go to Manhattan's Paramount Theater, at Broadway and Forty-Third, in the heart of Times Square, which was open twenty-four/seven. I would watch the same movie again and again. I think I watched *Some Like It Hot* ten times in a row, and it never stopped being funny.

I still had the limp and weak arm. When I went late at night they'd give me free popcorn. I'd sit in the balcony, as far from everyone else as I could get. When it was a Marilyn Monroe picture, the guy at the concession stand gave me extra napkins. It was his way of letting me know he knew I was jerking off in the balcony. Little did I know that that icon, the beautiful blond bombshell, would one day be a very good friend of mine.

At first, because I was young and inexperienced, my courier duties were strictly local, all Manhattan, mostly East Side. I went into places that kids usually don't see, and nobody said anything. Because I was dressed so nicely, people tended to think me older than I was. I was in and out of bars, restaurants, and nightclubs.

One of the places I visited regularly was the Copacabana, which on paper belonged to Jules Podell, but was actually owned by Frank Costello. I never asked what was in the envelopes and packages that I picked up and delivered, but I quickly got the idea. The people I was dealing with were running numbers, taking bets, and loaning money to degenerates who'd fallen into debt.

One famous incident that I witnessed as a kid was the fight at the Copa between members of the New York Yankees and some foul-mouthed out-of-town bowlers who were bad-mouthing and heckling that evening's entertainment, Sammy Davis, Jr.

Yogi Berra famously said of the brawl, "Nobody hit nobody," which was far from true. The Yanks cleaned house and, with a nod from Mr. Costello, they all walked away from the incident unscathed by the law.

From the start I was paid a hundred dollars a day. I was never to use my name. I was to say I was "The Kid," and, if necessary, "Mr. Costello's boy."

"Without a name, you can't be investigated," Mr. Costello said.

I guess I'd been working for Mr. Costello for a few months when he asked me if I was still living with my parents. Again, I lied and said yes.

"You're working nights. I don't want you to go all the way downtown after work," he said.

He pulled out a key on a steel ring. He said he had apartments all over town and that I could use one. Now I had my own place. I went and thanked Mr. Magnatti for everything. He was pleased that I was moving on.

I've been living in Costello apartments ever since. I had my new digs to myself at night, but during the day it was used for Costello business. There was a bank of phones where guys sat and took bets. They were hooked up to "The Wire," so track odds continued to update right up to a nanosecond before the start of the race. After the last race at Yonkers, the phone operators would leave, and I went to bed.

CHAPTER 2
Frank and Marilyn

The story of me and Frank Sinatra starts in the polio ward at Bellevue—no friends, no teachers, no nothing except for listening to the iron lungs all day and night. I guess I'd been there for about four months. I got there in August, and my birthday is December 12. I was getting really depressed. My nurse, Dolores, was my only human contact, and on my birthday she brought me a present.

"It comes from my uncle. I told him about you and he thought you might like it," Dolores said. She didn't say who her uncle was or what he did for a living, but the gift was the best I'd ever receive.

A transistor radio.

Up until that moment, all I could remember hearing were the intercom out in the hall—so and so report to such and such—and the sounds my fellow patients made, which were a nightmare that never ended.

"You turn it on by turning that dial on the side," Dolores said. "You have to keep it low so you don't bother the others."

I turned the radio on with my good thumb. It was a miracle. Music.

That radio became my sole connection to the outside world for years. I remember the first morning I had it. I listened to

the station WNEW. Announcers were talking about Frank Sinatra. He had a new album out, called *Sing and Dance with Frank
Sinatra,* and was rumored to be working on another to be
called *Songs for Young Lovers.* Disc jockeys talked about how
Frank had his own TV show on CBS on Saturday nights that
there were ads for. I wasn't sure what they were talking about.
I'd never seen TV.

That radio was a lifeline, my sole contact with the world outside of quarantine. That was how I learned that Frank Sinatra
and I shared the same birthday. I used to listen to all the singers,
and Sinatra was the best. He sounded like a guy who could be
your friend, hang out late at night, and have fantastic adventures.

OK, skip ahead. A few years later. I'm a teenager and running errands for Frank Costello. Mostly my job was repetitive.
I made predictable rounds. Part of my routine was picking up
and delivering envelopes inside the Plaza Hotel at the southeast corner of Central Park. I'd go in the lobby and up a staircase that led up to a barbershop and beauty salon where I
would pick up and drop off. (Don't try to do it today. They've
sealed off that staircase, but there are still a couple of marble
steps that don't go anywhere, leading into a wall.)

My next stop would be the Wyndham Hotel on Fifty-Eighth
Street. I would go out the Oyster Bar exit and through a passage-
way into the Wyndham. Standing there, menacingly, I thought,
was a policeman, who had his eye on me. I was afraid he was
going to stop and search me and ask me what a kid my age was
doing carrying around so much cash. It worried me. The next
time I saw Mr. Costello, I asked him about the cop.

He said, "That's our cop." He was there to make sure no one
jumped me.

That got me to thinking about how much money I was carrying around. It had to be millions over the course of a day.
You think of all the numbers and all the shylock payments that

needed to be divvied up into tribute. And the guy making book in every bar. Millions.

One day I was given a stack of envelopes and told to deliver them to the Copacabana. At that time there were several people there who got an envelope. They were taking bets out of the club. One envelope was for the Copa's bookmaker, who sat at the bar.

I got to the Copa early that morning, and there was a line outside made up of nothing but teenaged girls, which as a teenaged boy I found pretty interesting. But they didn't care about me. They were hoping to get a glimpse of a skinny big-eared singer inside who was rehearsing and doing a sound check for that night's show.

"Frankie," those girls said. "He's dreamy."

I told the guy at the door, "I'm the Kid," and he let me in.

That earned me a couple of mean-girl glares from the bobby-soxers.

I went downstairs and there was Frank Sinatra. I went up to the stage and watched.

Frank spotted me and looked over to Jules Podell, as if to say "Who's this kid?"

Podell said, "That's Frank Costello's boy."

I felt ten feet tall.

Frank continued rehearsing. I sat down and listened to a couple of tunes. When he took a break, I got up. Frank put a cigarette in his mouth, and I walked up and lit it.

I said, "Mr. Sinatra, I want you to know that you saved my life."

He said, "Oh yeah? How'd I do that?"

I told him about the polio ward at Bellevue and how Mr. Gambino sent me a transistor radio, and how his voice was my lifeline with the outside world, kept me sane until I could wait out my time in hell.

"Mr. Gambino?" he asked.

"Yes."

"As in Carlo Gambino?"

"Yes. Through that radio I learned about you, how you came from humble beginnings, your mother was a bar maid in Hoboken, your dad worked in a shipyard. We have the same birthday! Anyway, you gave me the inspiration to get out of there—and I just wanted to thank you."

"That's amazing," he said. "What's your name?"

I said, "The Kid."

"Who told you that? Who named you that?"

I said, "Mr. Costello."

"Wait a minute, Carlo Gambino gave you a transistor radio and Frank Costello named you the Kid?"

"Yeah."

He said, "Maybe I should get to know you. You sound more important than I am."

And we stayed friends forever. In fact, he baptized my son Luciano.

My job as courier for Mr. Costello went along without difficulty until one early summer day when I was fifteen and I felt a big hand on my shoulder. It was a truancy officer wanting to know why I wasn't in school.

According to the board of education I was a truant. They wanted me to go back and finish the second grade. I was fifteen, a little less than six months shy of turning sixteen—at which time I could legally drop out of school. It was a joke.

Mr. Costello hadn't seen this coming, but he was very smart, did a little research, and figured a way out. I could get around the truancy laws by enrolling in a beauty school. So, I was enrolled in the Wilfred Academy Beauty School on Seventh Avenue between Fifty-Third and Fifty-Fourth Streets.

Everyone knew why I was there. Nobody expected me to learn anything. The first few days I signed in and left, not allowing beauty school to interrupt my errands for Mr. Costello. Then a combination of fate and curiosity intervened.

It was maybe the end of the first week when some guys from the Lilly Dache Beauty Salon came in. Lilly Dache was a salon run by Kenneth Battelle (known in the biz as Mr. Kenneth), hairdresser to the stars. With Kenneth was his partner Marc Sinclaire, who was considered by *Vogue* magazine to be one of the world's top ten hairdressers.

They came to the Wilfred Academy looking for "shampoo boys" and I was selected. I realize now that I was picked because I was good-looking, not because I was particularly adept at shampooing hair—although I was later told I had a nice touch.

I told my teacher I didn't want to do it, and he explained the women were gorgeous and they tipped very well. As it turned out, I did better than tips. The job turned out to be quite an eye-opener.

Lilly Dache was not like salons that we know today, with a mirrored wall and a long line of chairs and sinks where women receive a wash and dress. This salon was for high society. Women wore blouses that cost a thousand dollars. Each client had her own little room, so I could wash her hair in privacy.

After a while, one head was the same as the next, but the view was always great. They'd take off their clothes in front of me. I'd help them on with a robe. I'd received some training. I always let the women feel the temperature of the water on their wrist before their head went in the sink.

I had already soaked one head and was about to lather when I realized I was washing the hair of Marilyn Monroe. She was in New York, living at the Waldorf Astoria—where I later learned Mr. Costello was footing the bill—and taking acting classes at the Actors Studio with Lee Strasberg.

Marilyn enjoyed the accommodations, but somewhere deep inside she must've known that she was indebted to Mr. Costello and one day he was going to ask her to return the favor. When that time came, it blindsided her. But that was all yet to come.

In that private shampooing room, it was Marilyn's voice that gave her away. She asked me my name and I told her. She asked me to give her an extra-long wash because it felt so good. Later, she invited me to come to her suite at the Waldorf, which led to me getting into a bathtub with her. We made love for an entire weekend. That was when I learned, among other things, what room service was.

(Years later, when I first met Marlon Brando, Marilyn long in her grave, I told him the story and he didn't believe me. Then I told him where her secret scar was. Then he believed me.)

When I met Marilyn, I was just a kid, but Marilyn was not. She wasn't a starlet looking for her big break. She was a mega-superstar. A Movie Star, maybe the biggest in the world, and she had been for years.

Considering that she'd gone from nothing to superstardom, a climb that started lower and reached higher than just about any other, she could never kick her built-in inferiority complex. She'd grown up trashy, a bastard child with two possible dads, and a little girl known for her beauty and already chronically used by men. When she was an adult, still brunette, she called herself Norma Jeane Baker, so she'd have the same last name as her mom. She was born Norma Jeane Mortenson and had learned from a painfully tender age that her youth, body, and beauty had tremendous value.

When Norma Jean was born, on June 1, 1926, in L.A. General, her mother, Gladys Baker Mortenson, worked for movie mogul Joseph Schenck (who would one day head both United Artists and Twentieth Century-Fox). When Gladys worked for him, he was making silent pictures with Fatty Arbuckle, Buster Keaton, and the Talmadge sisters, Norma and Constance. Norma, a major movie star of the silent era, was also Joe Schenck's wife. Gladys worked for Joe at Consolidated Film Industries, where women cut and spliced film according to an editor's frame-by-frame instructions. Gladys even cut film on a couple of Norma Talmadge movies. Norma sometimes visited the ladies, the cutters and the splicers, and brought cookies. Gladys considered Norma the world's most beautiful and possibly the nicest film actress. At a party, years later, an elderly Joe met Norma Jeane and she told him she'd been named after his ex-wife. Norma called him Uncle Joe and became a familiar guest at Schenck's mansion, called Owlwood, in the hills.

In his living room hung a larger-than-life oil painting of Norma Talmadge. The supersize portrait overlooked Joe's magnificent poker games, where pots for a single hand reached six figures and sometimes Norma Jean got to be the lucky girl who lit the cigars.

For a while he kept Marilyn in a bungalow out back with a tunnel so she could sneak into his mansion without being seen by those bastard photographers from *Confidential* magazine. Today, we'd call them paparazzi. And Marilyn became a major star working for Joe's Twentieth Century-Fox.

Now she was the biggest movie star on the planet and feeling unfulfilled. She'd given repeatedly great performances, both serious and comedic, yet Hollywood couldn't see past her tits and ass.

She wanted to ease up on her career as a movie star and work on her career as an actress. Toward that end she was learning "the method" at the Actors Studio, which had its headquarters on West Forty-Fourth Street in the Hell's Kitchen section of Manhattan, in a Greek Revival structure that originally housed the Seventh Associate Presbyterian Church.

The studio was founded by film director Elia Kazan (*On the Waterfront, A Streetcar Named Desire, East of Eden*) and others, and by the time Marilyn got there it was being run by Lee Strasberg, who taught "method acting," techniques first taught by Constantin Stanislavsky at the Moscow Art Theatre. Notable graduates of the school include James Dean, Marlon Brando, and Steve McQueen—although there are many.

Marilyn and I had many long talks and discovered we had things in common, for one thing an absent dad. When I was twelve I was in the hospital with polio. When she was twelve her mother put her in an orphanage. I told her about being moved to a bed by a window after years in quarantine and being able to see the Empire State Building, and she told me about her room in the orphanage in Burbank where she could look out the window and see the Warner Brothers water tower.

"I used to read every movie magazine I could get my hands on," she said. "I used to pick them out of the trash." She told me she was worn down by "the Hollywood scene" and she liked me because I was "so New York."

After our first wild weekend together, Marilyn and I became great friends. We had things in common and enjoyed each other's company. She would put on a disguise—a dark wig, big sunglasses, and a babushka—and we could walk together in Central Park and no one recognized her.

We walked across the Brooklyn Bridge, day and night, which had great views of Manhattan, Brooklyn, and New York Harbor. The legendary jazz tenor saxophone player Sonny Rollins busked on that bridge before and after gigs with Miles Davis, Thelonious Monk, and Charlie Parker. The most glorious of views was enhanced by the sweet sounds of that horn. It truly was magical.

We ate at great Italian restaurants, all very romantic for an L.A. girl. I've known rail-thin actresses who gave up show biz. "I'd rather eat than act," was the joke. Marilyn didn't seem concerned with dieting. She loved to eat, and a little flesh on her, of course, looked great.

There was a restaurant on Lexington Avenue between Sixtieth and Sixty-First Streets called Gino's where Marilyn and I would go. You had to be in Who's Who to get in on a Sunday night. Everybody was at Gino's. I could get a table because they knew I was with Mr. Costello—even though Costello always shied away from the limelight and never went there.

Marilyn and I could've easily gotten a table with the A-listers if she'd dropped the disguise. But being incognito was part of the fun. She liked being on the outside and watching.

From Gino's, we'd go to the Subway Bar, which was at the corner of Lexington and Sixtieth, right by the Brooklyn-Manhattan Transit (BMT) entrance. She loved being there and not being recognized. That was part of her dream, and it is common with people who become too famous. She wanted to slip back into anonymity so she could live her life in peace and out of the spotlight.

Of course, that was only part of her dream. She also wanted to stay famous, but as a great actress rather than a blond bombshell that had become a caricature of herself. I have a photograph of her that I took with a Brownie camera, of her in Central Park, with her disguise on, buying hot dogs. There is an innocent joy on her face, to be able to do a simple thing like buy hot dogs in the park without causing the slightest fuss.

By this time her good friend and benefactor Joseph Schenck had suffered a stroke and was no longer in a position to help her career. Things weren't quite so warm and fuzzy around Fox studio head Darryl F. Zanuck. She wanted real acting jobs, and he was busy making money portraying her as a sex symbol.

What Mr. Costello's lawyer discovered was that there was a "fat clause" in her contract, that if she gained weight past a certain point, her contract would be null and void. Coincidentally, Marilyn started putting on weight, and people thought it was because she was trying to get out of her contract—but it wasn't because of eating, it was because she'd become pregnant. The only two people at that time who could have been the father of the baby were Joe DiMaggio and me. She told Joe D.'s sister that it was Joe's baby, and she hoped they would remarry.

By the time I turned sixteen, I was friends with Frank Sinatra and Marilyn Monroe. I didn't associate the two of them in my mind back then, but in a few years they would be together in my memory in the most awful of ways.

Even after I turned sixteen, dropped out of school, and was no longer a shampoo boy, I continued to meet New York's most beautiful women, some already established and some future stars. It was the era when Audrey Hepburn and Grace Kelly were hanging around the lobby of the Barbizon Hotel at Sixty-Second Street and Lexington Avenue in New York. Parents who had fine daughters were sending them to New York to attend finishing school.

One day, Mr. Costello told me to go to the Barbizon and "get flowers for the table," which I was then to deliver to the Copa. So, I went to Carmine at the front door and said, "The old man wants me to pick up flowers for the table. What's he mean?"

Carmine laughed—and then gave me an envelope.

"You take a cab to the Barbizon Hotel and go up to the second floor and give that envelope to the floor monitor."

"Floor monitor?"

"Yes."

I did as I was told, went up there, and there was this guy and a girl behind a desk. I told them I needed to see the floor monitor about flowers for the table.

Turned out, the "flowers" were the young women from finishing school, many of whom had show-biz aspirations. Their job was to go to the Copa and give the place a sexy ambiance. They were not thrilled that they were being escorted to the club by a kid, but they went.

All of the Barbizon girls were eager to be chosen as a table flower because all the gossip columnists were at the Copa: Earl Wilson, Hedda Hopper, Dorothy Kilgallen, Walter Winchell. A mention in a column could lead to a job, which in show business was like a pot of gold at the end of the rainbow.

* * *

Here's a Mafia Secret that might surprise you, because no matter how you look at it, it's damn wholesome. Frank Costello never cheated on his wife. I know the image of the Italian man with the Madonna and the whore, the wife and the *goomada*, but Frank Costello was a one-woman man. He went to church, took a vow, and he took that kind of thing seriously.

Here's another secret: In a world known for its wild nightlife and sleeping till noon, Mr. Costello was home with his wife by ten o'clock every night. It wasn't just Costello, either. A lot of the older guys didn't play that game.

As the old, wise baseball pitcher Satchel Paige once said, "The social ramble ain't restful."

So, I had the respect of two of the godfathers but that didn't mean I was universally loved and accepted. The street guys, guys like John Gotti and Sammy "The Bull" Gravano, still teenagers like me—who were at the time errand boys for Gambino, hijacking trucks at the airport, and delivering envelopes to the Boss on Mulberry Street—hated me. They couldn't figure out who I was or why I was getting so much respect.

Gotti's jealousy got the better of him one Sunday in the Ravenite. There was a rule at the time that you had to have a button to be in the Ravenite on a Sunday. An exception was made for me because I was Frank's boy.

John Gotti, who was still in his late teens and was there to hand off an envelope and leave, was staring at me, trying to intimidate me. Carlo Gambino and Aniello Dellacroce noticed.

"Why you looking at the Kid that way?" Dellacroce asked.

"Who the fuck is he to be in here?" Gotti asked.

And Dellacroce smacked him, right across the face, and kicked him out of the club.

"Don't came back for sixty days, and don't forget to bring me my envelope every Sunday. I don't care how you get it here, but make sure."

I was a smart kid, and I knew there was nothing in it for me to get involved with those Howard Beach guys. They hated me and, what's more, they hated each other.

I didn't want to get too involved but I couldn't entirely avoid the Howard Beach goons either. I loved to dance. I would go around to church dances whenever I could. It was good for my polio.

I even made a buck or two off my skills when I was still a kid. I worked at the Fred Astaire Dance Studio teaching women to dance. The place was on the second floor of a building on Fifty-Seventh Street bear Fifth. I taught fox trot, mambo, and waltz, and got paid ten bucks for a two-hour lesson.

But, apparently, tough guys don't dance, and dancers draw bullies. So, these guys—I think they were from Howard Beach, absolutely Queens someplace—tried to pick a fight one night outside a dance in Corona, Queens.

I told them I was tired. I'd fight them the next night, same spot.

Spending years sleeping with a can of kerosene had taught me how to make a Molotov cocktail. I stole a couple of empty glass milk bottles, the kind the milkman used to leave on the stoop. I filled them with kerosene, stuffed the top with a rag, and then taped the top to keep the rag from coming out.

The street where the fight was to be had apartment buildings on it, with easy access to the roof. I took my milk bottles up there, so I was looking down at the gang that had picked on me at the dance.

I set the bottles on their sides for a moment so that the kerosene soaked the rag, and then I lit the rags and threw the bottles off the roof to the street below. They scattered. Next time I saw them I said, "Sorry I couldn't make the fight. I heard you guys had a fire."

I thought that would be the end of it, but these guys didn't want to give up. They'd been scared by the very kid they were trying to bully. Their only thought was to how could they up the ante. The next time I was at a dance with those guys, they all carried zip guns. (I never carried a gun as a kid. Guns meant nothing but trouble.)

One night I'm at a dance, again in Corona, Queens. I was dressed in a nice suit. Mr. Costello gave me a wardrobe budget and I always looked sharp. I showed up wearing a suit that the bullies couldn't afford.

At the end of the night, as I left the dance, a group of thugs got in my way, pulled zips, and, when I turned to flee, shot me twice: in the upper thigh and my ass. I don't know who they were. I figured Gotti put them up to it.

I managed to duck down into a storm sewer and hung on the ladder by my good arm. I was dripping blood, and hungry rats were collecting at the base of the ladder. First, I hid from the guys who shot me, then I hid from the cops who came after reports of gunshots.

I knew better than to let a cop see me with a bullet hole in me. Frank Costello told me rule number one was don't bring any trouble. I hung there feeding the rats with my blood until I was sure everyone had gone and climbed back up. I knew a "pharmacist" who took the bullets out.

After that, Mr. Costello decided to send me out of town. I would continue doing what I was doing, although sometimes I'd pick up packages in Las Vegas and deliver them to Chicago. Sometimes I'd go to New Orleans and pick up something that I was to immediately deliver to him. I was under strict orders not to deal with any street-level guys. Underbosses and bosses only.

Along with making sure no one knew my name, Mr. Costello also said that I should not be photographed: "If you see a photographer, turn your head away. I don't want anyone to know what you look like. Anyone asks you your name, what do you say?"

"I'm the Kid."

"No, really, what's your name? What do you say then?"

"I'm Frank Costello's boy."

"That's good. Yes."

I figured he was worried about kidnapping or something. I now know that the idea was to use me and, when necessary, hide me, lay low till the heat was off, so that my part in a complicated scenario could never be proved. In case his plan didn't work, I had prearranged legal help as well. (Of course, when Mr. Costello hid me, he hid me in complete luxury. I did not complain.)

And so, I went on a tour of America—and Cuba. One at a time I met every Mob boss.

CHAPTER 3
Tour of Bosses

In Las Vegas, I met a colorful character nicknamed "Mr. Entertainment," Jack Entratter. He ran the Sands Hotel and was responsible for booking the Rat Pack in that casino's Big Room. He was about forty years old when I met him and had been in the casino entertainment biz since he was very young.

Entratter started in casinos as a teenager, working as a reservation clerk for the French Casino in Miami. In 1940, when he was twenty-six, he came north and worked as a bouncer at New York's Stork Club, where he stayed and accrued power for twelve years until he had a controlling interest in the joint.

He booked the talent at the Copacabana, met the top showbiz names, and became a close friend of Frank Sinatra and his pals. At thirty-six, Entratter went to Vegas and became the general manager of the Sands, which at that time was considered not just one of the best hotels in Vegas, but in the world.

For Frank and the Rat Pack, Entratter built a nightclub into the Sands called the Copa Room. It was a classic Vegas room: late-night shows, top-name singers and dancers, comics working blue.

Gamblers were frequently bought drinks gratis. The food in the restaurants was top notch. And Entratter inspected it all to make sure it was up to snuff. He, himself, didn't drink or smoke—or sleep, it sometimes seemed.

Though he was active in Jewish causes—being one of the founders of the Jewish Federation of Las Vegas and president of Temple Beth Sholom from 1959 to 1963—Entratter had several associates who were suspected of gangland activity. Construction of the Sands, for example, had been financed with the help of the great Meyer Lansky and another Jewish gangster named Hyman Abrams.

The Sands was the first of the modern hotel/casino complexes to be built on what would become the Vegas Strip. The hotel was known for its sign out front, fifty-six feet high and asymmetrically cantilevered. The sign said Sands in an upward-slanting script, huge *S* in front, and in smaller letters below, "A PLACE IN THE SUN."

The sign was already well known when it became iconic in 1960 during filming of the freewheeling heist picture *Ocean's 11*. The stars of that picture—Frank Sinatra, Dean Martin, Sammy Davis, Jr., Peter Lawford, and Joey Bishop, that is, the Rat Pack—posed in front of the sign. The image became the most famous photo of the Sands, the most famous photo of the Rat Pack, and the most famous photo of Las Vegas.

At the Sands' 1952 opening, twelve thousand people showed up and each was given a Chamois bag with silver dollars in it. The opening day promotion cost the Sands $200,000, but it was well worth it, as the vig made up the difference in a matter of hours. In those days, silver dollars were used in the slot machines, then known as one-armed bandits.

At first, the hotel part of the complex was relatively small—but it grew.

My first out-of-town job for Mr. Costello was flying to Las Vegas to pick up a bag at the Sands Hotel. Mr. Costello told me, while I was there, I should keep my eyes and ears open for "loose talk."

"You always pick up on a Monday," Mr. Costello explained. "That's because you're picking up the skim. You take the package to Chicago, see a guy, they take some, give you back the rest, and you bring that here to New York and give it to Blackie."

I was old enough that Mr. Costello told me what was going to be in the package.

"It could be as much as a million dollars," he said. "If someone tries to rob you, give them the money—it's only money, there's more where that came from—but try to get the motherfucker's name."

And so, I bought a plane ticket to Vegas. Zero airport security back then. If somebody asked me my name, I said, "John Smith."

At the Sands, I was told to report to pit boss Milton Frank. You've seen the Scorsese picture *Casino*. Frank was played by Don Rickles. I was walking into the real-life version, completely dazzled by the bells and whistles. The rooms at the Sands Hotel were named after thoroughbred racetracks. The Outfit guys stayed in the rooms named after Illinois tracks.

Jack Entratter spent six million dollars of the Sands's budget on a private house on the property for high rollers to use as a party house. And that was what it became. The house had a pool that was surrounded by an eight-foot fence. With that privacy, the pool became the orgy site for the stars.

That pool was a happening place where hoods, stars, and showgirls mingled. The Rat Pack hung out. I saw some fantastic things. That was where I saw U.S. senator and future presidential candidate Jack Kennedy snorting cocaine off actress Juliet Prowse's stomach. She had fantastic legs.

Kennedy said Prowse was the first woman he'd ever seen with a shaved pussy. She said she shaved her pubes because she was a dancer.

After snorting the line, Jack looked up at Dean Martin and said, "Dean, this is better than that Percodan you gave me."

Percodan was an opiated aspirin.

Jack was feeling no pain.

There was already talk that he was going to be president,

which made me wonder what the world was going to be like with a drug-sniffing pussy hound in the White House. Well, we all found out.

Nobody paid any attention to me. I was well dressed, and too young to be threatening. They must've thought I worked there, and they made no effort to hide things from me. I saw famous actresses, award-winning actresses, having lesbian sex at poolside without a care in the world.

I picked up the package, following Mr. Costello's instructions to the letter, and flew it to Chicago. There I met boss Tony Accardo.

Accardo was American-born but clung to the ways of the Old World. He was the son of a Sicilian cobbler and his wife. Tony started out in the rackets as Al Capone's bodyguard. Tony got to quit school at fourteen rather than the legal sixteen. His dad needed him to get a job and help around the house. Dad forged a fake birth certificate.

Once on the streets, teenaged Accardo joined a ragged bunch of juvenile delinquents named the Circus Café Gang. His first chores as a gangmember were as lookout, mugger, and armed robber. But, as this was Prohibition, he soon evolved into a bootlegger.

Accardo was so good at tough-guy tasks that he attracted the attention of "Machine Gun" Jack McGurn, who recruited him into Al Capone's gang. Accardo earned major points with his boss in 1926 during a shoot-out when he took a bullet that was intended for Capone.

His first known kill was that of Hymie Weiss, leader of Chicago's North Side Gang, near the Holy Name Cathedral, in October 1926. About two and a half years later, Accardo was one of four Capone men who rubbed out seven members of the North Side Gang in the St. Valentine's Day Massacre.

Accardo's nickname was "Joe Batters" because he used a baseball bat for stuff other than hitting a baseball. He was big and would come at guys with one bat in each hand. *Boom, boom,* you had two broken arms. Destroying men with a bat became Accardo's signature.

Later on, when he grew old and big, he was known as "Big Tuna," after a photo was published showing him with a giant tuna fish he'd caught on a deep-sea expedition.

Accardo became known as a quiet and effective leader who usually did the thing that was best for business, and that was usually a nonviolent solution to beefs.

("It's always better not to shoot," Meyer Lansky once said—but not everyone agreed with him.)

Because Accardo was the way he was—keeping a low profile, tugging the brim of his hat over his eyes when a photographer was near, and never having to do jail time—it was relatively easy for him to move in on legitimate businesses, worm his way in through intimidation, and his empire diversified to include real estate (commercial buildings and shopping malls), truck and car dealerships, newspapers, hotels, paper and lumber factories, and travel agencies.

Accardo became underboss of the Outfit in 1943 when Frank Nitti shot himself. Soon thereafter, when boss Paul "The Waiter" Ricca was arrested and charged with extortion, Accardo became the Outfit's top cat.

As boss, he introduced innovations, some new rackets, and some updated old ones. He sold counterfeit cigarettes, no sales tax, replaced many of the city's ancient brothels with call girl services. Now the girls came to the customer, very convenient for the busy businessman.

In 1957, Accardo mostly stayed in his River Forest, Illinois, mansion (which had its own bowling alley). That was where I met him.

Not long after our meeting, a massive tax probe called Accardo to testify, and he invoked his Fifth Amendment rights 172 times—which might be the record.

In Chicago, I was introduced to the Outfit bigwigs as Frank Costello's Boy, then dealt with Nick Nitti (Frank's son), and sometimes Milwaukee boss Frank Balistrieri. Nitti and I, as you'll read, had all kinds of adventures together.

I also met the nightclub owners, the Fischetti brothers. They were originally from New York but moved to Chicago to be closer to their first cousin, Al Capone. The oldest Fischetti brother was Rocco, aka Rocky, aka Ralph Fisher. The others were Charles and Joseph. They made their first million as boot-leggers, and after Prohibition ran a gambling joint called the Rock Garden Club.

Sometime around the end of World War II, Frank Sinatra befriended the brothers, and it was through the Fischettis that Sinatra originally was mobbed up in Chicago. Frank accompanied the Fischettis to the so-called Havana Conference, during which they delivered a suitcase holding two million dollars to the exiled Boss of Bosses, Lucky Luciano. Later, Frank went to Chicago boss Tony Accardo and said he wanted to be with him.

Accardo called the Fischettis: "Your Italian songbird is here and says he wants to be with me and not you."

The Fischettis laughed.

Frank Costello heard about this and told Accardo, "Now we both got him. You take eight weeks and I'll take eight weeks." That was sixteen weeks that Sinatra had to work and got paid nothing. This was a pattern that followed Sinatra for his entire life. Near the end, he was still up there performing, with monitors all over the stage to help him remember the lyrics he'd been singing for fifty years. And he was doing it not because he wanted to, but because he had to. People wondered why he was doing this to himself. He wasn't. The Mob was making him do it, because the high rollers would come out to see him even if he was just humming while hanging upside down.

When I next saw Mr. Costello, he asked about loose talk, and I told him about Senator Kennedy and the drugs and the dancer. He said he'd never be caught dead in a scene like that. For one thing, he was a one-woman man. For another, as he put it, "You can't trust those Irish cocksuckers."

* * *

I wasn't back in New York for long. It was back to Chicago. I was picked up at O'Hare Field and driven to the Palmer House in Downtown Chicago, where I met for the first time Sidney Korshak, a man who stayed with me for the rest of his life.

I was to learn that Sidney Korshak was the Outfit's lawyer, a Chicago-born Jew who grew up in the Lawndale section of the Windy City's west side. He was a brainy guy and attended the University of Wisconsin in Madison before earning his law degree at DePaul University. He was introduced to the Outfit by Jake "Greasy Thumb" Guzik, Al Capone's right-hand man—and said to have a greasy thumb because he was always counting Capone's money. If you asked him, Guzik would say he was Capone's business and financial advisor. In Sidney Korshak, Guzik saw a lawyer who could do the Outfit a lot of good, so he personally introduced Korshak to the top guys.

Sidney wasn't the only power broker in the Korshak family. His younger brother Morris went into politics and became Chicago city treasurer and an Illinois state senator.

A list of Korshak's clients is like a Mob Hall of Fame: Al Capone, Sam Giancana, Frank Nitti, Tony Accardo, and Moe Dalitz. His power spread from Chicago to Hollywood, where he counted among his famous clients Robert Evans, Warren Beatty, and Hugh Hefner.

Some of the most powerful men in the movie industry went to Korshak for their legal advice: Universal chief exec Jules Stein and MGM top dog Kirk Kerkorian. He represented both Edmund "Pat" Brown, and his son Edmund "Jerry" Brown, both of whom went on to become governor of California. Corporations he repped included Hollywood studios.

Korshak's legend went beyond his legal skills, as he once simultaneously dated Jill St. John and Stella Stevens. Nice work if you can get it. And now he was in front of me with a slightly impatient expression on his face, which I found is common in lawyers.

He said, "You got a package for me?"

I said, "Yes."

I handed it to him.

"Do you know what's in it?" he asked.

"No," I said.

He opened it up and pulled out a package of money. He took the money and put it in his pocket. I could tell by the wrapper that it was $10,000 in cash. Also in there were two contracts. He pushed one of the contracts toward me.

"You sign here," he said.

I did.

"You know what this is?" he asked.

"No."

"You have just retained me to be your lawyer, and that means that, from now on, everything we say to each other is privileged information and cannot be revealed, even in court under oath. I don't care if the fucking FBI has tape now, they can't use it. I know your name. No one else does. Keep it that way."

I gulped.

While in Chicago, I learned the Outfit used a suburban Chicago hospital as a hideout. For years, during the 1960s, the Northlake Community Hospital served both sick people and wanted people. Fake patients included hit men, bank robbers, burglars, hijackers, and counterfeiters, all of whom checked in under a phony name and were discharged only after the heat was off.

The head of the hospital was Dr. Giulio Bruni, who was Tony Accardo's personal physician. The hospital was more than just a quiet place to rest for hoods on the lam. There were all-night card games involving catered food, party girls, and free-flowing liquor. Among those known to play cards there were Sam DeStefano, Sam Giancana, Rocco Pranno, and Charles "Chuckie" Nicoletti.

Hospital employees must have been selectively observant, as

no one ever reported unusual activity in private rooms under the supervision of Dr. Bruni, despite sex workers spending the night and delivery boys showing up at three in the morning with pizza.

Long before there were surveillance cameras everywhere, hospitals had them, with every entrance and exit to the hospital being monitored—it was next to impossible for a policeman or an enemy to get into the hospital without being noticed. If a cop did show up with the intent to investigate and possibly arrest someone, he was asked for a warrant. If he didn't have one, he was kicked the hell out.

I was impressed by how sewed up Chicago was for the Outfit. The gangsters were supported by a well-greased machine of politicians, cops, and judges.

It was a quick hop from the Windy City to the Motor City. In Detroit I met Giacomo "Black Jack" Tocco, who'd been the boss there forever. He was different from the other bosses I'd met and would meet. For one thing, he completed college at the University of Detroit and earned a bachelor's degree in finance.

For the most part he used his smarts to keep himself out of trouble. For years, Tocco's only bust was being a spectator at cockfights.

Years later he fell to a large RICO case—five years under investigation for racketeering, nineteen defendants including Black Jack—that sent him to prison for two years in 1998.

For forty years Tocco owned the Hazel Park Raceway. When a rumor persisted that Tocco had been in on the disappearance of Jimmy Hoffa, the FBI and a guy with a bulldozer showed up to dig at Tocco's racetrack but they came up empty. They are never going to find Jimmy Hoffa. Later on, I'll tell you why.

In Kansas City, I met Carl "Corky" and Nicholas "Nicky" Civella, the crazy brothers who ran that town. Nicky was the older, born Guiseppi Nicoli Civello in 1912 in Kansas City's Little Italy.

The infamous 1957 Apalachin meeting ended in disaster, but some business was accomplished before the raid. It was at that meeting that Nicky Civella was formally made the boss of Kansas City. During his younger years, Nicky had always sought to stay out of the spotlight, but that changed. Under his leadership, the Kansas City Mob expanded and grew in power.

I had more dealings with Nicky's brother Corky. They would become very important to me when I was interested in the development of Las Vegas real estate, as you'll see.

In Milwaukee, I was introduced to Frank Peter Balistrieri, who would go on to be boss of the Brew City, taking over for John Alioto, who was also his father-in-law. From the start, the Milwaukee Mob vowed allegiance (and by implication subservience) to the Chicago Outfit. If you wanted to run a racket anywhere in the Midwest you needed to get the permission of, and kick up to, Chicago.

When you think Mob, you don't necessarily think Milwaukee, but Balistrieri—known as "Frankie Bal" as a young man and "Mr. Big" when older—was one of the key guys regarding the Big Skim of Vegas. Truth is, Milwaukee had a rich criminal history during the twentieth century.

Frankie Bal's specialties were shylocking and sports book. His other racket was coin-operated machines, which included jukeboxes, cigarette machines, pool tables, and washer/dryers. He ran his growing business out of a corner table in the back room of Snug's Restaurant in the Shorecrest Hotel.

During the time I worked with him, both in Chicago with Nick Nitti, and in Milwaukee, Balistrieri was as ruthless as they come. Some of the murders Balistrieri ordered are still considered cold cases. The two that brought the biggest headlines were the whackings of nightclub operator Isadore "Izzy" Pogrob and jukebox distributor Anthony Biernat.

Sometime around puberty, someone said to him, "Hey, Mick, you should be a fighter."

Kids—that is, children—boxing was big in those days. There was an organized tournament for newsies, and the boys got their first taste of gloving up and getting into the ring, three two-minute rounds while chattering adults made bets at ringside.

Mickey didn't win the tournament, but he fared well enough to get his name in the papers, and a job as a sparring partner. He was fighting professionally as a bantamweight by the time he was thirteen.

He bragged about his boxing career in later years. Officially he only fought in seven prizefights and won none of them—three losses, four draws. But there were many more. He fought in four-round "smokers"—unsanctioned and illegal fights held in bootleg clubs. They were cockfights, only with kids off the street instead of roosters.

Cohen eventually became Bugsy Siegel's bodyguard, which put him on the fast track for success. In addition to guarding Siegel, Cohen was raking in the dough with his own bookie joint at the corner of Santa Monica Boulevard and Western Avenue. The place was cop-proof. The chief of the Hollywood bunco squad had a piece of the action. The joint was wired for the ponies during the day and operated as a casino at night.

There was no questioning his toughness, or his courage. The L.A. Mob boss Jack Dragna wanted him dead, bad. Mickey escaped every assassination attempt. Bullets were fired into his home. Dynamite once blew a gaping hole in his bedroom wall. Later he would take a shotgun blast to the shoulder. The attempts just made Cohen's fame grow.

I met him on that initial tour of bosses, gave him an envelope, and told him I was Costello's kid. Little did we know we'd meet again a few years down the road under the most awkward of circumstances.

In L.A., I also dealt with Johnny Roselli, and he became my friend. In Los Angeles, being Roselli's friend could open some very pleasant doors. I loved L.A. I was like a kid in a candy shop, out every night.

Sidney Korshak, whom I had retained as my lawyer, was always in L.A. because he owned a joint there called Le Bistro on Rodeo Drive.

Before my first arrival, Korshak told his staff: "There's a guy coming in known as The Kid. When he comes in, he sits at my table and he's on my tab."

I went to Le Bistro and every movie star in the world was hanging out there. I was going there almost every day. I had a pocket full of money, but they wouldn't take my money.

When I would see two or three beautiful women having lunch or whatever, I'd give money to the waiter and pick up the tab for the ladies. I made a few friends that way.

One day, Sidney came up and asked me, "How much do you weigh?"

"What kind of a question is that?" I asked.

"I think it's a good question. You've been picking up so many checks around here I figured you must weigh five hundred pounds by now."

My most memorable visit during that initial tour of Mob leaders was to Havana, where I delivered a package to Meyer Lansky. Castro was getting closer by the day and Lansky was just beginning to get concerned.

But I got to see the Riviera Hotel and Casino in its glory. I learned just how much the Mob lost when they lost Havana. And why there would be such a violent reaction when attempts to get Havana back seemed to be sabotaged by the White House.

CHAPTER 4
The Jewel That Was Havana

All during my tour of the U.S.A., city to city and back again, I was dazzled by what I saw, overwhelmed by the size of the personalities I was meeting. Sometimes I would just be in awe, and that was how I felt around Meyer Lansky. So much Big Man energy radiating from a physically small man.

When I arrived in Havana, it was during the part of Lansky's life that he enjoyed the most. He used to boast that he didn't need to be a criminal in Cuba. Gambling was legal and he didn't rip off his customers. Sure, there was a vig built into the system, but that was to be expected, and perfectly legal.

He ran a place where American men and their wives (or girl-friends) could come and indulge themselves in ways that were then unheard of in the United States. Remember, Vegas as we know it didn't exist yet. This was the template.

Lansky had been laying the groundwork for a move to Cuba for decades. During the 1930s he befriended Cuban dictator Fulgencio Batista, and worked with Batista to clean up the island's gambling industry. But government in Cuba was volatile, Batista fell out of power, and Lansky returned stateside.

Years later, in March 1952, Batista headed up a coup and re-gained control of Cuba. Batista was a vicious killer, a man who routinely offed his enemies, who had their bodies displayed to discourage dissent.

If Lansky knew about Batista's reign of terror, he kept it quiet. He would later say that it really didn't matter to him who ran Cuba, as long as they let him do his thing. (It never occurred to him that the next leader of Cuba might not accept his bribe. It didn't compute.)

While Batista was away, gambling in Havana retreated back to the bad old days of clip joints and hustle games. In fact, next to Tijuana, Mexico, Havana was considered the sleaziest trap for American tourists. There were no donkey shows, but there was a Nymphet Ranch near the airport where pigtailed "virgins" (some in their early thirties) optioned and re-optioned their first-time rights.

The Havana clip industry took a tumble when one of the tourists who got clipped turned out to be a friend of Richard Nixon, the U.S. vice president at the time.

One of Batista's first moves was to increase protection of tourists by law enforcement. His second was to get Lansky to return and again use his considerable power to push the con artists out and reimagine the Cuban gambling scene as one that could be trusted by tourists.

"I want you to turn Havana into the Monte Carlo of the Caribbean," Batista said.

"It would be my pleasure," Lansky said.

Lansky negotiated his fee and went to work. His first move was to take over the Montmartre Club, fire all the crooks who worked there, bring in his own people whom he knew to be honest, clean the joint up, and declare it safe for tourists.

His second move was to contact those who operated the crooked casinos and tell them that bad things might happen if they didn't shape up. The Lansky name remained magic in Havana. He was a famous gangster in the U.S., but in Cuba he was the new sheriff in town who kept the crooks away from the gambling casinos.

If you came to town with the ambition of owning and operating a hotel/casino, you had better be a friend of Lansky. You could tell who Lansky liked by who were allowed to compete with him—guys like Santo Trafficante, and Moe Dalitz.

In conjunction with the Cuban government, Lansky took over the Nacional Hotel, installed a Lansky-approved gambling room, and hired singer Eartha Kitt to headline the opening night floor show. When the Mob bigs hung out together, they stayed at the Nacionel Hotel and played cards by the pool.

Lansky had the Montmartre and the Nacional to keep him busy, but he wasn't satisfied. Lansky had a dream. In Havana, during the spring of 1956, he would build his masterpiece:

The Riviera Hotel: The biggest hotel/casino complex outside of Vegas.

He'd owned pieces of hotel before, the biggest being the Flamingo in Vegas, and he'd operated illegal carpet joints in the U.S., but this would be the first time a hotel was his own baby. Much of the construction cost, reportedly eight million dollars, came from a state-run development bank, the Bank for Economic and Social Development, set up by President Fulgencio Batista.

Lansky's investment partners included many of the top hotel men in the world, not to mention the interests of Sam Giancana, who was having "Sugartime" with Phyllis McGuire of the McGuire Sisters when he wasn't running Chicago rackets. Phyllis apparently had a thing for Dan Rowen of *Rowen and Martin's Laugh-In*, which almost got the comedian killed. Giancana also had a mistress named Judith Campbell, who was one of JFK's girlfriends.

When construction was near complete, Lansky moved into the Presidential Suite at the top. He owned and operated the Riviera, except not on paper where he was listed only as "kitchen director." For the record, the hotel's president was Harry Smith, a Canadian hotel man. T. James Ennis, a Cuban hotelier, was managing director.

That isn't to say that Lansky didn't take his role as kitchen director seriously. When the hotel opened, he joyously gave special guests a tour of his kitchen, the construction of which he had personally supervised.

The plush, spectacular Hotel Havana Riviera opened on December 10, 1957. It stood twenty-one stories, had many rooms with a view of the nearby Caribbean, and was covered with mosaics.

The opening-night headliner at the Riviera cabaret was Ginger Rogers, who once danced as well as Fred Astaire only backward and in heels. Lansky wasn't a major fan. He complained that she could "wiggle her ass" but couldn't "sing a goddamn note."

At first, Lansky wanted to hire locals to work in the casino but couldn't find anyone with adequate experience. So, he ended up recruiting pit bosses, dealers, etc. from his American carpet joints.

Lansky told me that when the Riviera first opened, business was sluggish. Havana had such a grubby reputation that classy people didn't want to go to Cuba. Then a fabulous idea was handed to him.

At that time Steve Allen, first host of *The Tonight Show*, had a Sunday evening variety show on NBC—*The Steve Allen Plymouth Show*—that usually lost its time slot in the ratings to *The Ed Sullivan Show* on CBS. To change things up, Allen's staff spent weeks arranging for them to do a live show from the Havana Riviera, with an all-star lineup.

In those early days of television, moving the show was an ordeal, complicated and expensive, and a gamble as there was no guarantee that any more people would watch the show from Havana than if they did it at the Hudson Theater on Broadway. Ed Sullivan's fans were religious about him.

To move Allen's show, they had to fly into Cuba sixteen tons of lights and five miles of cable. A cast and crew (with wives) of sixty were flown down.

Lansky recognized that the TV show, whether it beat Sullivan or not, was going to give the Riviera the kind of publicity you couldn't buy, so he gritted his teeth and held his tongue when the TV people came in and took over for a few days. When the producer whined about the "cost of all of this," Lansky shrugged and kicked in $25,000 toward the effort. Allen then stepped back and watched his variety show turn into a commercial for the Riviera.

"Is there any hotel plug in this script?" someone asked at a preproduction meeting.

"Is there any script in this hotel plug?" Allen shot back.

The most difficult part of the setup was lighting. TV needed intense lights back then, and because so much of the hotel was being shown during the show, both interiors and exteriors, all five miles of cable were used. Everywhere you looked there were lights. A poolside restaurant had been transformed into a control room. There were a disturbing number of "Danger—High Voltage" signs. Everywhere you turned there were anti-theft security guards, giving everyone the side eye.

Also on the show were Allen's bandleader, Skitch Henderson, ventriloquist Edgar Bergen with his pals Charlie McCarthy and Mortimer Snerd, and comedian Lou Costello (without Bud Abbott). Allen's wife, actress Jayne Meadows, made a cameo. Allen regulars Bill "Jose Jimenez" Dana (who did not do his silly Hispanic bit while in Cuba), Don Knotts, Louie Nye, and Tom Poston were on hand. The announcer was Gene Rayburn, who later became a household name as host of *The Match Game.* Rayburn deserved combat pay as he did commercials while standing precariously on the pool's diving board, the wind audibly whipping in his microphone.

Things did not go off without a hitch. During rehearsals Don Knotts buckled to the humidity and passed out. Locals didn't like Skitch Henderson's casual wardrobe, thinking his sweater and jeans looked too much like a revolutionary. It didn't help that Henderson had a beard like Castro's.

Allen found Lansky and said, "You might want to make an announcement in the casino that anyone who is not with their spouse should go elsewhere during the show."

Lansky had the announcement made, there was laughter, and then more than a few slinky departures.

Come showtime, the wind approached gale force and a storm blew in, which the show, presented live, pretended not to notice. The show began with a view from the hotel's front entrance. A limo pulled up out front and the entire cast got out, introduced as they ran by the camera and into the hotel. Last to arrive was the host, Steve Allen, riding a cart pulled by a donkey. Despite the obvious wind, Allen read the cue card and said it was a "romantic and starry night."

Allen moved into the main showroom and opened his monologue with, "Welcome to Havana, ladies and gentlemen, home of pineapples and Meyer Lansky." The joke received only nervous laughter. The rest of the jokes did better, but it was Lansky's first and last mention.

"The Riviera is so luxurious, each morning they change the view."

"I don't want to say the Riviera is fancy, but Conrad Hilton is a bellhop."

Steve Lawrence lip-synched "Begin the Beguine" as he strolled around the Riviera's casino (as nothing but married couples stood in the background grinning) and hotel lobby, showing off the iconic architecture to its fullest advantage.

The va-va-va-voom singer/actress Mamie Van Doren sang a song beside the egg-shaped pool about having sand in her shoes. In the background four brave trick divers, shivering in the chill, dove into the pool. Off screen they immediately got out, were draped with towels, and given a bottle of rum to pass around.

Van Doren, too, lip-synched, beginning the number in a metallic evening gown, moving like a cat behind a changing screen to emerge in a one-piece bathing suit. There was much intrigue off screen as Van Doren's dressing screen kept blowing over in the wind but miraculously stayed up while she changed behind it. Being a trouper, Van Doren finished her number by diving in the pool and emerging at the edge with wet hair and a sparkling smile. The instant her scene was over she, too, went for the towels and rum.

As Allen had promised Lansky, order would come out of the chaos, and once the red light went on, the show went off without a hitch. It was a technological achievement above and beyond the hectic scene at the Riviera, as it was also the first live TV production from Cuba, "beamed over the horizon" to Miami for relay to New York.

The sixty-minute commercial that Steve Allen had given him had been a tremendous boon to business. What better way to get classy people to come to Cuba than to show them the elegance of the Riviera?

Reservations came in before the show was even off the air.

From then on, planes arriving at the Havana airport were filled with Americans in shades looking for Lansky's sin city. The show may not have beaten Ed Sullivan in the ratings, but it put a dent in Sullivan's lead, and resulted in just the reaction Lansky had hoped for. Everyone wanted to swim in that pool where Mamie Van Doren sang, everyone wanted to gamble in the casino where Steve Lawrence was. The hotel was booked solid, zero vacancies, for the first half of 1958. Business was so good that Lansky became a primary driver of Havana's economy with ownership of bars, restaurants, the marina, and even the airport.

Lansky had been worried about attracting enough rich Americans to grubby Havana. The joint made $3 million in its first four months.

Less than a month after *The Steve Allen Plymouth Show* came to Cuba, Lansky returned to New York to take care of some business. NYPD detectives shadowed him from the airport as Lansky got into a cab and headed for Manhattan. The going was slow as there was a snowstorm, but eventually Lansky and his shadow reached Times Square. Lansky got out and police immediately nabbed him. He was placed under arrest—charged with vagrancy, which was a joke—and he had to spend the night in jail before a lawyer could arrive and post $1,000 bail.

Meyer would have been content to stay in Havana and run his hotel for the rest of the days. It was his dream come true, running a sophisticated and trustworthy casino where the rich and the famous would show up packing wads to choke a horse and lose, lose, lose—customers could run up a debt, but when they did, instead of washing dishes for a month in Meyer's kitchen, they would scratch out a check for thirty grand and retire to the bar to lick their wounds.

It was paradise! At the Riviera, in fact, Lansky had never had a customer who couldn't pay his debt. He had regulars who lost so predictably that Meyer comped them left and right, free room, free food and drink. Only chips cost money.

There was even a family-like warmth between the Boss and the hundreds who worked at the casino. Meyer was a great boss. Not outwardly greedy in any way, he had invented a system that made money so freely that there was no need to be. Everyone could be happy, and they were.

The only thing that stood in the way of his happiness and infinite prosperity was Fidel Castro, whose move to take over Cuba began in late 1956 when he and eighty others—including his brother Raul and Che Guevara—battled the Cuban army guerrilla style from Playa Las Coloradas in southeast Cuban through the Sierra Maestra mountain range, which was where the skirmishes were taking place when the Riviera opened in Havana.

It was in December 1958, just short of a year after the TV show aired, that Castro's now much larger army of rebels defeated Batista's army and took the city of Santa Clara. As this occurred, the New Year's Eve Party at the Riviera was raucous.

Batista was apparently not the type to go down with his ship. He and his family fled while Castro was still many miles away, first to a friendly air force base, then in three planes to the Dominican Republic.

Even before Castro arrived, the citizens of Havana turned on the Riviera. They invaded it, trashing everything they could get their hands on. Farm animals ran around Meyer's kitchen. The rioters left as quickly as they came but left the place trashed.

Castro and his men eventually fought their way to the capital and took over the governmental buildings.

These were days when Lansky thought the situation was salvageable. That he'd pay Castro to leave him alone, and that would be that. But Lansky's customers were all American. He had no idea (or interest in) how he was perceived by Cuban citizens.

With Castro in charge, the Riviera was seen as a symbol of Batista's government, the oppression of the Cuban people, and of a powerful America that would use them when convenient but not give back.

Then came the day in January 1959 when Fidel Castro stated during a speech that he wasn't just going to kick the American gangsters out of Havana, he was going to have them shot on sight.

That was Lansky's cue to get the hell out of Dodge. He chartered a plane for the Bahamas, never looking back. By the time Castro came by to see the former wonderland, there was goat shit in the roulette wheels.

Castro held the hotels hostage for a time, and one at a time allowed them to reopen for business. But the damage was done. American tourists were through going to Havana to do their sinning. It was too dangerous.

Lansky let it be known that he was in the market to sell the Riviera, but naturally there were no takers. Americans were going to need another place to do their sinning, someplace like Nevada.

* * *

As a quick postscript, there was a stretch during which Castro ran Cuba but still courted American friendship. He came to New York and was given a hero's welcome by some. This irked Lansky, who'd done a lot of reading about third-world dictators, and whose life had been threatened by Castro. He was convinced that it was only a matter of time before Cuba turned Communist and sided up with the Soviet Union. In May 1959, Meyer gave his prediction regarding Castro to the FBI, said he thought it his patriotic duty to do so. Special agents politely listened and then filed his report away. To act upon anything Lansky said would have caught flack from J. Edgar Hoover because of Lansky's American rep as an enemy of the people. Years later it was clear that Lansky, more so than anyone else, had seen through Castro. Every word of his warning to the feds came true.

For Meyer Lansky, the question was, what next? He'd sunk all his money into a project that he'd been forced to abandon.

"I crapped out," he later said. And his health deteriorated. A heart attack in 1960 put him in an oxygen tent for a month.

By that time, America had a new, young, and handsome president who didn't even know how to pronounce Castro's island. He called it "Cuber."

As I've said, I never had much respect for my dad—but I had a grandfather I loved. He told me that my fancy clothes I was getting from Mr. Costello were all well and good, but I should have a skill to fall back on in case the wiseguy business fell through.

So, I was a bricklayer for a summer. Then I went back to delivering messages and packages to bosses.

Thanks to me, my father became an executive with the musician's union. I did a major favor for James Caesar Petrillo of the American Federation of Musicians. So, to pay me back he asked me if there was anyone in my family who was a musician.

"Why do you ask me that?"

"You do a lot of things for me, no questions asked. I want to do you a favor," he said.

"My father's a sax player . . . not very good, but . . ."

My father was such a buffoon. He took the *O* off his name and billed himself as Lou Russ, so he could play at all the Jewish weddings. The guy was a bum. A little bum. But he was made an executive with Local 802 because of me.

It was maybe the last nice thing I did for my father while he was alive. After he died I had Senator Orrin Hatch from Utah organize a color guard for his funeral. My sisters laughed at me because I insisted on a twenty-one-gun salute. They were saying, "You are so nuts."

I heard it was impressive. I don't know. I didn't go.

During the Kennedy and Nixon presidential campaigns, Mr. Costello sent me to make my regular stop in Vegas to deliver envelopes (each package bore the initials of the intended recipient). To put it mildly, the Vegas Strip was under construction. With Havana gone, the boys moved to Vegas to build their casinos.

Moe Dalitz was Lansky's guy in Las Vegas. Dalitz was born December 24, 1899, in Boston, but grew up in Detroit. As a youth he had deep-set and well-shadowed eyes over a beak of a nose, and an easy smile that could go cold as ice in the blink of an eye. He was all nose and Adam's apple as a kid but in adulthood grew into his face. He never grew tall, however, topping out at five-three.

As a young man he worked in his parents' laundry and first turned to crime when he was nineteen after the Volstead Act, which banned the production or sale of alcoholic beverages, went into effect. The family business made a quick transition. Box trucks purchased to haul laundry now hauled booze.

He worked his way up the syndicate and while still in his twenties was a member of the Purple Gang—the notorious

Jewish Mob of bootleggers and hijackers that terrorized Detroit throughout Prohibition. He controlled a huge chunk of a booze empire that encompassed Canada and Mexico, and a large portion of the U.S. You couldn't drink in Galveston, Texas, without Moe getting a slice.

When Prohibition transitioned with a thump into the Depression, Moe again shifted gears and went into gambling. He knew that in tough times men became desperate and fixated on get-rich-quick schemes—and where better to flex than over a roulette wheel?

He opened a parlor in Detroit. Moe was afraid of nothing, but there was too much competition in Detroit so he relocated to Cleveland. As had occurred during his booze days, his business grew and grew, spreading throughout Ohio and into Kentucky.

Dalitz enlisted in the Army after Pearl Harbor, rose to the rank of lieutenant, and was discharged after VJ Day. After the war, Dalitz invested in Nevada real estate, a charter member of the Vegas Club.

He was one of the visionaries who saw a gambling parlor as big as a city, a humongous cash machine, cheaper and more lucrative than building your own mint, bells and whistles worthy of a carnival midway—and all perfectly legal!

He proved that he really was afraid of nothing in 1964 when he had a beef with the world heavyweight boxing champion, Sonny Liston, a bear of a man with a fearsome punch. It happened in the Beverly Rodeo Hotel in Hollywood. The men were not exactly nose to nose, as Moe's nose only came up to Liston's belly button, but Dalitz nonetheless reminded Liston that he might be able to fight, but that did not mean he was bulletproof.

"Touch me and you're dead in under twenty-four hours," Dalitz said, and the boxer, who had a reputation as a bad man, backed down.

By that time Dalitz was among the four hundred richest men in America (according to *Forbes Magazine*).

* * *

During the JFK presidential campaign, I was teaming up with Frank Sinatra and working with the unions to get Jack Kennedy elected, because Jack promised he'd get the Havana casinos back in Mob hands. Every Mob family backed JFK.

If you talked to a Kennedy family historian today, they'll tell you that Joe Kennedy, JFK's dad, was never involved in smuggling or bootlegging during Prohibition, but that's bullshit. I know because Frank Costello told me. He said that he and Joe Kennedy were partners during Prohibition and each made thirty or forty million dollars selling booze.

Mr. Costello once said it plain as day: "I helped Joe Kennedy get rich."

Joe Kennedy asked his old partner Frank Costello to use his influence to help his son John become President of the United States.

Costello said, "What's in it for me?"

Kennedy said, "The first thing Jack will do when he becomes president is invade Cuba."

That was a deal. Joe K. would get his kid in the White House and the Mob would get their Havana casinos back. There was nothing Costello and his fellow bosses wanted more.

Well, as the world knows by now, John Kennedy was elected president, in a squeaker over Richard Nixon, winning only with the help of the Outfit in Chicago, who tipped the scales in Illinois in Kennedy's favor.

John then appointed his brother Bobby as his attorney general. Bobby hated their dad (he was a mama's boy), disobeyed his brother the president, and went to war against the Mob.

I went to JFK's inauguration. They gave Mr. Costello a ticket. He asked me if I wanted to go and I said sure. I was seventeen years old and sitting ten rows from the podium.

People were looking at me and saying, "Who is this kid?"

Jack gave his great "ask not what your country can do for you" speech.

Eighty-six-year-old Robert Frost, the legendary poet, read a poem called "The Gift Outright."

Frank Sinatra and Peter Lawford organized a pre-inauguration ball at the D.C. Armory. To give you an idea of how powerful Kennedy was with the show-biz community, he got Broadway theaters in New York to take the night off so performers could travel down to D.C. and participate in the preinaugural show. The ball doubled as a fundraiser to help pay for the Kennedy campaign, which had run over budget.

The Rat Pack was there, except for Sammy, who was asked by Kennedy's people not to come because he was married to a white woman (May Britt). Sammy's love life had been controversial throughout the campaign, and Sammy waited until after the election to marry Brit, but they were man and wife by the time of the inauguration and not invited.

At the end of the ball, JFK took the microphone and said, "The happy relationship between the arts and politics which has characterized our long history I think reached a culmination tonight."

At the inauguration ball, the invocation was given by Cardinal Cushing, America's top Catholic, and other men of the cloth offered their prayers as well, representing Greek Orthodox and Protestant churches, and a blessing was offered by a rabbi.

Superstars of the arts world were there. In addition to Frost, poet Carl Sandburg, novelists John Steinbeck and Ernest Hemingway, and painter Mark Rothko were on hand.

Little did I know that the youthful new president only had two years and 306 days to live. The oath of office was administered to JFK by Supreme Court Chief Justice Earl Warren, who three years later would helm the "investigation" into Jack's assassination.

Both events, the ball and the swearing-in ceremony, had to deal with nasty winter weather. All living ex-presidents were invited but Herbert Hoover didn't make it because his flight was grounded by a blizzard.

It was cold and snowy on the night of the ball and the next day, thousands of volunteers were called in to remove snow from Pennsylvania Avenue so the inaugural parade could go on as scheduled.

I'd been around the country meeting every Mob boss there was. I'd met the Rat Pack and Jack Kennedy and too many women to count, and I was still a minor.

One day, late fall in 1961, Mr. Costello says, "You're going to turn eighteen pretty soon, Kid. What do you want?"

I said, "I want to be a millionaire." I was joking.

"You got it," he said. And he made it happen.

I told him I'd like to open a nightclub. Seemed like fun.

"Where?"

"Miami. Seventy-Ninth Street Causeway."

So, I bought a piece of a club in Miami called La Disc, right on the causeway, which was happening with a strip of restaurants and clubs. I owned but didn't manage. I still worked for Mr. Costello.

At the same time as I was building La Disc into something great, I ran a big-money gin-rummy game for suckers in Cabana One at the Miami Beach Fontainebleau Hotel. Frank Sinatra always performed there for a week in the winter, and there were snowbirds everywhere. All year-round you could find Mob guys hanging around the lobby. Cops could have just come in and rolled them all up, for consorting with each other. There was a thousand-dollar buy in. The guy outside tending the huge circular bar was the bank, selling and cashing in chips. Inside the cabana, the games were crooked. Mirrors were set up. Cocktail waitresses circled the tables and spoke to us in code.

I had La Disc on the causeway for years. Show-biz royalty performed there: Frank, Dean, and Sammy, Rickles, funnyman Shecky Greene, and Liza Minnelli. I hired fearsome bruisers to work as bouncers so troublemakers were outside on their ear before they knew what hit them.

Many years later, the joint made the papers when Richard Nixon and his running mate Spiro Agnew, fresh from being nominated for president and vice president at the 1968 Republican National Convention at the Miami Convention Hall, had their victory party at La Disc.

Nixon was in the Mob's pocket and not squeamish about having a party at a connected club. If they didn't already know, people figured out that Nixon was mobbed up when he commuted Jimmy Hoffa's prison sentence. Considering what happened, Hoffa would've been better off behind bars.

My partners at La Disc, Carmine Black and Charlie Alaimo, were made guys with the Genovese family. They broke the rules and sold blow out of the club. When the pair was summoned to New York, they thought they were getting a pat on the back for being great earners. Turned out, the bosses knew about their cocaine side hustle and they were *erased*. Black fell from the roof of a Brooklyn tenement and Alaimo disappeared.

That left me on my own in Miami, sole owner.

I had to answer a few questions, too. Mr. Costello wanted to know if I knew about the drug deals going on in the club. I didn't and he believed me. But life didn't go on as before. The Bureau of Narcotics was watching La Disc twenty-four/seven. I got sick of it and walked away from the club.

CHAPTER 5
The Murder of Marilyn Monroe

By 1962, my jobs for Mr. Costello were international—Central and South America, the Caribbean where I was having adventures that seemed out of a James Bond novel. I still dropped off and picked up, but now there were times when I thought I might be transporting something other than cash. I didn't ask. Some sort of valuable commodity. I met Manuel Noriega down there, a connection that would come in very handy years later.

John Kennedy had been in the White House for a year and a half, a very long year and a half of the Mob tapping its collective toe impatiently. And Castro was still entrenched in Cuba.

Bobby was busting mobsters left and right.

Something had to give.

Joe Kennedy had promised he'd get the casinos back first thing, but it didn't happen. Joe was in a wheelchair. Did Jack even know what his dad had promised? Questions ate at Mr. Costello. Was old crooked-as-the-day-is-long Joe Kennedy no longer in charge of his brood? Had Jack and Bobby gone rogue? Or was it just Bobby, the mama's boy, who didn't care what his invalid dad had promised?

And Bobby wasn't just at war with the Mob, he was prosecuting a nasty, mean-spirited campaign versus organized crime, one that he saw as his destiny, one that he hoped they'd make a Hollywood movie about someday, attacking the very entity that helped get his brother elected. It was like he had a death wish.

Mr. Costello's suspicions about those "Irish cocksuckers" became all too true not long after the inauguration. You couldn't trust them. He said the Kennedys had "no measure of loyalty." Until the Kennedys used the Mob to gain power and then went to war against it, I'd never seen Mr. Costello mad. Good thing, too. When he angered, he was terrifying.

And it got worse.

It started with the Bay of Pigs Invasion in April 1961, which featured U.S.-trained Cuban exiles hitting Cuban beaches. It was a massive failure because the promised air cover was canceled by President Kennedy, and there was a slaughter on the beach. Jack had made the Costello shit list for certain.

Castro sided up with Moscow just as Meyer Lansky had predicted. Khrushchev put nuclear missiles in there, and the world teetered on the brink of war.

As all of that was going on, Mr. Costello still had me traveling from boss to boss. After five days of picking up and dropping off, I was spending weekends at the Sands Hotel in Las Vegas—so I could take out the skim on Monday morning.

During the early summer of 1962, Frank Costello couldn't hold it in anymore.

"I don't care if the motherfucker's got a drool cup, I'm giving him a piece of my mind," Mr. Costello said.

He called his old booze partner Joe Kennedy, who remained incapacitated by a stroke. Frank yelled at Kennedy about the promises he and his kids had not kept. Whether Joe could understand or do anything about it, we don't know, but he received a warning from the Ambassador: "It's been a year and a half. Joe, the clock is ticking. You and I both know what happened at the Bay of Pigs. You don't get Castro out of Havana, we start taking out your sons."

When the wanted response didn't come, Mr. Costello formulated a plan, one that had worked like a charm in keeping the FBI off the Mob's case. Mr. Costello, via Dallas oil magnate Clint Murchison, indulged FBI director J. Edgar Hoover's gambling addiction, saw to it that he always won, and if that wasn't enough, he had a film made of Hoover at a drag party wearing a dress and calling himself Mary. That film was in the possession of Sidney Korshak.

Despite the fury that Mr. Costello felt toward the Kennedys, his first plan was nonviolent. He would set the Kennedys up in a sex scandal that would force them to keep their promises.

The plan was to be executed on the last weekend of July 1962. I know, because I was there.

Earlier in the month, Mr. Costello called me to a meeting at the Peacock Alley, a bar at the Waldorf.

"We're setting up Jack and Bobby," he said.

The brothers were to be invited to the Cal-Neva Lodge, a rustic resort on Crystal Bay, along the north shore of Lake Tahoe, directly on the Nevada-California border. There were tunnels that ran from the lake to the lodge, remnants of Prohibition when that was how they brought the booze in. The bungalows and the lodge's inner walls were all covered with copper mesh, which was said to disrupt electronic surveillance devices.

At the Cal-Neva they would set up the Kennedys, using a sex lure and filming the extra-marital sex inside a bungalow—footage that would go straight to Sidney Korshak. The wired bungalow—film with sound—was Cabin #3. It was known as "the girls' cabin."

Trafficante and Lansky were going to have their Havana casinos back pronto. The Kennedys would have to get rid of Castro or fall to a sex scandal. He didn't name the "sex lure," and I didn't bother to ask. Any woman would do. The Kennedys marketed themselves as good Catholic boys; a sex film would have ruined them.

One of the lodge's main design elements was a dividing line painted on the outside and inside, right down the middle of the main building, so everyone knew what state they were in at all times.

The place was owned on paper by Frank Sinatra, but actually by Sam Giancana, who stayed on the California side, as Sinatra would have lost his gambling license had he been caught on the Nevada side.

Giancana, a convicted felon, had his name in the so-called Black Book. But all he had to do was stay on the California side of the line and the authorities couldn't touch him.

(At some point Giancana must have wandered onto the Nevada side and got caught because Sinatra did lose his license in 1963, and Giancana being on the Nevada side of the premises was the reason.)

Enforcement of the Black Book was pretty civilized: If you were a convicted felon and were caught in a Vegas casino, they'd give you forty-eight hours to pack up and get out. After that, the casino's license was in jeopardy. When a felon wanted to gamble at Cal-Neva, the joint would set up a private game for him in his California-side bungalow that no one needed to know about.

Mr. Costello continued giving me my instructions: "There's going to be a meeting there. You are to be my eyes and ears," he said. He was blunt. If the Kennedy boys didn't show, they were dead. If Sinatra didn't show, he was dead. Everyone better show up or they were dead.

One of the last things he said to me, almost as an afterthought, was, "Marilyn Monroe is going to be there—and I want you to stay away from her."

"Why?" I asked.

"She's part of the plan."

Uh-oh.

Mr. Costello was cashing in the chip he earned by paying Marilyn's rent for a year at the Waldorf. He was so angry he wasn't content to ruin the Kennedys, he wanted to film a pornographic masterpiece.

I hadn't seen Marilyn much lately. She'd gone back to L.A. But she'd made the papers plenty, and I knew she wasn't doing well. As July 1962 came to an end, her primary employer, Twentieth Century-Fox, wasn't talking to her.

After years of being clear eyed, Marilyn's gaze had developed a glaze in 1962, and the problems she'd had getting to the set on time during the shooting of *Some Like It Hot* only grew worse when it came time to make *Something's Got to Give* with Dean Martin. Marilyn found it impossible to get up in the morning and was fired from the movie. Now Dean was suing for his whole salary, saying it sure as hell wasn't his fault the picture was scrubbed.

Something with Marilyn was off. I sensed it too when she went to Madison Square Garden that May in a painted-on dress and sang, "Happy birthday, Mr. Pwesident," in an affected babytalk. It was a little much even for her.

When I met her, she had had it with Hollywood and was going to see Strasberg's Actors Studio. She was close friends with Susan Strasberg, Lee's daughter. I heard that Marilyn went to live with the Strasbergs and during that time had a baby girl. As far as her acting career went, Marilyn was doing the right things. She was thirty-six and would need to transition into middle-aged parts, a transition that many a sex symbol failed to make. But, if she couldn't get up in the morning, it would all go away and she'd be another unemployed middle-aged actress, a dime a dozen.

It was Friday night, July 27, when I got there and hung out at the pool. Singer Buddy Greco—his big hit was "Oh Look A-There Ain't She Pretty" fifteen years earlier—was performing at Cal-Neva that weekend. He was also by the pool.

Frank Sinatra came out bare chested. He looked at me for a second or two, figuring out why I was there.

Then he said, "How ya doin', Kid?"

Peter Lawford came strolling in, he didn't sweat, and with him was a woman in all green, slacks, a blouse, and babushka. She also wore dark glasses, a disguise I recognized immediately. It was Marilyn.

For the Big Plan, everyone would be staying in bungalows. Like in an English sex comedy, there would be a lot of tippy-toeing from one to the other. The plan was for Marilyn to have three-way sex with both Kennedy brothers in her bungalow, a session that would be filmed by a hidden movie camera operated by Sam Giancana himself. What could go wrong?

As it turned out, the plan didn't have a chance—for the simple reason that it was too ambitious, and far more complicated than it needed to be. Why did it have to be Marilyn? Wouldn't any willing female have done the trick? And it didn't have to be both brothers, blackmail evidence on one would have forced co-operation from both. It was a plan birthed from anger, and that was its fatal flaw.

It wasn't hard to figure out the exact moment when Marilyn found out that she was part of a plan to ruin the Kennedys. Frank Sinatra gently took her away from everyone and whispered in her ear in private. She began to scream bloody murder.

Even though I'd been told to stay away from her, I wandered over by where Frank and Marilyn were to see and hear what was going on.

By the time I could hear her, she was saying, "These Kennedy brothers. I am done with them. They're using me like a piece of meat! They want the world to think they are good Catholic boys. It's a charade! Bobby got me pregnant six weeks ago and made me have an abortion!"

Marilyn wanted nothing to do with the blackmail plan, a possibility that Mr. Costello hadn't considered. Like most men, he thought of her as a thing, tits and ass, a sex lure. He did her a favor, now he wanted one back.

President Kennedy, perhaps sensing a trick, sent his regrets. "Sorry, can't come to the orgy, have to lead the Free World, carry on without me, chums," or something like that. But Bobby *showed up* and when Marilyn saw him, she became freshly agitated.

Love was not in the air. Bobby was wary of Marilyn, who was intoxicated and furious. She said she was thinking of going to the press and letting everyone know what Jack and Bobby were really like. She yelled loud enough that even Buddy Greco heard some of it.

Once I realized that the plan wasn't going to come off, I left Cal-Neva and reported back to Mr. Costello that it was scrubbed. Nobody'd cleared it with Marilyn ahead of time and she wasn't into it.

Marilyn was just one of the problems. The president was a no-show. I told Mr. Costello I was troubled by Marilyn's mental state that weekend. She was drunk and high.

My heart was breaking for her when I heard her say those things, things she couldn't take back. I thought of all the long walks we'd taken through Central Park and across the bridge and she'd tell me that all she wanted was to have a baby. She didn't even care whose it was.

I told Mr. Costello some of the things she'd said.

"She said 'abortion'? She said that word out loud so people heard?"

"Yes."

"They're going to kill her," Mr. Costello predicted.

I later heard that Marilyn wanted to get the hell out of Cal-Neva but no one there was willing to take her. She called Joe DiMaggio, her ex-husband and former New York Yankee baseball star, and asked him to come get her. DiMaggio called his friend Frank Sinatra and asked what the hell was going on. Frank said it was nothing, to stay away, and DiMaggio left Marilyn swinging in the breeze.

It haunts me to think about that conversation. What if Joe DiMaggio had come to save her, took her away and protected her? She might've had a chance to live a full life.

How she got back to L.A. is a mystery to me. When I left the party, Marilyn was asleep in her bungalow and the only two men around that I knew of were Frank Sinatra and Sam Giancana.

That's what makes Don Rickles's story so interesting. When Don Rickles was old and sick, he told a story about Frank Sinatra that he'd never told before. Frank was bipolar. When he was drinking he could be strutting around like God's Gift, and the next second he could be weeping over something or other; one second he's six-four, the next he's a little kid. Top of the world, Ma. Head in the oven. So, I believed Rickles when he said that he was with Frank one night when Frank was drinking heavily, and Frank went into a crying jag and confessed to being part of Marilyn Monroe's murder.

The blackmail scheme didn't work, and it ended up costing Marilyn her life. One week later she was dead, injected (I was told) in her pubic area with air by a doctor under Bobby's orders. Considering the drugs in her, this was overkill, and an indication that the killers wanted to make damn sure she stayed dead.

According to my friend Mark Shaw, who's writing a book about Marilyn's murder, Joe had a sister who was very fond of Marilyn and kept in touch with her after she and Joe separated. She spoke to Marilyn during her last days and quoted Marilyn as saying, "They're going to kill me."

"Who?"

"Bobby." No last name necessary.

A lot of sources still list Marilyn's death date as August 5, 1962, but it was actually the fourth. In Hollywood there was a longstanding tradition of studio people and fixers getting to unseemly crime scenes before the LAPD or county sheriff had a chance to respond. It was tradition that the "first responder" was usually about the eightieth responder, and that was the case here.

As for my observations of activities at Cal-Neva, no one else who was there wanted to talk about it. Sinatra didn't mention it until he was very old and sick. The guy who best corroborated the events was Buddy Greco, who noticed that Cal-Neva was more star-studded than usual the weekend before Marilyn's murder—but Greco didn't know what was going on, just the roster of players, and the fact that Marilyn was pissed off at the Kennedys.

As for the murder of Marilyn, one of my best sources was Joe DeCarlo, a manager and club owner of Sicilian blood who I knew very well. I knew Joe through backgammon. The club where all the celebrities went to play was called Pips—because the piece you move around the backgammon board is called a pip. I was known for a while as one of the better backgammon players in the world. I traveled everywhere. I played backgammon in Monte Carlo, Monaco. I played Omar Sharif for a million dollars. That was when I had my boat, the 146-foot *Riva*. I had it parked outside the Hotel de Paris. I was twenty-one years old.

So, I knew Joe DeCarlo through Pips, and he'd been around. He'd once been acquitted of murder with codefendant Mickey Cohen. He once had dinner at the White House (Jimmy Carter administration) with Cher on his arm. And he knew about Marilyn's death.

Once, Joe DeCarlo was watching a TV show that said Bobby Kennedy had an alibi for Marilyn's murder. That set him off. He knew. Bobby and Peter Lawford went to Marilyn's house. Their intent was to talk her out of having her tell-all press conference. They begged her to shut up. Marilyn told them to get lost.

"So they sent people there," DeCarlo said. "They had it handled, no needles, anal. A drug enema."

I found out the same way everyone else did that Marilyn Monroe had died: on the news, in the papers, the official version. I couldn't believe what I was reading, because I knew it wasn't true, but this is what they said:

Officially, Marilyn died of a barbiturate overdose in her

home at 12305 Fifth Helena Drive in the Brentwood section of L.A. during the evening of August 4, 1962, Saturday night, and her body was discovered just before dawn on August 5. Her long-established problems, assumed to be a combination of mental illness and substance abuse, had prevented her from completing a picture for close to two years. Authorities, it was said, traced Marilyn's last hours. She spent her final day at home and received four visitors, who came at different times. They were publicist Patricia Newcomb, housekeeper Eunice Murray, psychiatrist Ralph Greenson, and photojournalist Lawrence Schiller, who discussed with Marilyn the possibility of selling nude photos of her taken on the set of *Something's Got to Give*, the film from which she'd been fired, to *Playboy* magazine. She also received a visit from her massage therapist, and had received a massage.

She made several phone calls to friends, and when deliveries were made to the house, she signed for packages. One phone call she received was from Joe DiMaggio, Jr., son of her ex-husband. Clearly, the DiMaggios, with the possible exception of Joe, Sr., were more concerned than most about Marilyn's well-being. Marilyn was concerned with their welfare as well. Joe, Jr. called to tell her that he'd broken up with a girlfriend that Marilyn didn't like. Marilyn was pleased and Joe, Jr.'s happy breakup was one of the pieces of news she relayed to Dr. Greenson when he later visited.

Still according to the official version of Marilyn's last hours, she received a phone call at eight p.m. on the evening of her death from film star, Rat Packer, and presidential brother-in-law Peter Lawford, asking Marilyn to attend a party he was throwing later that night. Lawford later reported that he was alarmed by the conversation because Marilyn was slurring her words and seemed heavily intoxicated considering the hour.

According to Lawford, Marilyn was fading off to sleep as she signed off, and she reportedly said, "Say goodbye to Pat [Lawford's wife, the president's sister], say goodbye to the president, and say goodbye to yourself because you're a nice guy."

After that she fell silent.

Lawford tried calling her back, but she didn't pick up. Lawford was so concerned, he worked the phone. He called his agent, who called Marilyn's doctor. He called Marilyn's lawyer, Milton "Mickey" Rudin, and finally called Marilyn's housekeeper, who assured Lawford that Marilyn was fine.

Marilyn's doctor thought Marilyn was in a particularly fragile state and urged the housekeeper to spend the night at the house and keep an eye on her. The housekeeper stayed but didn't keep an eye on Marilyn, as Marilyn reportedly locked herself in her bedroom.

At three a.m. Murray "sensed that something was wrong." She could see that the light was on under the door, but Marilyn didn't respond when she knocked. She was worried enough to go outside and try to see her through her bedroom window.

Murray didn't like what she saw and at 3:30 a.m. called Dr. Greenson, who came over immediately. Joining Murray outside Marilyn's bedroom window, the psychiatrist saw Marilyn lying face down on the bed, covered with a sheet and clutching her telephone receiver.

Dr. Greenson broke the window, climbed in, and discovered Marilyn dead. Dr. Greenson called Marilyn's primary physician, Dr. Hyman Engelberg, who arrived at 3:50 and confirmed she was dead. Two more hours passed before the doctors called the LAPD.

That's the official story. Marilyn had emptied her pill bottles into her belly and died. But there were facts that story couldn't support. For example, the statements of June DiMaggio, Joe's niece and a good friend of Marilyn's for eleven years. June said that after Marilyn's body was found, there was an attempt to contact Joe, but he couldn't be found, so they contacted June's mom, Joe's sister-in-law Louise, in an attempt to find him. Unexpectedly, the woman said she knew what had happened to Marilyn. She had been on the phone with Marilyn the evening before when intruders interrupted their conversation. They pulled Marilyn away from the phone but the receiver wasn't hung up. There were sounds of a struggle and then silence. Louise said that she knew who killed Marilyn, Marilyn had said who it was that was breaking into her house, but the woman refused to say it. She was terrified and wanted to protect her family. She got a chance to prove her point as the FBI traced Marilyn's last phone call and questioned her but she revealed nothing, intentionally anyway.

"I want my family to live," Louise said.

Every newspaper led with the fact that Marilyn was found nude, as if even her death had been overwhelmed by her sexuality.

Enter deputy coroner Thomas Noguchi, who performed Marilyn's autopsy on the same day her body was discovered. The coroner, despite the quantity of drugs in her and her shrink's testimony that she was prone to suicide ideation, refused at first to indicate a manner of death.

There was a superficial coroner's inquest. Chief Coroner Theodore Curphey and his office were assisted by a panel of psychiatrists—Norman Tabachnick, Norman Farberow, and Robert Litman, all veterans of the L.A. Suicide Prevention Center. The panel of experts was to determine how and why Marilyn committed suicide.

It's pretty clear that officials had made up their minds regarding their conclusion before the evidence was in. No one mentioned homicide.

Dr. Noguchi's autopsy report supported the anal-overdose theory. There was a "purplish discoloration" in Marilyn's lower colon. There was also an analysis of the autopsy that claimed swallowing that many Nembutal tablets at once would have killed Marilyn instantly, yet she lived for another couple of hours.

Examining the crime-scene photos, one notices that there is no drinking glass on Marilyn's night table. Nobody takes that many pills orally without water, and no one who has taken that many pills washes out the glass in the sink. They set it down and prepare to die. So, where was the glass?

Another mystery of the autopsy was the discovery of chloral hydrate in Marilyn's system, the key ingredient in a Mickey Finn, and a drug that no doctor would admit to having prescribed her. Her physician said he couldn't imagine any doctor prescribing her chloral hydrate.

This was a baldfaced lie as there exists a June 7, 1962 prescription for chloral hydrate to Marilyn, signed by her doctor, with instructions to use as directed. Plus, ten chloral hydrate tablets were found in Marilyn's bedroom

Interestingly, Dr. Noguchi's autopsy report did not contain the word "suicide." Only when his boss, Dr. Curphey, filled out the Certificate of Death were the words "Probable Suicide" added. No one asked Dr. Curphey why he hadn't performed the autopsy himself instead of delegating it to an assistant.

(The late Dr. Cyril Wecht, who loved to reveal the flaws in political cover-ups involving coroners, said that in his life he'd read sixteen thousand autopsy reports and only one ever put the word "probable" in front of "suicide.")

Dr. Noguchi testified that based on advanced rigor mortis, he estimated Marilyn died between 8:30 and 10:30 p.m. on Saturday night. He found massive quantities of chloral hydrate and pentobarbital in her blood and liver, and there were empty bottles of those medicines on the night table next to Marilyn's bed. Either drug, independent of the other, was present in a fatal quantity.

The only real question—officially, that is—was did she overdose on purpose or by accident, and the experts agreed that accidental death was unlikely because of the quantity of drugs. She'd taken *all* the pills. Her Nembutal prescription had been filled just the day before, so there had been twenty-five pills in the bottle before she swallowed them. Her death had to be on purpose.

Dr. Litman was asked if the fact that there was no suicide note might be an indication that death was accidental and he said no, that less than half of suicide victims leave a note.

Dr. Greenson told the coroner that Marilyn, during the last years of her life, had become dependent on uppers, downers, and booze, while experiencing depression, anxiety, and insomnia. In her last days, Greenson added, she had been unkempt, which wasn't like her.

"She seemed disinterested in her appearance," Dr. Greenson said.

He added that Marilyn had dealt with suicidal thoughts in the past, but she had always called for help, not always to him but always a close friend, and she'd been rescued. In 1960, Marilyn had come apart at the seams and needed to be institutionalized at the Payne Whitney Psychiatric Clinic, in New York, including four days in a padded cell and forced baths. Joe DiMaggio came and rescued her.

In addition to her padded-cell hell, Marilyn had been hospitalized for an additional month in 1961, and the official reasons for those stays were an operation for endometriosis (uterus) and a cholecystectomy (gallbladder).

Before taking anything Dr. Greenson says at face value, consider the sworn statement of Beverly Hills police officer Lynn Franklin that on the night Marilyn died, he stopped a speeder near Brentwood who turned out to be Peter Lawford. In the passenger seat in front was Marilyn's psychiatrist Dr. Greenson, and *Bobby Kennedy was sitting in back*. Police Chief Daryl Gates of the LAPD also recalled seeing Bobby in L.A. the day Marilyn died, conflicting with Bobby's "alibi" that he was in San Francisco that day.

Publicist Patricia Newcomb testified that Marilyn had seemed in a good mood on the last day of her life—but not all the time. She and Marilyn had also quarreled. It was Newcomb's opinion that Marilyn had been in a foul mood because she'd not slept well the night before. Newcomb noted that, despite the spat, all was well by the time she left Marilyn's house and that Marilyn's last words to her were, "See you tomorrow. Toodle-oo."

The coroner found "no evidence of foul play."

The three shrinks from suicide prevention submitted a written report following the inquest. Based on their investigation, Marilyn "often expressed wishes to give up, to withdraw, even to die. She'd made a previous suicide attempt by overusing sedative drugs."

The story that Marilyn, perceived as the sexiest woman in the world, had committed suicide had a terrible effect on the people of L.A. County who were fighting their own battles against depression. The suicide rate in L.A. rose dramatically that August.

The seeds of doubt regarding Marilyn's autopsy report were sewn within days of her death by investigative reporter, and syndicated newspaper columnist, my friend Dorothy Kilgallen, who was asking unanswered questions in her column as early as August 8.

Kilgallen wanted to know why Marilyn's bedroom was such a mess despite the presence of housekeeper Eunice Murray.

"It's a small house and should have been easy to keep tidy," Kilgallen wrote. She asked why Marilyn's bedroom door was locked that night when it usually wasn't. And why, if Marilyn was having trouble sleeping, was her bedroom light on?

"Most people sleep better in the dark," Kilgallen wrote.

Kilgallen also asked why the big delay in calling the police. Murray thought something was wrong and investigated at three a.m., but the police weren't called until six.

She wrote, "The real story of Marilyn's death hasn't been told, not by a long shot."

Privately, Kilgallen told friends she believed the Kennedys were involved.

On August 27, Kilgallen reported that the weekend before Marilyn's death, a housekeeper found Marilyn unconscious on

the floor of her Cal-Neva cabin, and that the next day she was
flown to California in Frank Sinatra's private plane—with
Peter Lawford but without Frank.

I'd already left Cal-Neva by that time, but it certainly could
have happened that way.

Even before Marilyn died, Kilgallen was reporting that some
of the people closest to her were not what they seemed. In an
August 1, 1962 column, she wrote that Marilyn had told a magazine reporter that she couldn't be an actress until she convinced herself that she was a person. Kilgallen then wrote
directly to Marilyn, saying she *was* a real person, and "I don't
care what your psychiatrist says"—a reference to Dr. Greenson.

In 1984, an FBI document dated August 3, 1962 was declassified. The document reported on two phone conversations
overheard via a wiretap, one of Kilgallen and her close friend
Howard Rothberg, the other between Marilyn and Bobby.

Rothberg told Kilgallen that Marilyn had been quite the society girl as of late, attending A-list Hollywood parties at which
she intimated she was through with the Kennedys and had
some very big secrets to tell. She mentioned "bases in Cuba"
and spoke of Jack's plans "to kill Castro." She said she had it all
written down in her "Diary of Secrets." (Interestingly, Marilyn
was also theorizing at those parties that flying saucers were
real, based on something JFK had told her about his visit to a
secret Air Force base. He said he'd seen "things from outer
space." JFK told Marilyn that he wanted the public to know but
his "hands were tied.")

Kilgallen investigated Marilyn's history with the Kennedys. If
she'd known what I knew, she could've cut to the chase—but
she started at the beginning. Marilyn could've met Jack as early
as 1957 at a Ball at the Waldorf. Jack was there with Jackie, Marilyn with her last husband, Arthur Miller. But the first confirmed meeting between the icons came at Bing Crosby's house
in March 1962, less than five months before she died. On May
19 she was at Madison Square Garden singing "Happy Birth-

day" to Jack, wearing a memorable dress in which she couldn't sit down. (That alone could have pissed off Jackie. She couldn't watch and hear Marilyn sing that song to her husband and not *know*.)

Kilgallen was at the Garden Party and wrote in her column, "It seemed like Marilyn was making love to the President in front of forty million Americans."

Also declassified, but more problematic as evidence, is an undated FBI memo with all source material redacted. Because of the information it contains, it must've come from a phone tap of Marilyn's phone, and possibly Bobby's as well.

The memo confirmed that Marilyn and Bobby were having a "sex affair," that their trysts had been arranged and condoned by Peter Lawford and Bobby's sister Pat, and that Bobby was hoping to have a Hollywood movie made about his anti-Mob war, jealous that the studios made a movie about Jack (*PT 109*) but not about him. This gave him an excuse to be in L.A. as much as he was.

When Marilyn was sacked by Fox for failure to show up for work on *Something's Got to Give*, she called Bobby from her house to the Justice Department in D.C. with the news and he reassured her that she shouldn't worry, that he would take care of everything.

Bobby repeated apparently earlier promises to divorce his wife Ethel so he and Marilyn could be together. But he forgot his promises as soon as he made them. He didn't help her with her studio and of course he didn't divorce Ethel.

Marilyn was catching on and her next call to Bobby was sharper in tone. She "threatened to make public their affair." After that, Bobby stopped taking her calls. That was the end of the FBI memo.

Marilyn's funeral was held on Wednesday, August 8, arranged by Joe DiMaggio, Marilyn's half sister Berniece Baker Miracle, and her business manager, Inez Melson. This committee

decided to invite only close friends and family. To open the funeral to Hollywood would have resulted in a wild parade of
thirsty stars.

The limited invitation list, however, did little to lessen the
spectacle of the event, as hundreds of curiosity seekers and
mourners gathered around the perimeter of the Westwood Vil-
lage Memorial Park Cemetery. The service, presided over by a
local minister, took place in the cemetery's chapel.

There was an open casket, with Marilyn wearing a green
Emilio Pucci dress while holding a small bouquet of pink
roses. Lee Strasberg delivered the eulogy. A phonograph was
set up and a record of Judy Garland singing "Over the Rainbow" was played, Marilyn's favorite song.

She was interred in a crypt along the cemeteries Corridor of
Memories. DiMaggio paid a lump sum at a local florist and
arranged for red roses to be placed at her crypt three times a
week for twenty years. Hugh Hefner paid $75,000 for the crypt
next to Marilyn's so, when the time came, he could spend eternity next to her.

In her will, Marilyn left the bulk of her money, including
future royalty income, to the Strasbergs. She remembered
her half sister and her secretary and set up trust funds for the
education of a friend's daughter and to take care of her aging
mother. She donated a large sum to psychiatric institutions
and groups.

The first researcher to theorize in public that Marilyn had
been murdered was Frank A. Capell, a staunch right-winger
who self-published a pamphlet in 1964 entitled *The Strange
Death of Marilyn Monroe* in which he argued that Marilyn had
been killed as part of a Communist conspiracy.

Although that conclusion was nonsense, the details of Capell's
theory were harder to dismiss. He claimed that Marilyn had
had an affair with Bobby Kennedy, a shocking notion at that
time, and that Bobby, who was by Capell's way of thinking a

Communist, had her killed after she threatened to cause a scandal. That part was true.

Capell saw communists everywhere, a leftover from the Red Scare of the 1950s, and wrote that Marilyn's doctors and one of her ex-husbands, playwright Arthur Miller, were Communists, too.

Perhaps accidently accurate, Capell's scenario struggled when traced back to its source, i.e., it didn't seem to *have* a source. Capell said he got the info from newspaper columnist Walter Winchell, and Winchell said he got the story from Capell.

The pamphlet did contain some information from eyewitnesses that official versions had ignored. First and foremost, there were the statements made by LAPD Sergeant Jack Clemmons, acknowledged to be the first cop at the scene of Marilyn's death.

He said that he'd been told to keep his mouth shut in 1962, but now, two years later, was willing to talk about what he saw. He said that when he arrived the housekeeper Murray was washing Marilyn's sheets.

Clemmons, like Capell, had a political agenda and had vowed to expose "subversives." Capell and Clemmons were indicted in 1965 for perjury, libeling a political enemy in a sworn affidavit. The source of this Bobby-did-it theory was such that the public failed to latch on to it.

Clemmons, agenda or no, made some interesting points. He said it was impossible to eat as many pills as Marilyn was supposed to have, without vomiting, and there was no indication of vomit at the scene. Such evidence might've been destroyed, he said, noting again that the housekeeper Murray was doing laundry, washing Marilyn's sheets when he arrived.

By 1973, Bobby was dead, no one was looking for Communists crawling out of the woodwork anymore, and the re-emergence of the Marilyn-was-murdered theory took a firmer hold—but only briefly.

Famous novelist Norman Mailer published *Marilyn: A Biography* in 1973, and in it repeated the claim that Bobby and Marilyn were having an affair and speculated that the FBI or maybe the CIA had killed Marilyn to put pressure on the Kennedys. America was ready to believe it until a few weeks later when Mailer went on a network TV interview program and, perhaps buckling to pressure, claimed that he'd made up the story about Bobby and Marilyn in hopes of increasing book sales.

In 1976, Anthony Scaduto published *Who Killed Marilyn?* under the pen name Tony Sciacca. He largely repeated earlier claims, including those he'd made the year before in *Oui* magazine, but added a new wrinkle: that Marilyn kept a diary, the "Red Diary," in which she kept secrets she'd learned from liaisons with the Kennedys.

Scaduto added that somewhere there was proof Marilyn had been murdered because her house had been wired by Jimmy Hoffa to gather anti-Kennedy evidence. Again, the source for this shocking info was unclear.

In 1982, Milo Speriglio published *Marilyn Monroe: Murder Cover-Up*, claiming that Jimmy Hoffa and Sam Giancana killed Marilyn. New info came from Lionel Grandison, who worked for the coroner's office in 1962 and said her body was extensively bruised, a fact that was covered up, and that he had seen the "Red Diary," could confirm that it existed, and that it had mysteriously disappeared.

Mark Shaw, who has previously written two books about my friend Dorothy Kilgallen (whose mysterious death we'll delve into later), is now researching Marilyn's demise. He has shown that Bobby Kennedy and Peter Lawford were at Marilyn's house for six hours after she died and before police came.

Shaw's story comes from a pair of hitmen who claimed to have done some "dirty work" for the Kennedys and who had the inside dope on how Marilyn died. According to this source, Marilyn was calling the White House trying to talk to Jack.

Jackie was pissed, went to Joe and said she needed a divorce. Marilyn had to go—and the Kennedys authorized it.

On the night Marilyn died, Bobby opened Marilyn's bedroom window and his men climbed in. The men were not identified by name, just as "Bobby's guys." She was out of it, so they grabbed her and positioned her, ass up. They took her medication, diluted it into a solution, then using a hypodermic syringe, injected it into the mucous membranes of her bowels, a massive dope enema, shot directly into her bloodstream for immediate effect. In other words, Marilyn had a needle mark, but it wasn't where Dr. Noguchi was going to look.

In addition to Bobby, the hitmen said, Peter Lawford was involved "and the poor son of a bitch was never the same."

That story, in which Jackie knew about Jack's affair with Marilyn and wanted the score settled, failed to corroborate, or oppose, my knowledge of the motive, which was to keep Marilyn from holding a press conference and talking about the abortion Bobby made her have.

It would be career suicide for her, but she was self destructive so she just might have done it. If Jackie was a factor, as in the hitmen's tale, nobody said that in front of me at the Cal-Neva.

The noise over Marilyn's death became so great that, by the 1980s, L.A. County District Attorney John Van de Kamp ordered the Los Angeles coroner's office to "review the case."

Oversights were discovered. Marilyn's intestines were never examined. In a case in which how the drugs got into the woman's system would be important, this was inexcusable.

Plus, Dr. Noguchi admitted that he only sent Marilyn's blood and liver to the lab for toxicology testing and should have sent samples from all the internal organs. He also admitted that "much of the controversy" over Marilyn's death might have been cleared up if he'd only been thorough.

"I didn't follow through as I should have," he said, and his regret was apparently real as two weeks after the autopsy he went back to the toxicology lab and asked if the missing tests could still be performed. He was told the organs had been destroyed and the case closed. Go away. The results of the 1982 "investigation": they found "no reason" to change the original findings.

So, surprise, surprise, no new evidence was found, but Dr. Noguchi did admit that it was a case in which he might've gotten it wrong.

He said, "The case is a giant jigsaw puzzle . . . with a dozen pieces missing."

In 1985, housekeeper Eunice Murray agreed to an interview with the BBC and told more of what she knew than she ever had before: "I was not supposed to know the Kennedys were a very important part of Marilyn's life, but over a period of time I was witness to what was happening."

"Was Bobby Kennedy in Marilyn's house on the day she died?" the BBC interviewer asked.

"Oh, yes. Sure. I was in the living room when he arrived. She was not dressed."

CHAPTER 6
JFKill: The Kid Who Knew Too Much

I spent the rest of 1962 and most of 1963 running errands for Mr. Costello. The plan to blackmail the Kennedys into keeping their promises hadn't worked out. The new plan would be far more direct. As Mr. Costello had told Joe Kennedy, time was running out fast on his boys.

I was nineteen now and had all the money a young man could want as I began another tour of the country, dropping off and picking up. On November 18, 1963, at a meeting in Peacock Alley, Mr. Costello gave me a plane ticket.

"I want you to go to New Orleans and talk to the Little Man," he said. That meant Carlos Marcello.

I flew to New Orleans, landed at Moisant Field, and cabbed to Mosca's Restaurant in Avondale, Louisiana, outside New Orleans. Marcello was the Boss of New Orleans (which also included all of Louisiana and much of Texas) from 1947 to 1983. Because the Black Hand—the original name for the American branch of the Sicilian Mafia—made the Louisiana Bayou one of their first outposts in the New World, Marcello liked to say that he was father of the oldest Mafia family in America. He had a point.

Marcello was born Calogero Minacore in 1910 in Tunisia, one of nine kids, to Sicilian parents. He came over on the boat when he was still an infant. He wasn't like the hoods in New York, many of whom worked the streets before they were old enough to sell newspapers. He lived and worked as a child on a run-down sugar plantation, and it wasn't until he was a teenager that he arrived in New Orleans's wild-and-wooly French Quarter and almost immediately turned to crime.

Before long he ran a gang of teens that committed armed robberies, mostly rolling the drunks of Bourbon Street. Try the absinthe, go home without your wallet. It's all part of the adventure.

The Marcello empire expanded into drugs, and Carlos did ten months of a longer sentence, then cashed in a chip. Louisiana governor Huey Long waved his hand and Marcello was released. You got to have friends.

Around then, Marcello went into the gambling business with Frank Costello, a relationship that continued for the rest of their lives. By the early 1950s, Marcello was a big enough gangster to testify before the Kefauver Committee, pleading the Fifth again and again for the better part of a long afternoon.

By the 1960s, Marcello was one of the mobsters that Bobby Kennedy was, to coin a famous phrase, "eating for breakfast." In April 1961, right around the time of the Bay of Pigs Invasion, Marcello was arrested.

Bobby was a real jerk. Marcello asked Bobby not to arrest him in front of his family, but he was arrested in front of his family. He asked Bobby that his grandkids wouldn't have to see him handcuffed, so Bobby ordered that the cuffs be put on in front of the kids.

Marcello said to Bobby, "You know you are a dead man."

"Are you threatening me?" Bobby said in his Bugs Bunny voice. "Are you threatening a sitting attorney general?"

"No, I'm not threatening you. I'm telling you. I'm gonna kill you."

Marcello was deported by the attorney general's office, put on a plane without an opportunity to pack, not so much as a toothbrush, and dumped unceremoniously beside an air strip in the middle of the Guatemalan jungle.

The Justice Department got away with that because at Marcello's deportation trial it came out that he'd entered the U.S. illegally via Guatemala, so back to Guatemala he went.

That, to put it in a nutshell, was the kind of sadistic guy Bobby was. Marcello spent a couple of days in the jungle, searching for someone to assist him. To add to his agony, he fell and broke a rib.

It took Marcello four months but he managed to get back into the U.S., hitching a ride with CIA pilot David Ferrie back to the States. (If you saw the Oliver Stone movie *JFK*, the character of Ferrie was played by Joe Pesci.)

Anyway, as you might imagine, by the time Marcello got back to Louisiana, now an outlaw, he plotted to take care of his problems the old-fashioned way, with bullets. He immediately began to scheme against his archenemy, the president's brother, the attorney general. The plot was not to take out Bobby, but the president.

"Kill the head and the arm dies, too," Marcello said.

His other famous quote was, "Take the stone from my shoe," which has long been considered a reference to what was about to happen in Dallas.

Of course, I knew none of this.

When I arrived at Mosca's Restaurant in 1963 to meet with Marcello, the joint was empty. He was in the back and had his own private men's room back there. I had to go and I had to wait because there was someone in there. In a minute or two the guy came out, a skinny fellow, and we bumped into each other as I tried to get in. I would realize later that the skinny man coming out of Carlos Marcello's private restroom was Lee Harvey Oswald.

I ate a meal with Marcello. He touched his right earlobe with his forefinger. It was my cue to lean in because what he was about to say was meant for me and me only.

He said, "I have a message for Frank Costello."

"I will deliver it," I said.

"Tell him, 'It's on.' "

"It's on?"

"Yes, just that. He will understand."

"It's on," I repeated one more time, and he nodded.

On Wednesday, November 20, 1963, I delivered the message to Mr. Costello.

"It's on," I said.

He nodded his understanding, then said, "You, my boy, are going on a trip."

"Where?"

"Europe. I will make arrangements. You sail Friday noon-time."

He handed me an envelope that I later found out had $30,000 in it, spending money for my time away.

I was leaving the country for an unspecified time. I didn't know right away what it was all about. I never questioned the instructions Mr. Costello gave me. I trusted him completely. I was like, where do you want me to go? You want me to go to the Moon for you? All right.

He filled out the papers for me. As he had friends with the International Longshoremen's Association, he got me papers saying I was a merchant marine. That enabled me to board the ship without showing my passport.

And so, on the morning of Friday, November 22, 1963, I boarded the SS *Independence*, an American-built passenger liner that had been shuttling people back and forth across the Atlantic since 1951.

As I arrived at North River Pier 84 at the foot of West Forty-Fourth Street, I had my luggage with me. I schlepped it on board and asked which way to the staff quarters. Mr. Costello had given me the name of a contact on the ship and when I said it, they went and got him.

The contact—who knew I was Frank Costello's boy—told me

I wouldn't be living with the crew, but rather with the passengers. He took me up to U Deck where the fancy quarters were.

Passengers on the *Independence* stayed in cabins designed by Henry Dreyfuss. There were apartments and penthouses. The shops were designed to imitate shopping on Fifth Avenue, and the public spaces featured a 125-foot window on the observation deck. The old wood bars were carved with old tattoo designs.

I was amazed at my suite. The guy and I went out on the balcony and looked out over the Hudson River on the west side of Manhattan.

"This is some boat," I said.

"Ship," he corrected, and he listed some of the famous people who'd been passengers: "Harry Truman, King Saud, Alfred Hitchcock, Walt Disney."

"Looks like you could shoot a movie," I said.

And he said they'd already thought of that. "Cary Grant made a movie on this ship."

Just then, two noisy kids came out on the balcony next to mine and they were making a racket.

"These kids next door to me?"

The guy said, "Yeah."

I said, "Ohhh, got anything quieter?"

The guy, "Well, she said you were going to be on this cruise and that you should have this suite."

"Who's *she?*"

"Princess Grace."

That was Grace Kelly. She was an old friend. I knew her because she was friends with Costello, and I was happy that she remembered me now that she'd quit Hollywood and gone royal. The two kids were hers. She only had Albert and Caroline at the time.

We shoved off right on schedule, noon on the dot, and slowly pulled out of the pier and headed south through New York Harbor. We'd been underway for a half hour, forty minutes, and we were going under the Verrazano-Narrows Bridge when a message came over the public address system:

"The president has been shot."

They didn't say he was dead at first, just that he was shot. I went on deck. The ship stopped. Pilot boats were pulling up alongside. I watched as they took a few dignitaries off.

The next morning, I found a copy of a newspaper and there was a picture of Oswald under arrest. Immediately I knew I'd seen that guy before. He was the fellow who bumped into me coming out of Carlos Marcello's private men's room in the New Orleans restaurant.

I could feel the blood draining from my head. I had to go to my room and lie down. I thought I was going to faint. I instantly made the connection between "It's on" and what had happened.

I didn't want to be a part of this. I loved Jack Kennedy. He was a beautiful guy and man, could he party. He was still going when the sun came up. It's weird seeing a guy do coke and Percodan and later he becomes President of the United States.

On the way to Europe, I ate at the captain's table every night. That was Captain Pennington. You can imagine the dining room on the night of November 22, our first night at sea. It was like a morgue. They killed the president. What's going on?

Grace was at the table. We were all in shock—me, maybe more so, because I knew I knew something important, and I was leaving the country in the hopes no one would ever find out what it was.

Grace Kelly was a smart cookie, and she had an inkling about what was up. I didn't have a good reason for going to Europe. Mr. Costello said I should, that's all I knew. Grace had been on the inside for a long time, and she knew the kind of things the boys were up to, and she had a feeling she knew who was behind the assassination.

But, being a smart cookie, she didn't say anything. And she knew that I knew the president. During the time he was a senator, Frank Sinatra spent every weekend with him, for months, grooming him, or so it seemed.

When the ship arrived in Barcelona, Spain, I was met by a guy named Vito. He was standing on the pier with a sign that read "The Kid." Vito was about fifty and shaped like a Johnny Pump.

Man, did Vito show me a good time. I remember I had my wardrobe on the ship, but once I got off, Vito said to leave all that stuff behind. Instead, he gave me $10,000 to buy a wardrobe for the strip.

Everything was new, expensive, and luxurious. Nobody knew who I was or why I was there, and they were smart enough not to ask. To keep it that way, Vito made sure we never stayed in one place for long, and he made sure that I never wandered off without him. He wanted to be able to eyeball me at any moment.

I realized why I had to be sent abroad for my safety. Mr. Costello was worried that the FBI had Marcello under surveillance and would know who he met with during the days before the association.

I was on the lam and laying low, but I hardly thought about it. I concentrated on the great food and great women. I saw a lot of Italy. I visited Palermo, Sicily, where my people came from. While in Palermo, I stayed in a suite at the Villa Igiea and met the local godfather. It was twenty-two months before I returned to America, September 1965, but it was a great twenty-two months.

Upon my return, Mr. Costello put me back to work as if nothing had happened. The subject of why I'd had to be away for twenty-two months did not come up. My first job, after returning Stateside, was to deliver an envelope to Meyer Lansky, who was in Miami.

While down there I stayed at the Fontainebleau on Collins Avenue. I registered as Dr. Jay Adams, Jewish physician, and found that maintaining my cover was more complicated than I'd thought. I had to treat a patient at one point—I got lucky and the illness, a stomachache, was not serious. Then I had to wiggle out of a most enjoyable relationship with a Jewish woman.

In 1963, Marcello was arrested and charged with immigration fraud. On the day Kennedy was killed in Dallas, Marcello was acquitted. And thus allowed to stay in the country. But by that time the FBI had their sights on him.

During the lead-up to the assassination, Marcello was in frequent contact with CIA pilot David Ferrie, the odd hairless man who flew Marcello back to America—and who, it turned out, taught Oswald as a teen with the Civil Air Patrol. Marcello and Ferrie were together on Marcello's six-thousand-acre estate, known as Churchill Farms, on the two weekends before the assassination.

Taking out JFK did not stop the federal harassment as Marcello had hoped. In 1966, he snapped and smacked an FBI agent. Cost him six months. By 1980, the feds claimed to have 1,350 recordings of Marcello's conversations, acquired through court-ordered electronic surveillance.

According to G. Robert Blakey of the House Select Committee on Assassinations (HSCA), Marcello implicated himself in the JFK assassination three times on tape. Those recordings remain sealed by court order, so we don't know precisely what he said.

In 1982, Marcello was convicted of labor racketeering and attempting to bribe a federal judge. He went to prison but was released in 1989 when an appeals court threw out his conviction.

One HSCA witness was a Las Vegas private investigator named Ed Becker, who said that Marcello told him about a plan to assassinate JFK that included using "a nut" to deflect blame from the Mob.

Marcello himself testified before the HSCA. He admitted to

hating Bobby Kennedy's guts and vividly described his adventure in the Guatemalan jungle, but denied knowing anything about the assassination.

FBI special agent Joseph Hauser went undercover in 1979 to investigate Marcello's crime organization. According to Hauser, Marcello admitted to knowing Oswald and Oswald's uncle, Charles "Dutz" Murret (his mom's brother), and that Oswald worked for him in 1963 as a runner for his betting operation. (Which could have been why I ran into him coming out of Marcello's private men's room.)

An independent FBI report quoted an informant as saying Oswald received money from a Marcello capo named Joe Peretto in a New Orleans restaurant called Town and Country, which was managed by the Boss's brother, Anthony Marcello.

In 1980, Agent Hauser talked to Joseph Marcello about the way the Kennedys hassled the Marcellos, and Joseph reportedly said, "Don't worry, we took care of them, didn't we?"

An FBI teletype dated March 3, 1989, says Marcello, then a prisoner in Minneapolis for conspiracy to bribe a judge, mistook his prison guards for his own personal bodyguards and recalled being driven from New York City after a meeting with Tony Provenzano, a Genovese capo and Teamster exec, a meeting during which they discussed "getting Kennedy in Dallas."

The evidence was enough that the HSCA concluded Marcello had the "motive, means, and opportunity to have President John F. Kennedy killed."

The committee noted that, unlike any other suspect in the assassination, Marcello could be easily linked both to Lee Harvey Oswald and Jack Ruby, the alleged assassin and his killer. Oswald's uncle Dutz Murret worked for Marcello. Oswald's mother had dated several men who worked for Marcello. Ruby also had several business associates who were Marcello men, a necessity as Ruby ran a strip joint on Marcello's turf.

JFK had many enemies and some of them had already

worked together, so combining forces was easily done. My friend Johnny Roselli admitted to being a liaison between the Mob and the CIA in efforts to take out Castro. Because of the Bay of Pigs Invasion, we know that Cuban exiles were working with the CIA to topple Castro.

Another guy involved was John Martino, a kid from Jersey who started out as a numbers runner and worked his way up to casino manager in Havana working under Santos Trafficante. Martino was arrested by Castro and did three years in a Cuban cell. When he returned to Miami he worked with CIA guys on anti-Castro schemes. He admitted to knowing in advance that JFK was to be hit in Dallas, and verified that Jack Ruby was part of that world, too, as if anyone ever had any doubts.

Ruby, Martino said, helped smuggle casino profits from Cuba to the U.S. Ruby smuggled guns into Cuba by boat. While running the Carousel Club, he procured women for Dallas oil magnates. How the Warren Commission ever sold Ruby as a "lone nut" is beyond me. Take a look at Ruby's phone records, info the commission tried to bury in its twenty-six volumes of evidence: October 30, 1963, Ruby called a Marcello capo named Nofio Pecora. On November 7, two weeks before the assassination, he received a seventeen-minute collect call from Robert "Barney" Baker, who was muscle for Jimmy Hoffa.

When Johnny Roselli was whacked (and we'll get to that), Trafficante said, "Now only two people are alive who know who killed Kennedy—and they ain't talking."

On his deathbed, Trafficante called Dallas a mistake. "Carlos [Marcello] fucked up. We should not have killed Giovanni. We should have killed Bobby." He must have meant, killed Bobby first.

For those of you unfamiliar with the events of that weekend in Dallas, Texas, November 22–24, 1963, here's a quick rundown:

President Kennedy and his glamorous wife Jackie joined Texas governor John Connally and his wife, Nellie, in an open limo for a motorcade that meandered through Dallas from Love Field, where Air Force One had landed, to a convention site where JFK was to give a speech. The vice president, Texan Lyndon Baines Johnson, rode in a car back in the motorcade and started to duck even before the first shot.

The careful research of author Vince Palamara regarding the Secret Service during the Kennedy Administration has demonstrated—proven, in fact—that JFK was uniquely insecure when he was shot. The Secret Service, normally right up on the bumper of the president's vehicle during motorcades, dropped back before the shooting sequence. Weirdly, one Secret Service agent was left behind at the airport, his hands in the air saying "Hey, wait for me." A lot of the crew was pretty hungover. JFK's security was *most lax when most needed.*

As the president's limo passed at snail speed through Dealey Plaza, there was gunfire. A shot struck JFK in the throat, another struck his back, and a third shot was a direct hit to the upper right forehead, taking off much of the right side of Jack's skull, and blowing a large hole in the back of his head. Presidential brains sprayed over the back of the limo, into the windshields of the following motorcycle cops, and onto Elm Street. A large chunk of his skull was later found in the street by a small boy named Harper. Governor Connally was also wounded with a through-and-through wound in his back, chest, and wrist. That bullet came to rest in his thigh.

The official version of facts was that Lee Harvey Oswald was the lone gunman and fired three shots with a cheap mail-ordered Mannlicher-Carcano rifle from the sixth floor of the Texas School Book Depository Building, which was above and behind the president during the shooting sequence.

An eight-millimeter film of the assassination made by tailor Abraham Zapruder shows the entire assassination sequence from in front of the legendary grassy knoll. The film shows Jack's head slamming backward when hit with the fatal shot, unlikely if that bullet had come from above and behind.

The film also offers the timing of the shots, that there were only six seconds between the first and last, time for a lone nut with a faulty rifle to fire only three times. There was a lot of damage for three shots.

Plus, there was solid evidence that at least one shot missed everything and slightly wounded a spectator on the far side of the plaza. That left two shots: one the fatal shot to Jack's head, and the third—the "magic" bullet—which must've caused all the other wounds to JFK's back and throat, and Connally's back, chest, wrist, and thigh.

That magic bullet, so the story went, was found in Parkland Hospital, practically pristine, yet X-rays showed chunks of metal still in Connally's wrist. (This mathematically disproves the lone-nut theory, as we now have three-plus bullets, thus a second shooter.)

The doctors at Parkland Hospital, where the dead president was brought, told the truth, had no reason to lie, and explained to the world that JFK had been shot from the front. But the lone nut was behind him, so JFK's body was snatched from Dallas police by the Secret Service and flown to Bethesda, Maryland, where it was given a fishy military autopsy, during which, surprise, his wounds moved so that he appeared to have been shot from behind.

In the meantime, the patsy Oswald, who may or may not have been in on the plot, fled like a rabbit. At the very least Oswald knew he was in deep trouble when JFK was whacked out in front of the building where he worked. According to the official version of events, Oswald went home, got a handgun, had a confrontation with a Dallas cop, J. D. Tippit, shot the cop dead, fled into a movie theater, and was arrested in that theater, the Texas Theater, which was showing an Audie Murphy war picture. These were not the actions of an innocent man.

Oswald was questioned for two days and never admitted to anything. On Sunday morning, as Oswald was being transferred from the city jail to the county jail he, like the president before him, found himself uniquely insecure at the moment of greatest danger, as he was paraded before America, blindingly lit by TV lights.

Jack Ruby, a Jewish Chicago hood sent by Tony Accardo to Dallas to straighten out the nightclub and girls business, walked right into the police station basement where the transfer was taking place, put his .38 police special in Oswald's belly, and shot him to death on live TV.

Those of you who are old enough vividly remember that weekend. It cast a dark cloud over America. Many Catholics were in Mass when it happened. Priests sent their flock home. "Pray this isn't World War III," they said. Only 9/11 in the many years since can match November 22, 1963 as a day of American fear and grief.

Dallas was the perfect city in which to whack Jack. They hated him there. (Kids in Dallas schools cheered when they heard the president had been shot.) Dallas was where Big Oil was, sick of paying Kennedy taxes.

The local cops, some of them in the KKK, hated Kennedy's progressive attitudes toward civil rights. Some Dallas cops were also in the anti-Communist John Birch Society and would be sure to look the other way if anything came off hinky.

The FBI wouldn't be interested in figuring out who did it. J. Edgar Hoover hated the Kennedys more than anyone. He was sick of taking orders from that beer-drinking frat boy, the president's brother. Besides, Hoover had only recently and begrudgingly admitted that the Mafia existed. The FBI wasn't going to figure out what really happened in Dallas.

The setting-up of the patsy was a key part of the plan. Oswald had been a screwy kid with a screwy mom, a truant, a U.S. Marine, defected to Russia (then the Communist Soviet Union) promising to divulge info regarding U.S. supersonic aircraft technology (which he may have actually known because of his top-secret Marine duties in Japan), and while in Minsk married the daughter of a Russian intelligence officer. After getting through the red tape, he and wife Marina crossed the Iron Curtain and returned to America to live in Louisiana and Texas as an impoverished young couple with a growing family. Since returning Stateside, the Oswalds had received several visits from an FBI agent, keeping tabs on them.

The spookiness continued. Some think the man who came back from the USSR wasn't the same as the one who went, but a Russian sleeper spy, an Oswald look-alike. A man impersonating Oswald went to Mexico City and tried to get permission to enter Cuba, where the Soviet-backed Fidel Castro was in charge. This was a clear attempt to make the assassination appear to be a Communist conspiracy. Back in Texas, the real Oswald got a job, thanks to a friend of his wife, a woman with her own spy ties, in a building on Dealey Plaza overlooking the future presidential motorcade route.

Bottom line: Oswald had a very shadowy CV. He was not only an excellent patsy for a lone-nut scenario, but, depending on which way the wind blew, he could be sold as part of a Communist conspiracy as well. (As we saw in the Marilyn case, Communist conspiracies were still big.)

When Oswald died in custody, many of the investigating bodies responded first by covering their own asses. Even the KGB, the Russian intelligence agency, wanted to distance themselves from Oswald, a man who'd told them he knew U.S. military secrets he'd learned while a marine.

That black cloud caused by the assassination lingered, largely because what happened that day in Dealey Plaza was a poor match for the official version of events. Every cop, every fed, every Secret Service guy on the scene knew it was a cross fire. Yet they sold the lone-nut theory to much of the world.

The new president, LBJ, said he wanted to squelch all this nonsense that there was some sort of plot to kill Kennedy. He appointed a panel of distinguished Americans, some of whom really disliked the president, to "investigate" the assassination. This was the Warren Commission, named after Supreme Court Chief Justice Earl Warren. The commission produced *The War-*

ren Report, which said Oswald was a lone nut who killed JFK and Tippit, and wounded Connally, and Ruby was another lone nut who, in turn, killed Oswald.

The Warren Commission did a magnificent job of covering up, but nonetheless left many loose threads. Conspiracy theories sprouted like weeds. Some said the CIA killed JFK. Others thought it was the Mob. With Johnny Roselli, theorists realized the two theories did not need to be mutually exclusive. In Johnny Roselli, the two groups found common ground.

I mention this because the day would come when Roselli would admit to me that he was the rifleman who shot JFK in the forehead.

"I shot from a storm drain," he said. He had the best shot because for several seconds the motorcade was coming directly toward him, and because he was atop the knoll he was above the car and could put his crosshairs on JFK's forehead without worrying about hitting the Secret Service agents in the front seat of the car or the wives of the politicians sitting next to their men.

A look at the infrastructure of Dealey Plaza confirms the accuracy of the story. In 1963, at either end of the triple overpass, which was straight ahead of the motorcade during the shooting sequence, there were storm drain openings large enough for a man to crawl inside. The opening on the south side of the bridge has since been paved over, but the one on the north end is still there—and this is the one Roselli was in. From this spot, he could have sighted the president through the balustrade. The deed done, he ducked back into his hole, pulled the grate closed, and disappeared through a tunnel. The Texas-sized drainage tunnel Roselli ducked into was later explored by an assassination researcher (Jack Brazil) and found to come out near the Trinity River, a fifty-four minute crawl away.

Further evidence that the fatal shot came from the spot

where Roselli claimed to be was the crowd's reaction after the shots. Many ran precisely to that spot to see what happened up there on the bridge. The smell of gunpowder was in the air, puffs of smoke had been seen by spectators, but there were no signs of a shooter.

After Jack Kennedy was whacked, there was much talk about potential witnesses to a conspiracy dying in unusual ways. I suppose a lot of it is true. Some of those accidents were really accidents—but not all of them.

CIA agent John Garrett "Gary" Underhill told a friend after the assassination, "They tried it in Cuba and they couldn't get away with it. Right after the Bay of Pigs. But Kennedy wouldn't let them do it. I know who they are. That's the problem. I can't stay in New York." On May 8, 1964, Underhill was found shot dead, a bullet wound behind his left ear. The case was declared a suicide, despite the fact that Underhill was right-handed.

Only hours after Jack Ruby whacked Oswald, three journalists searched his apartment. They were Bill Hunter of the *Long Beach Press*, Jim Koethe of the *Dallas Times Herald*, and attorney Tom Howard. We don't know what they found, but soon thereafter Hunter was shot dead by a policeman in the pressroom at the Long Beach, California, police station. The cop said it was an accident. Koethe announced that he planned on writing a book about the assassination, but he never had a chance because on September 21, 1964 he was killed when a man broke into his apartment and broke his neck. Tom Howard died of a heart attack in March 1965.

Guy Bannister (played by Ed Asner in the movie *JFK*), and CIA pilot David Ferrie were a key part of setting up Oswald as the patsy. When New Orleans district attorney Jim Garrison started digging into Oswald's Louisiana connections, both Bannister and Ferrie were dead before they could be brought into court.

Roger Craig was a cop on duty in Dealey Plaza at the time of the assassination, and said he saw things that didn't match the "official version" of what happened. Immediately following the shots, he ran directly to the storm drain that Roselli had already ducked back into. Craig then turned and headed back toward the Texas School Book Depository building, where he saw Oswald run down to the street and get into a Nash Rambler station wagon that resembled the car driven by a Mrs. Ruth Paine, with whom Oswald's Russian wife Marina was living at the time. Craig survived until 1967 and managed to testify in New Orleans as to what he saw but was shot to death soon thereafter while walking across a parking lot.

It didn't end in the 1960s. When the HSCA held hearings in 1976, scheduled witnesses began dropping like flies—including, as we'll see, Johnny Roselli, who knew more than anyone. George de Mohrenschildt, Oswald's friend and mentor, "shot himself" with a shotgun on the eve of his testimony.

Point is, those who saw things they shouldn't and knew too much—like me—were being eliminated. Mr. Costello sent me to Europe so I would survive the purge.

One famous witness who knew too much was my friend, the famous newspaper columnist Dorothy Kilgallen, who we discussed earlier because she was a friend of Marilyn's and didn't believe the official story of Marilyn's death.

Kilgallen had a column in the morning paper talking about the entertainment world, and was one of the most famous women in the country because she was the smartest celebrity panelist on the very smart game show *What's My Line?* Presented live, the show came on at ten thirty in New York on Sunday nights. Watching *WML?* was how America ended their weekends.

Killgallen had been famous for years by the time she excelled at the quiz-show game. As a young fresh-faced lass, she'd become America's first hard-nosed "girl reporter." She was born in Chicago in 1913, daughter of a reporter. At age nineteen she covered FDR's first presidential campaign. Three years later, she covered the murder trial of Richard Haupt-mann, who kidnapped and killed the small son of aviation hero Charles Lindbergh. At age twenty-three, she became the first woman (as a passenger) to fly around the world in an air-plane. She was only the second woman ever to circumnavigate the world using any mode of transportation, with Nellie Bly being first. Kilgallen finished the trip globally famous, wrote a bestselling book about her experiences (*Girl Around the World*). Her career skyrocketed. Ernest Hemingway called her the world's greatest woman writer. She got the "Voice of Broadway" column in the New York *Journal-American,* and hosted a daily morning chitchat show on New York radio. She was the basis for the smart-alecky female reporter in hundreds of Hollywood movies, the basis for Superman's raven-haired girlfriend Lois Lane. She wrote one of the first-ever true-crime books based on her reporting of several high-profile murder cases.

I first met her because Marc Sinclaire, my old boss at the Lilly Dache Beauty Salon, did her hair, and I used to see her all the time at the Copa. She often sat with Earl Wilson. We sat and had many conversations. She had a reputation for not pulling punches and some of the things she said about Frank Sinatra pissed him off. Frank could get nasty when he was sulk-ing. Once Kilgallen slammed him for something—punching photographers, Mob friends, whatever—and he got mad.

Another time, on stage in Vegas, between songs, drink in hand, Frank lit a cigarette and then said into his mic, "If you run into Dorothy Kilgallen . . . I hope you're in your car."

Kilgallen got herself in real trouble a year and a half after Marilyn's murder when she decided to investigate JFK's death. As her game-show fans knew, she loved solving puzzles, and the JFK assassination was a big one.

She wrote in her column that America deserved the truth, and the conclusion of the Warren Commission, that both Lee Harvey Oswald and Jack Ruby were lone nuts, was "laughable."

She wrote that the famous backyard photo, showing Oswald

holding a rifle, a handgun, and a fistful of Commie propaganda, was an obvious fake.

"This story isn't going to die as long as there's a real reporter alive," Kilgallen wrote.

She'd been working hard on the assassination as a crime story. She'd been to New Orleans, asking about Marcello, and was planning to return. She'd gone to Miami where Mob guys and anti-Castro Cubans worked together.

She acquired a tape of police radio activity at the time of the assassination and heard Dallas police chief Jesse Curry, who was in the motorcade, say, "Get a man on top of that overpass and see what happened up there." That, as you now know, was where Johnny Roselli was, shooting through the bridge's balustrade and ducking down into his hole. Kilgallen didn't know about Roselli, but her journalistic instinct began to tingle when, during interviews, Curry said that, during the shooting sequence, he was certain the shots came from the Texas School Book Depository (TSBD) building, where Oswald was. Why had he changed his tune?

She noticed other weirdnesses. A Dallas policeman, Seymour Weitzman, said the rifle he found on the sixth floor of the TSBD was a 7.65 Mauser. By the next day, all agreed that the rifle was a Mannlicher-Carcano, identical to one Oswald allegedly mail-ordered under a fake name.

She had contacts in such high places that she received a 102-page transcription of Jack Ruby's testimony for the Warren Commission, and put Ruby quotes in her column, before a copy of that testimony showed up on LBJ's desk. Those columns didn't launch a new investigation into the assassination, but they did launch an investigation into Kilgallen and her friends. Suddenly, Kilgallen and her inner circle had their phones tapped. They taped Kilgallen telling a friend that she "would die" before revealing her source.

Because she knew Barney Ross, the former boxing champion who was Jack Ruby's best friend growing up, and because

Ruby watched *What's My Line?*, she had the inside track on get-ting an audience with the defendant. In fact, the first time she appeared in the Dallas courtroom, Ruby was completely starstruck and asked his lawyer Joe Tonahill if she'd speak with him. So, there in the courtroom, Ruby told Kilgallen that he hoped to be acquitted because he felt he had a lot to con-tribute to society.

"I want to do something to help people," he said.

Others were nearby and listened in.

But Kilgallen was not happy with this public audience. She got exclusive permission from Judge Joe Brown to interview Ruby in his Dallas jail cell one-on-one, during a lunch recess. The interview lasted about ten minutes and during that time Kilgallen and Ruby sat face-to-face in serious conversation.

We don't know what was said during that interview, but Kil-gallen came out bragging that she was going to "blow the lid" off the JFK assassination case. She told her friend and hair-dresser Marc Sinclaire that she wanted to tell him what she was working on, but it was dangerous stuff and she didn't want to put him at risk.

She was found dead on the morning of November 8, 1965, in her East Sixty-Eighth Street town house, of "a combination of alcohol and barbiturates," naked but for a bathrobe, false eyelashes, and a floral hair accessory. She was in a bed in the guest room of her apartment, a place where she never slept.

One of the first to find her lifeless body was Marc Sinclaire, the same guy who years earlier had picked me to be a "sham-poo boy." He told police that Kilgallen was sitting up in bed and he could tell she was dead immediately. He'd seen her the morning before, and knew that she removed her makeup and dressed in comfy clothes for sleeping.

Now, in death, she had full makeup on, false eyelashes, not a hair out of place. There was a book lying on top of the bed, open but upside down from Kilgallen's vantage point. Sin-claire knew it to be a book she'd finished reading weeks be-fore, because she'd discussed it with him.

Though it was cold in the apartment, the air-conditioning was on. The body was in the precise center of the bed, and though there was a glass on the night table, Kilgallen would not have been able to reach it from where she lay.

Kilgallen's toxicology report indicated a deadly cocktail of barbiturates in her brain: secobarbital, amobarbital, and pentobarbital (Nembutal).

Police may or may not have investigated but announced that no evidence was found of violence or suicide. It was an accident, they said. She reportedly gave a copy of her Ruby notes to her good friend Margaret Smith, but Smith died two days after Kilgallen and those notes have never surfaced. (Looking back on it, it is significant that Dorothy and Marilyn Monroe died in very similar ways. Both in bed, both OD'd, both with Nembutal in their systems.)

The best witnesses, for what they were worth, were Evelyn and James Clement, Kilgallen's maid and butler, who heard her come in early Monday morning with a male guest, not unheard of apparently even though she was married. Later, the servants heard a door shut and assumed this was the guest leaving. Who he was, they had no idea.

Kilgallen's death was definitely murder. When she died, she was about to print her theory that the Mob had something to do with JFK's death, and that Marcello had taken part in the orchestration of the scheme—both things I knew to be true, which meant others did, too.

But it'll never be a "historical fact." The CIA is never going to admit that they teamed up with the American Mafia and executed a coup d'état that brought a new administration into the White House, ended (temporarily anyway) an anti-Mob campaign by the feds, and started up a munitions-consumptive war in Vietnam that made a handful of defense contractors really rich.

Yeah, I'm going to write about it. Why not? I liked Jack Kennedy. Why should his hit be a secret?

Now Dorothy Kilgallen was dead, murdered—a murder to

shut her up, a murder made to look like suicide—so much like Marilyn's murder three years earlier that it sent a shiver up your spine.

When Ruby's lawyer, the flamboyant Melvin Belli, heard that Kilgallen was dead, he said, "They've killed Dorothy: now they'll go after Ruby." Thirteen months later, Ruby was dead in his cell of a wildly galloping cancer.

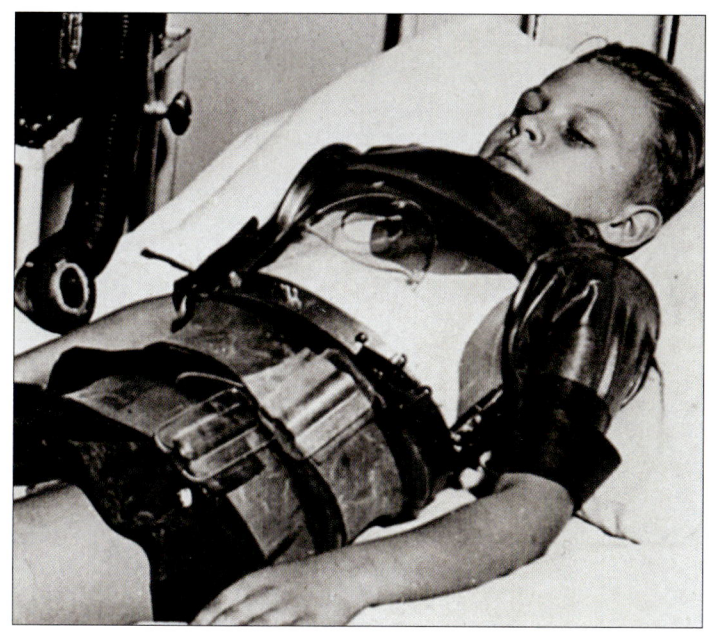

When I was a kid,
this was my world.
Author's collection.

When I looked out my Bellevue window
I could see the Empire State Building,
a sure sign that there were things out there
in New York bigger and more fantastic
than anything I'd known.
Author photo.

From the time I was seven until I was twelve,
I lived here, in Bellevue Hospital,
in pediatric quarantine.
Author's collection.

That's me, Gianni Russo, movie star.
Author's collection.

According to legend, Roselli met Al Capone when both were among the 104,943 people who attended the Jack Dempsey–Gene Tunney rematch on September 22, 1927 at Soldier Field in Chicago, the famous "Long Count" fight in which Tunney got up off the canvas to win by unanimous decision.

Capone was impressed with Roselli's combo of intelligence and ice-cold blood. Capone assigned Roselli to be his L.A. watchdog, and to be a liaison between the two cities. During this period, Roselli moved in on the offshore gambling ship *Monfalcone*. Like any good pirate, Roselli proclaimed himself the captain now, and put the Mob firmly in control of the floating casino.

The Boss in L.A. was Joseph Ardizzone when Roselli first got out there. But Ardizzone survived two hit attempts and was advised to retire in 1931, at which time he disappeared for good. The new boss was Jack Dragna. Roselli was valuable to Dragna at first, because he knew both the hoods on the street and the corrupt mayor's office where palms were efficiently greased.

Roselli was part of a union holdup of the movie industry and paid a price, indicted for racketeering in 1943, charged with extorting $2.5 million from Loew's Inc. (MGM), Paramount, Twentieth Century-Fox, Warner Bros., and the International Alliance of Theatrical Stage Employees.

The deal was, the Hollywood moguls had to pay up or the projectionists, whose union the gangsters had taken over, would strike. The indictments included the guy who'd taken over the Outfit when Capone went to jail, Frank Nitti—and coincided with Nitti's suicide.

Roselli's reaction to his own indictment was less dire. He had been drafted into the Army, and was stationed at Camp Cooke, California. He'd made it through basic and was training with a tank battalion when informed of his indictment. He flew across the country to answer the charges in a New York court. While he waited, he lived in luxury uncommon for a soldier in the Waldorf Astoria.

CHAPTER 7
Sirhan Sirhan and Handsome Johnny

My friend "Handsome Johnny" Roselli (sometimes spelled Rosselli; he wasn't particular) was born Filippo Sacco on July 4, 1905, in Esperia, Lazio. He came over on the boat and settled with his family in Boston. We should take his Fourth of July birthday with a grain of salt. Sometimes immigrants took the Fourth of July as their birthdate to ease their assimilation into American society—and little Filippo was traveling with his mother.

"You see? My boy is a Yankee Doodle Dandy!"

He lost his father to the 1918 Spanish flu epidemic. He was thirteen. After that he started getting into trouble. Busted for dope in 1922, he fled to New York, laid low for a while, and moved to Chicago, where he changed his name to Roselli.

Like most hoods during Prohibition, Roselli was a bootlegger, drove a truck—but he was smart and soon moved to L.A. where he was a smuggler, shining lanterns at offshore liquor barges.

Through Roselli's charm and influence, his smuggling evolved from sneaky to brazen. Everyone with an interest in stopping him was in Roselli's pocket. When Prohibition ended, Roselli stayed in L.A. and shifted his efforts to girls (that is, prostitution) and gambling.

Frank Costello, the Ambassador, the man who saved me.
Author's collection.

Ex-boxer and future Genovese boss Vincent Gigante indirectly changed the course of my life when he shot Frank Costello in the head but missed his brain.

Frank Costello on the night he was shot. You can see the blood on the shoulder of his coat. Only days later he told me I worked for him now.
Author's collection.

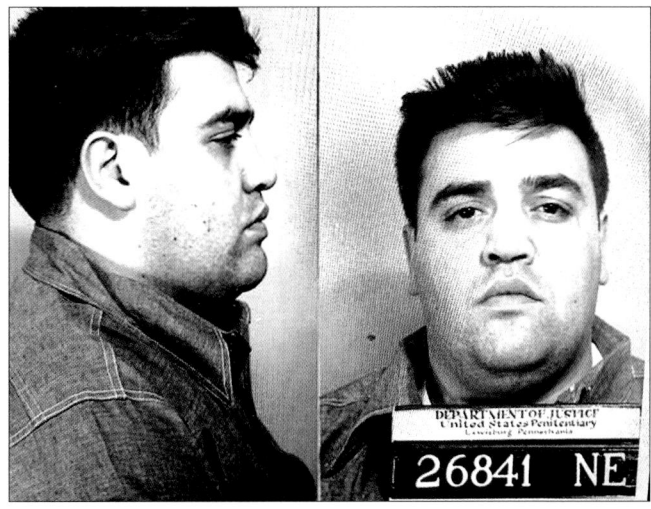
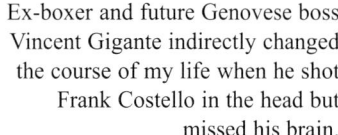

DEPARTMENT OF JUSTICE
United States Penitentiary
Lewisburg, Pennsylvania

26841 NE

Marilyn Monroe.
Author's collection.

So that I would avoid the truant officer, Mr. Costello enrolled me at the Wilfred Academy Beauty School on Seventh Avenue between Fifty-Third and Fifty-Fourth Streets. Through that gig I met some of the world's most beautiful women, including Marilyn Monroe.
Author's collection.

I first met Jack Kennedy when he was a senator and partying hearty with the Rat Pack in Las Vegas.
Author's collection.

Marilyn Monroe lip print, May 1962.
Author's collection.

Frank Sinatra as he looked when we met. Those were different times. Note the coonskin cap sitting on the piano.
Author's collection.

The wild crown princes of showbiz, the Rat Pack. Left to right: Frank Sinatra, Dean Martin, Sammy Davis, Jr., Peter Lawford, Joey Bishop.
Author's collection.

Frank and me.
Author's collection.

Sinatra and the boys worked tirelessly to get JFK elected, but once Jack was in the White House, he forgot who his friends were—a fatal mistake.
Author's collection.

JFK used Mob help and the Rat Pack to get elected, all with the understanding that once in office he'd kick Fidel Castro (pictured here) out of Cuba and return the luxurious Havana casinos to the gangsters.
Author's collection.

Mr. Costello planned on controlling the Kennedys through blackmail. In the long run, bullets did the trick for Bobby (left) and Jack (right). Only Teddy in the middle lived to be old. · *Author's collection.*

Marilyn buys hot dogs in Central Park.
Author's collection.

Marilyn is high. Frank is sad. That was the way it was at the end. She was off, and you could feel the tragedy unfolding.
Author's collection.

The married President of the United States sharing an intimate moment with the world's biggest movie star. Threats to expose their relationship placed Marilyn in extreme danger.
Author's collection.

That's me and Marilyn on that fateful weekend at Cal-Neva.
Author's collection.

My friend Johnny Roselli.
He told me what really
went down in Dealey Plaza
on November 22, 1963.
Author's collection.

Front row at one of my singing
performances in Chicago.
That's Nick and Yolanda Nitti on the left,
Clarice and Tony Accardo on the right.
Author photo.

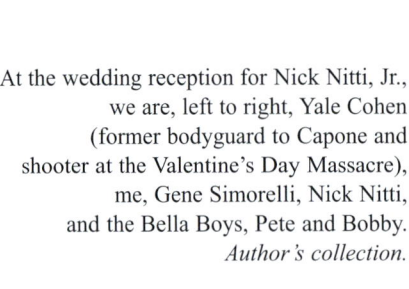

That's me on the far left, our private pilot
Captain Ferrara in the middle, and Nick Nitti
on the far right, with his kids Sandra and Ricky.
We're throwing coins into a fountain.
Author's collection.

At the wedding reception for Nick Nitti, Jr.,
we are, left to right, Yale Cohen
(former bodyguard to Capone and
shooter at the Valentine's Day Massacre),
me, Gene Simorelli, Nick Nitti,
and the Bella Boys, Pete and Bobby.
Author's collection.

I know for a fact that Oswald didn't act alone, as implied by this composite photo that purports to show him carrying two murder weapons and Communist propaganda. *Warren Commission, Exhibit 133-A.*

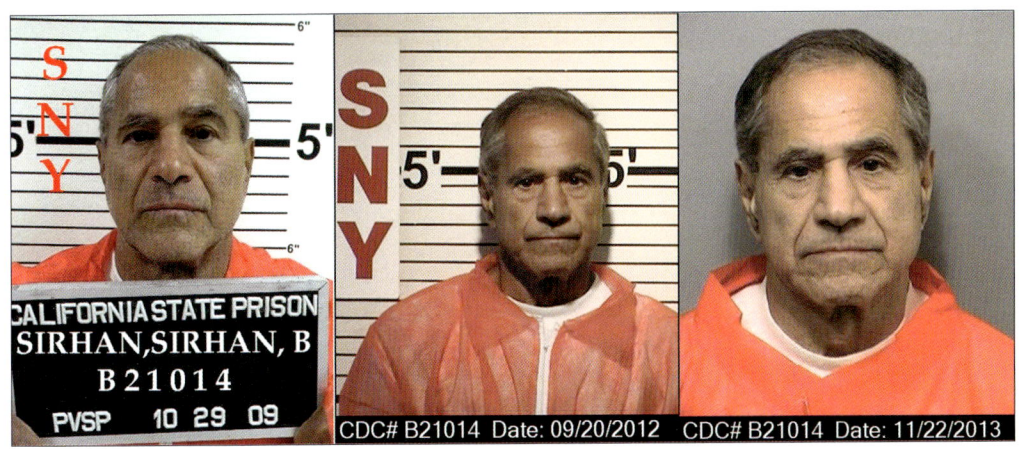

I also know for a fact that Sirhan didn't act alone.
He was hypnotized, brainwashed, and still doesn't remember shooting at Bobby Kennedy.
Author's collection.

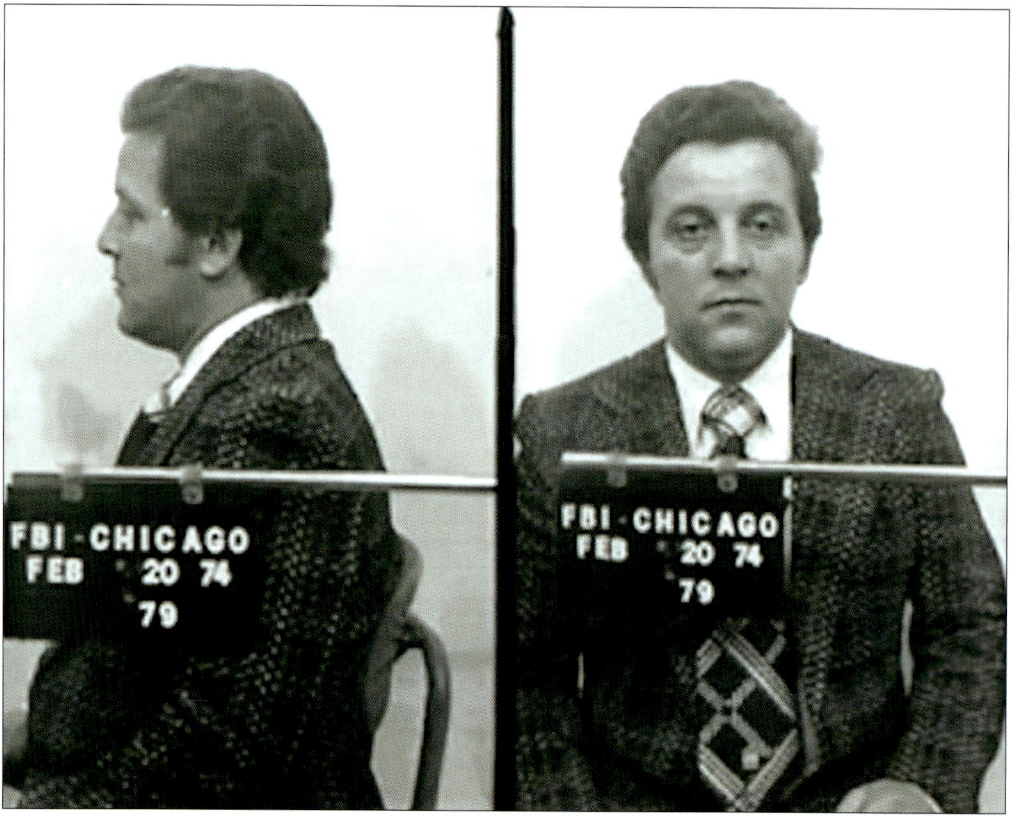

Tony "The Ant" Spilotro
was assigned to protect
the Outfit's casino skim
but had no control of himself.
I had the misfortune of seeing
his demise.
Author's collection.

Tony Spilotro's Nevada
Black Book entry,
which barred him from
casinos across the state.
Author's collection.

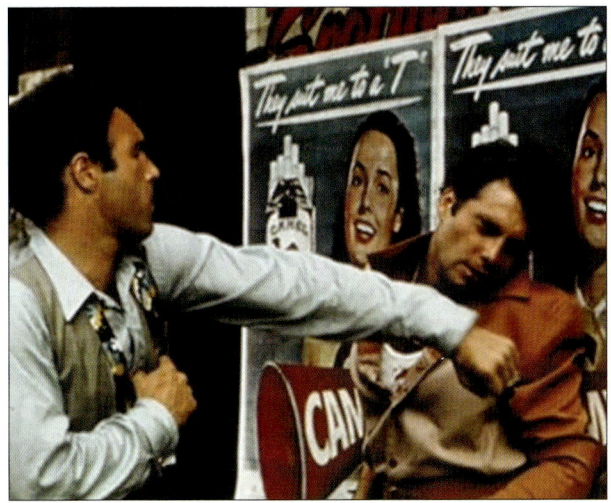

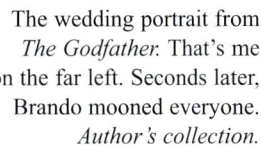

A still from *The Godfather* as Jimmy Caan beats me up. It looked real because it was. He broke a few of my bones. *Author's collection.*

The wedding portrait from *The Godfather.* That's me on the far left. Seconds later, Brando mooned everyone. *Author's collection.*

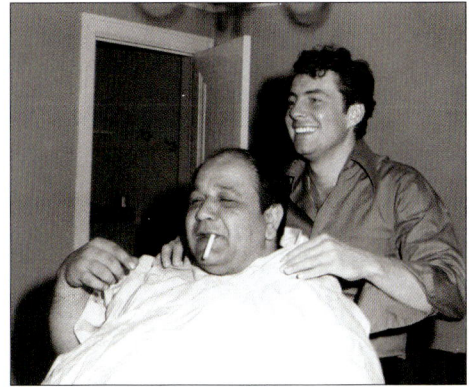

A lighter moment on *The Godfather* set, me giving Richard Castellano (Clemenza) a trim. In the movie it was the other way around. *Author's collection.*

Al Pacino and me on the twenty-fifth anniversary of *The Godfather.* *Author's collection.*

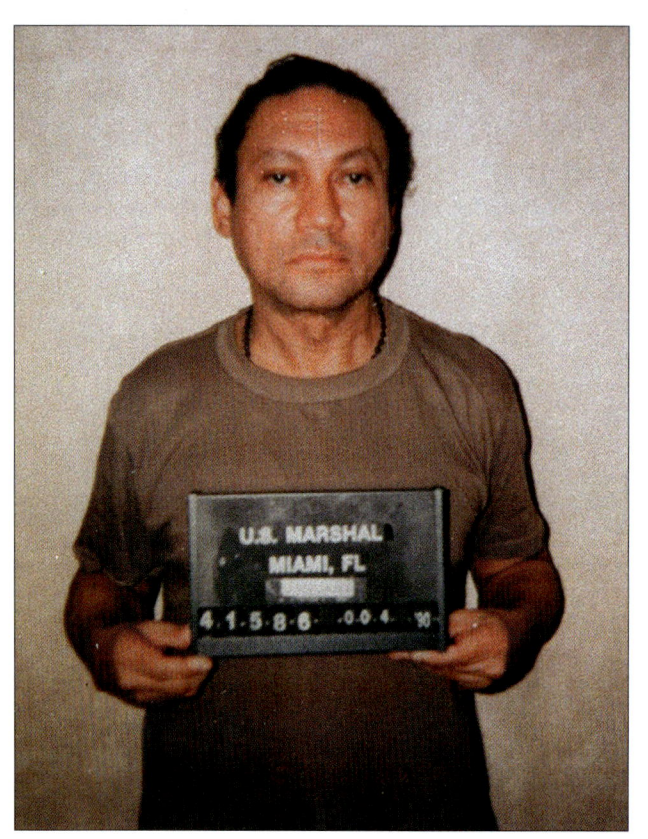

Manuel Noriega was
Chief of Military Intelligence,
a position he used to move drugs.
Lots and lots of drugs.
Despite this, early in his career
he worked hand in hand with
the CIA to tamp down anti-American
sentiment in the third world.

I knew John Gotti from the time
we were kids and he was kicked
out of the Ravenite for
disrespecting me. He didn't play
by Mafia rules, killing without
permission and playing to the
press like a thirsty starlet.
He was a prime example of what
ruined the American Mafia.

Here I am with Pope John Paul II. As you'll read, I did a lot of work for the Vatican. *Author's collection.*

Me and Robert DeNiro. *Author's collection.*

Me and the Donald have been friends since long before he became president. *Author's collection.*

Me and Elizabeth Taylor. *Author's collection.*

Nice pussycat! Here I am messing around with Siegfried and Roy's leopard, Sabu. I was terrified. *Author's collection.*

The "King of Cocaine,"
Pablo Escobar.
My adventure with him
will curl your hair.

My nightclub,
Gianni Russo's State Street,
was a fabulous success.
Almost everyone made it
out alive.
Author's collection.

Frank Costello's tomb in St. Michael's Cemetery.
Author photo.

Others indicted with Roselli were George Browne and Willie Bioff, the B&B boys who first set up the extortion of the movie moguls. Those moguls agreed to pay B&B in exchange for a promise that the unions they controlled would not ask for a raise and never strike. So, the payoffs were worth it.

Roselli went to the fed pen in 1943 and got out in 1947. Got knocked down, got up again. Life got easier in the mid-1950s when Dragna died and Roselli's lawyer, Frank DeSimone, took over the Outfit's West Coast operations.

Roselli had a lot of influence in Hollywood, much more so than his legit job title would indicate. Officially he was a producer at Monogram Pictures, a bargain-basement studio that would later become Allied Artists, where they made quick and cheap movies like Bowery Boys and Charlie Chan pictures.

After his release from prison, Roselli—like Meyer Lansky, Bugsy Siegel, and Moe Dalitz—shifted his focus to Las Vegas. The Mob wasn't getting Havana back, so Nevada would have to be the next playland.

I'd met Roselli before, but it was our meeting in 1967 that made me an eyewitness to shadow history, things that really happened but don't make it into the "official" history books. Secrets.

I was twenty-three in 1967 and still making the rounds. Roselli and I had gotten to be friends. On this day I was to meet him at Hollywood Park racetrack, which despite its name was actually in Inglewood, next to the Forum, the indoor basketball arena at the time. They tore it down in 2014, and it's now the site of SoFi Stadium where they play football. None of it is anywhere near Hollywood.

Roselli was a sharp guy, always finely dressed, and he had a table right on the finish line. I knew where to find him. On this day he had this little guy with him. The guy stood maybe an inch or two taller than five feet. He was dark-skinned and had dark bushy hair.

"This is Sirhan," Roselli said. "He's our guy."

I didn't ask questions.

When Sirhan left to go to the john or something Roselli turned to me and said, "I'm his babysitter."

I found out later that they had the little guy hypnotized, easily triggered by posthypnotic suggestion, and he was programmed to be a fall guy.

With Sirhan still away, Roselli stuck his nose in his program as if he were furiously handicapping, and he said, "I got a story to tell you, Kid. I'm the guy who killed JFK."

My eyes went wide.

He told me about the storm drain. He said that there were at least five shooters in Dealey Plaza when the president's motorcade passed through. "Every family wanted to have a gun on hand," he said. He was there repping the Outfit in Chicago. "Other guys fired, but I'm the one who put the bullet in JFK's head that killed him. I poked my head up out of a storm sewer and shot him from in front."

As Roselli spoke, he got up and I followed. We walked together to the fifty-dollar window.

"What would have happened if you missed?" I asked.

"Oh, there was plenty of backup," Roselli said. "Not just in Dealey Plaza, further along the route, all the way to the Trade Mart, at the convention center where he was going to give a speech. There was CIA. Texas authorities. Someone was going to shoot that motherfucker that day—but I'm the one who did it."

He flashed me a psychopathic smile. His teeth were the whitest I'd ever seen.

"What about Ruby?"

Roselli said he met twice with Jack Ruby in small hotels in Miami in October 1963.

"He was one of our guys, too," Roselli said.

I didn't understand why Roselli was opening up to me in this way. It worried me. If he was telling me, he was telling others as well, and that kind of thing had a way of coming back to haunt a guy.

By 1967, gangsters had figured out that Dallas had not, as anticipated, solved the Kennedy problem. Bobby had shaken off his grief and was ready to pick up where Jack left off, leader of the free world, a post from which he could continue his war against the Mob.

So, another assassination was in order.

Sirhan Sirhan was Palestinian and psychologically malleable. Through hypnosis and other brainwashing techniques, they convinced him that if Bobby Kennedy were elected president he would annihilate Palestine.

Sirhan, I learned along with everyone else, was born in Jerusalem in 1944. A Jordanian citizen, he came to America when he was twelve, settled in California, and graduated from Pasadena City College. He was first a blip on U.S. intelligence radar when he protested Robert Kennedy's support for Israel in the 1967 Six-Day War.

I was twenty-four by the time Sirhan's programming was put to its desired use, on June 5, 1968, as Bobby was campaigning for the Democratic nomination for that November's presidential election. Bobby, the cold-blooded killer of my friend Marilyn Monroe, still had the world bamboozled, the good Catholic boy, the crusader for justice. Marilyn was in her grave screaming about the abortion, but no one could hear.

He had just won the California Democratic primary and seemed well on his way to becoming the Democrat nominee for the presidency, with a great chance to, as his brother had, beat Richard Nixon in the fall election.

Bobby, who got his brother killed by attacking the very forces that helped get Jack elected, gave a victory speech at the Ambassador Hotel in Los Angeles. He promised to stop the Vietnam War, which made him very popular with young people.

He finished his speech, big cheer, lots of excitement, flashed a couple of peace signs, and was led by security into the hotel's kitchen area, which was crowded with people trying to get close to Bobby. And who was in that kitchen but Sirhan, the little guy I'd met at Hollywood Park.

Sirhan pulled a gun, his eyes spiraling in a hypnotic daze, and fired wildly in Bobby's direction. Several people were hit. Kennedy fell mortally wounded, and the tiny man with a gun in his hand was wrestled to the ground by Kennedy security, his thumb broken as he was disarmed.

But had Sirhan actually been the one to kill Bobby? Ballistics said no. Eyewitnesses said Sirhan never got closer than a few feet from Bobby, while the bullet that ended up killing him was fired at point-blank range. Though Sirhan was always facing Bobby, the fatal bullet entered behind Bobby's right ear.

It felt like the same guy was writing the script for both Kennedy assassinations. Jack was shot in front by a patsy who was behind. Bobby was shot from behind by a patsy who was in front. But whereas Oswald must've known something about what was going on and had to die, when Sirhan was snapped out of his trance, he had no idea what he'd done or why. He was programmed to forget his own programming, and thus was allowed to live. They weren't afraid of him talking because he'd be unable to say anything that made sense.

From day one, eye- and earwitnesses at the site of the RFK hit have insisted that they heard more than one gun during the shooting sequence. One of them, Nina Rhodes-Hughes, said in 2012, "What has to come out is that there was another shooter to my right."

Despite those who heard two guns, and the crime scene where there were more bullet holes than acknowledged bullets, Sirhan was the "kook" who took the blame. Unlike Oswald, he was tried, convicted, and imprisoned. Sirhan, like Oswald, had a résumé (and ethnicity) that in itself convicted him in the minds of Americans.

After being shot, Bobby lay on the floor for seventeen minutes. His right eye was open, the pupil shifted to the right, and his left eye was closed. He could move all four limbs and appeared to be in a semiconscious state. It would be forty-five minutes after the shooting before Kennedy arrived at L.A. Central Receiving Hospital. Unlike JFK, RFK lingered for twenty-six hours after he was shot. He was transferred to a Good Samaritan Hospital intensive care room after surviving almost four hours of brain surgery, with his family at his side. Doctors said that a bullet in Kennedy's brain had been removed. The bullet had smashed into his brain, piercing the brain stem with lead and bone fragments. Another, in his neck, was left alone with plans to remove it only if he grew stronger. Of course, that never happened. Following surgery, doctors warned that even if he survived he might never again be "normal."

The press said Sirhan was a dirty little Arab. Despite his background, Sirhan was not a Muslim, although most Americans didn't distinguish Middle Eastern men. He was, in fact, a fervent Christian, belonging to both the Baptist and the Seventh Day Adventist churches, and was also reportedly a member of the secret society known as the Rosicrucians.

Following Sirhan's arrest and initial interrogation, LAPD's Chief Thomas Reddin said the shooter had confused the department. "It's a strange case because at this point we don't know what triggered it [the murder]."

"Chief, have you personally spoken to Sirhan?" a reporter asked.

"I have—for about fifteen minutes. I found him articulate but not forthcoming about who he was or anything regarding the shooting."

"When he was being articulate, what was he articulate about?" Same reporter.

"We talked about current events. This would indicate he is a newspaper reader."

"Which current event?"

"He spoke of Lutz Kische, the East German border guard who escaped to the west over the Berlin Wall."

A different reporter asked, "What was his demeanor when you spoke with him?"

"He was stretched out in a chair. He seemed relaxed, not nervous at all."

"Was anything of importance found in his pockets when he was searched?"

"We found four one-hundred-dollar bills and two newspaper clippings, both anti-Kennedy in nature. One of the clippings contained a list of Kennedy's speaking engagements."

"Chief, do you think this was an Arab conspiracy?" There you go. That's how Americans think.

"We're not ruling anything out at the moment."

The press conference was held in the big police auditorium to accommodate the hundreds of press, print and electronic, who were there to cover the shooting. So many TV cameras were plugged in and running at once that the police station blew a fuse, causing a pause while cops scrambled to get the lights back on.

Sirhan, they announced, lived with his brother Joe Munir Sirhan on East Howard Street in Pasadena. They traced Sirhan's gun to an eighteen-year-old man from Marin County just north of San Francisco, who said he sold the gun to a bushy-haired man named Joe who worked in a Pasadena department store.

Somewhat controversially, a judge set Sirhan's bail at $250,000, which worried some. What if Sirhan was released and Kennedy died? It turned out to be a moot point as no one came forward to pay the bail.

As I was reading this in the newspaper back in 1968, I knew this guy was the one I'd met at Hollywood Park, so I was interested when that racetrack came up in the story.

Sirhan, police said, was positively identified by fingerprints he gave to authorities as a juvenile and a student at John Muir High School. The prints were necessitated when he applied for a job at Hollywood Park as an exercise boy. He'd also worked for a time at Santa Anita racetrack as a groom.

The papers referred to him as a jockey wannabe. Maybe.

What we do know is that he was plucked out of the stables and enrolled in a CIA mind-control program called MK/ULTRA, which literally programmed him to shoot RFK.

By two in the morning on June 6, Kennedy was dead, and police had searched Sirhan's home, and found his diary. Written in it was, "Robert Kennedy has to be assassinated by June 5, 1968"—that date being the one-year anniversary of the Six-Day War between Israel and the United Arab Republic.

Sirhan continued to act bizarrely while incarcerated, filling journals with scribbles and nonsense. Thinking back to the Oswald case, Los Angeles made special sure to keep Sirhan safe.

During his trial, some thought his strange behavior amounted to no more than malingering, an attempt to demonstrate a diminished capacity to distinguish right from wrong.

Sirhan was convicted in a California courtroom of first-degree murder on April 17, 1969 and sentenced to death. That sentence was later commuted to life imprisonment.

To this day, during his attempts to impress the parole board, his lawyers argue that he has no memory of killing Bobby because he was a victim of a mind-control program, a brainwashing administered by the Rosicrucians or a "political organization."

Sirhan has always maintained that he has no memory of confessing to Bobby's assassination, which he reportedly did only days after his arrest, a confession during which he claimed he acted alone and was drunk when he pulled the trigger.

Suspicions that there was more than one shooter in the Ambassador Hotel that evening started in earnest during Sirhan's murder trial. The postmortem surgeon who performed Bobby's autopsy is familiar to our story, Dr. Thomas Noguchi, who'd autopsied Marilyn. Now, having been promoted to L.A. County chief medical-examiner-coroner, he worked over the body of her killer.

At Sirhan's trial, Noguchi testified for the defense that he agreed with the crime-scene investigators' assessment of the murder. Despite the fact that Sirhan never got closer than a couple of feet from RFK, the fatal shot was fired at point-blank range, about one to one and a half inches from Kennedy's ear.

This testimony led researchers to look again at the shooting to determine who was in a position to shoot Kennedy from that close. What they learned was that behind and to Bobby's right was a security guard named Thane Eugene Cesar, who of course denied firing his gun during the assassination sequence, but also offered various versions of his movements. He denied even pulling his weapon, but multiple witnesses said that he did pull his gun, and one eyewitness, Don Schulman, a runner for KNXT-TV, said he saw Cesar fire his gun. Research revealed that Cesar had "made no secret of his hatred for Bobby Kennedy."

I wasn't there, I don't know what happened. Dan Moldea, a Bobby Kennedy assassination expert without peer, interviewed Cesar and came away believing he was innocent.

Cesar said, "I'm on the right side of him and what I'm doing is taking my hand and pushing people back because Kennedy was having a hard time walking forward. I saw flashes and reached for my gun but did not fire. At his closest, I believe Sirhan was two feet from Kennedy." An eyewitness who saw Cesar with his gun out and in his hand corroborated that he did not fire.

"I thought he would shoot Sirhan, but he didn't," the witness observed.

Moldea thinks Noguchi got it wrong, and in the chaos of the shooting sequence, it was Sirhan who shot Bobby from behind while in front.

One thing I know for sure. I'd seen Oswald with Carlos Marcello, and I'd seen Sirhan with Johnny Roselli. Whatever else you want to theorize, they were not lone nuts. The patsies were more important than the shooters, as they needed to strike an immediate negative chord with the American people, the Communist kook (Oswald) and the little Arab (Sirhan).

* * *

Now we skip ahead seven years. Roselli was subpoenaed by the U.S. Senate Select Committee on Intelligence, and on June 24 and September 22, 1975, Roselli testified. Not only didn't he take the Fifth, he began to blurt out truths. My earlier worries that Roselli had forgotten he was supposed to keep secrets proved to be correct. He was aging poorly and turning into an old blabbermouth.

He spoke of CIA involvement with mobsters—Santos Trafficante, for example—joining forces to whack Fidel Castro.

Just days before Roselli's second appearance before the committee, June 19, 1975, Sam Giancana was murdered in his home, shot to death in his basement, shot by someone he knew and trusted, someone he'd invited in for the sausage and peppers he was cooking.

In true gangland style, Giancana was shot seven times in the face, and around the mouth as a sign of "talks too much." The murder weapon was later found on the banks of the Des Plaines River. It was a silenced Suramatic semiautomatic .22 pistol.

It's my opinion that Giancana wasn't hit because of what he knew about the Kennedys but because he couldn't control Anthony "Tony the Ant" Spilotro—but I'll get to that.

Giancana's execution scared Roselli into temporary silence. The following year, 1976, Roselli was subpoenaed again, this time to talk about Dallas. I heard that and I thought the jig was up.

But Roselli went missing before he could appear. He was last seen on July 18, 1976, and on August 7 he was found by a fisherman in a fifty-five-gallon steel fuel drum floating in Dumfoundling Bay near Miami.

I was an eyewitness to the discovery of Johnny Roselli's body, a fact that I hadn't thought about for a few years but was reminded of in March 2024 when I spent some time with the man I was with. He's still kicking so I can't mention his name.

At the time of our final Johnny Roselli sighting, he and I

were having breakfast on a patio overlooking the north side of Dumfoundling Bay. Johnny Roselli's barrel came afloat. We could see it out there, bobbing around. They killed him somewhere else and by the time they tried to put him into the drum rigor mortis had set in. They had to use a saw. He was disassembled and put into the drum in pieces.

They took the drum out on a boat and pushed Roselli overboard, but they screwed up and the weights that were supposed to anchor the body to the bottom of the bay came loose and up came Johnny, just offshore as I sipped espresso on the patio with my friend.

We not only could see the bobbing drum, we could see *JR* spray-painted on it, so we figured out who was inside. We got up and ran out of the place. The last thing we needed was to be in the vicinity of Johnny Roselli's mortal remains.

The drum was first reported at eleven a.m. by fishermen who were driving along the Intercoastal Waterway east of Biscayne Boulevard at 189th Street. Some swimmers between North Miami Beach and Golden Beach got close enough to smell the thing and fetched a marine patrol boat with a hook. The boat towed the drum to the shore. A tow truck backed up to the shore, hooked the drum, and pulled it onto the land where it leaked a foul sludge.

There was brief talk of calling the police or the medical examiner or someone like that, but the men decided to first crack the drum open, just in case it was a false alarm—although it sure didn't smell like a false alarm.

The tow-truck driver volunteered that he had just the right tools to open that thing like a can of soup. And he did. When the top of the tub was removed, inside was a gray-and-white blob with a stench that knocked them back.

One man had the courage to look into the drum steadily and register what he saw. The legs had been removed from the rest and shoved into the drum along the sides. Several men vomited.

The remains did finally make it to the coroner, Dade County medical examiner Dr. Ronald Wright, who revealed that death was by asphyxiation. Attempts were made to get fingerprints off the corpse. Results were negative, except for a few ridges off one of his thumbs.

The body had at least one visible gunshot wound.

When the coroner figured out who they had, *the* Johnny Roselli, not only did the press crash down on them like a tidal wave of India ink, but there was lengthy questioning from all of the organizations in the Alphabet Soup, CIA, NSA, FBI, DEA, Secret Service, a different intelligence service every day. I was glad I'd hightailed it away from there.

The death was big news. Roselli was last seen at one o'clock in the afternoon of July 28. He'd been wearing golf clothes, had his clubs in the trunk of his 1975 Chevrolet Impala, and was driving away from his sister's home in Plantation, Florida. He told his sister he was playing eighteen and would be back for dinner, but that didn't happen.

His car was later found abandoned in the parking lot of Miami International Airport near the Delta Airlines passenger area.

During the late 1960s, Mr. Costello said he had a job for me in Vegas.

"I'll have some things for you to do in L.A., too," he added.

He said I should stop in Chicago and talk to Tony Accardo.

"He may have things for you to do, too. Do what he says, just as if I told you."

"Yes, sir."

I headed for the airport.

In Chicago, Accardo gave me an envelope to deliver in L.A.

"Where you going after L.A.?" Accardo asked.

"Vegas," I said.

"Good. When you get there, report to the Las Vegas Country Club. You will be expected."

I hadn't been to Vegas since I was a kid. I loved it then and, as a young adult, I loved it even more. The glitz, the glamor, it was all me. At the country club I met with Moe Dalitz, Jack Entratter, Carl Cohen, and Herman "Hank" Greenspun. Dalitz was Meyer Lansky's guy in Vegas, Entratter was the on-paper owner of the Sands, ghosting for Mr. Costello. Cohen was one of the owners of the Sands. He came out of the Cleveland Mob. Greenspun was publisher of the *Las Vegas Sun* newspaper. They gave me carte blanche and I split my time between staying at the Sands and Caesars Palace, and as usual everything was on the house.

In Vegas, I met a nineteen-year-old woman, fell in love, and got married. I bought a house in L.A. and an apartment in Vegas and shuttled back and forth. She stayed in Vegas. I went into business with my new father-in-law and opened a jewelry store on the Strip.

Like a bar owner hiring B-girls to encourage customers to spend, we hired professional women to pick up rich tourists and convince them to buy jewelry for them, at my jewelry store. When it came time for the men to go home and return to their wives, our girls returned the jewelry to us, so we could sell the same pieces again and again. One necklace sold fifty times.

Next, I opened up Gianni's Wig World. That was when I was first bitten by the show-biz bug. I began to make TV and radio appearances to promote my stores. That led to one Vegas TV station offering me my own variety show. The show did okay, not spectacularly great, and lasted for a couple of years.

Life in Vegas was wild. I got to know Elvis Presley and went on a wild out-of-town search for banana-and-peanut-butter sandwiches with him.

Frank Sinatra and I hung out quite a bit. One night we were in Palm Springs having dinner at a joint called Ruby Dunes. By this time I was familiar with his mood swings. He'd get a few drinks in him and he'd fight anybody. Not a good habit for a guy as famous as that. When everybody knows you, it means the idiots know you, too, and that can be annoying.

I'd see him get like that and I'd say, "See you later, Frank. Time to go."

One time he tried to smack me. We weren't even having an argument. I disagreed with him, and he saw that as betrayal. We were at the Galleria Bar in Caesars Palace, which at that time was completely mobbed up.

Howard Hughes had purchased the Sands (more about that in chapter 11) and the Mob guys built Caesars Palace, and they took all of the talent with them.

Well, not all.

The Mob guys told the Hughes guys, "Here, you can keep Wayne Newton."

Frank and I were talking about Joe Louis, who at the time was a punchy old man who Frank took care of. Joe Louis had been a great American hero and Frank wanted the old guy to have dignity. Now, I wasn't about to disrespect Joe Louis to Frank Sinatra, but he was running down the Brown Bomber's fights and he left out Billy Conn, the guy who could run but he couldn't hide. I corrected him, and he tried to smack me, and I grabbed his arm. I took his right hand between my hands and I said, "Frank, try it again and I'll rip off your arm and shove it up your ass. Who do you think you're talking to?" Then, after a pause, I added, "Come on, Frank. I love you, man. Cool it." And I felt him relax.

CHAPTER 8
Why They're Never Going to Find Jimmy Hoffa

The Mafia has been hell on Union leaders who wouldn't do the right thing. The most famous example of this is Jimmy Hoffa, who was erased from the face of the earth on July 30–31, 1975. He had been the most powerful and corrupt union leader on Earth, King of the Teamsters, and Teamsters were King!

Hoffa was a Detroit kid, hit adulthood just as the stock market crashed and the nation plunged into the Great Depression. Hoffa was a natural organizer of men. As a teenager, he led a rebellion by workers at a grocery store warehouse where conditions were cruel.

The Teamsters Local 299 hired Hoffa as an organizer in 1932. Hoffa, of course, became a Teamster for life, rising steadily in the ranks in a very public way. He worked his way into America's heart when he stood up to Bobby Kennedy on live TV during a Senate committee hearing on corrupt unions.

Under Hoffa's leadership, the Teamsters became the most powerful union in America. Trouble came when the Mafia came for their skim: Hoffa balked. Mob guys moved in, got themselves elected as union officers. Hoffa waved his fist—but not for long.

His disappearance became instantly legendary. Within hours of his last sighting, front-page headlines rocked every daily newspaper in the country: JIMMY HOFFA MISSING. And he remains American culture's favorite missing person, edging out Judge Crater and D. B. Cooper.

Hoffa was last seen wearing a dark blue sports shirt, dark blue trousers, and sunglasses, standing outside the Machus Red Fox restaurant on Telegraph Road near Maple in Bloomfield Township, Michigan, a northern suburb of Detroit.

Interestingly, no one inside the Machus Red Fox remembered seeing Hoffa on that Wednesday. Management confirmed that he had no reservation at the restaurant at any time that day.

All eyewitnesses who saw him saw him outside. He stood up close to the side of the restaurant and looked as if he were waiting for someone. That was ten a.m. on Wednesday, July 30. At 2:30 p.m. Hoffa called home and said the person he'd expected to meet had not shown up.

And yet he was picked up. And then he was gone.

At six p.m. on Thursday, with Hoffa off the board for more than a day, his family reported him missing. Police found Hoffa's 1974 Pontiac Grand Ville hardtop in the parking lot of the Machus Red Fox. It was empty and unlocked, no signs of a struggle. It stood to reason, though, that Hoffa left his car in the parking lot and got into another car as a passenger, so there may have been duress.

The disappearance wasn't a total shock. There'd been foreshadowing. Teamsters Local 299 had endured a series of violent events, a plague of troubles, in the month before Hoffa's disappearance. The Mob was going to have its way.

Michigan governor William Milliken told a gaggle of pressmen that it was his understanding that Hoffa had intended to meet Detroit Mafia kingpin Anthony Giacalone at the time he was last seen. Who actually picked him up was anyone's guess. No one saw Hoffa getting into a car.

*   *   *

Since the day Hoffa vanished, there has been a relentless search for his remains, with regular, almost constant rumors as to where they are. The most famous was that Hoffa had been shot to death with a silenced .22 pistol in Michigan, disassembled with a power saw and a meat cleaver, frozen, and mixed into the foundation under the end zone at Giants Stadium closest to section 107 in the Meadowlands, New Jersey.

Nope. I can tell you for a fact that's not what happened, and that's not where he is.

Frank "The Irishman" Sheeran claimed that he killed Jimmy Hoffa, shot him twice in the back of the head, cremated his body in an incinerator in the Detroit suburbs. Nope.

Authorities dug here, dug there, but I can tell you right now, they are *never going to find him.* And here's why:

What apparently no one at the restaurant saw was that Hoffa was picked up in a burgundy-colored Buick, not a Mercury Marquis as has been reported. The hit was done in a very imaginative way. They had it set up on a freeway. A moving truck, with the back open, rear ramp dropped so it was just off the ground, moved into position so it was driving in front of the Buick.

Behind the Buick a tow truck moved into place. It was not a regular tow truck, but a sizable truck with a hook on the back. In one fluid motion, the rear truck pushed the Buick right into the back of the front truck, the ramp was drawn in, and the rear of the front truck slammed shut.

So now, Hoffa, and apparently a driver who wasn't informed of the plan in its entirety, were trapped in the front truck, which had a device attached that ran from the exhaust pipe to the interior, so that as it drove the rear compartment filled with deadly carbon monoxide. The men in the burgundy-colored Buick were asphyxiated.

It took time, but they had time, as that moving truck drove seven hundred miles, traveling south of Lake Erie, a route that was longer but eliminated the crossing of the Canadian border. Unobserved, Hoffa's stiff was moved all the way through Indiana, Ohio, Pennsylvania, and New Jersey—and finally across the Bayonne Bridge, over the Kill Van Kull, and onto Staten Island. The truck drove into a chop shop where I knew the guys, a large "body and fender" place.

The Buick was removed from the back of the rigged moving truck, which immediately left and began its return drive to Michigan. The Buick and its contents were crushed into a two-by-four-by-four cube, using a process so hot that any tissue containing DNA was burned away.

The guys who ran the shop were big along the waterfront: ex-pugilist Alex "The Ox" DeBrizzi—aka Al Britton, his boxing name—who was for a time treasurer for the International Longshoremen Association (ILA). He used to keep the ILA treasury in a jar at home. DeBrizzi was a soldier for his crime family for three administrations: Mangano, Anastasia, and finally Gambino. His big rackets were extortion, gambling, and a side hustle in drugs.

The other guy was Michael D'Alessio, another Gambino guy who'd been running gambling and other rackets on Staten Island for generations. I knew D'Alessio because my friend Tommy Bilotti, who I'd known since we were kids in Little Italy, ran errands for him when he was a kid.

The Staten Island boys didn't dispose of the cube. They decided to auction it off, and sure enough every well-to-do hood in America wanted to own the "remains" of Jimmy Hoffa, which became American folklore within hours of Hoffa being snatched.

A friend of mine bought the cube. I can't tell you who he is, because he's still alive and I don't want to be found dead. Let's just say he lives in Florida. He bought the cube and mounted a four-foot-by-six-foot piece of glass on top, to make it into a coffee table, which he keeps in his basement, the smoking room. It looks like an art piece. It's very interesting.

Sometimes, if you're visiting him, he'll say something like, "Let's go downstairs and have a cigar with Jimmy Hoffa."

The Hoffa disappearance is familiar, but there were others involving mob/union disputes as well, maybe lesser known, and they were wild.

Take Elmer "Al" Bramlet, a guy I met when I was making the rounds for Mr. Costello. He was the secretary-treasurer of Las Vegas Culinary Workers Local 226, and president of the Nevada AFL-CIO. He was murdered in 1977 after two Vegas restaurants were bombed when they refused to unionize their kitchens.

Bramlet was a Southern gentleman, born in 1917 in Jonesboro, Arkansas, son of a railroad worker. His family moved to Joliet, Illinois—suburban Chicago—when he was fourteen and right after that he took his first job in the culinary field, washing pots.

He worked his way up in kitchens from Chicago and Miami to New York and L.A. He finally took the top job at Local 226 in Vegas. Known for his moustache and cigar, he ruled 226 in 1954 when it was a struggling, small organization, maybe 1,500 members.

Bramlet made it huge, 22,000 strong, until in 1976 it was large enough to shut down the Vegas Strip with a strike that crippled the resorts, costing the local economy about $26 million. That didn't win the union any friends. The gangster response was: Who are these guys to shut us down?

Bramlet was also feeling heat from the frustrated rank and file, disgruntled with the way Local 226 treated them. Workers at several restaurants in town had negotiated with management only after kicking Local 226 out of the room. The talk was that Bramlet had "sold them out" during contract negotiations. A few months earlier, the National Labor Relations Board in San Francisco voted to decertify Bramlet's union respresentation of a place called Harold's Club.

Then there were the feds, who'd figured out that Local 226

had loaned $29 million to Dunes Hotel executive Morris Shenker out of a fund managed by Bramlet. Uh-oh.

On February 24, 1977, sixty-year-old Bramlet had just returned to Vegas from a business trip to Reno, and telephoned his daughter from the airport, saying he would be home shortly. He never made it.

A flight attendant on the Hughes Airwest flight from Reno to Vegas remembered Bramlet being on the flight and commented that he slept most of the way—an indication perhaps that he wasn't expecting trouble.

The boys snatched him minutes after he landed. Bramlet was abducted outside McCarran Airport by three men, handcuffed and gagged with duct tape.

The instant cops heard that Bramlet had been snatched, they had a pretty good idea of what was up.

"I hope we don't have a Hoffa case on our hands," one investigator said. But they did. Luckily, Bramlet would be easier to find, that is, findable.

Bramlet's new wife—they'd been married for less than three months—the twenty-seven-year-old Barbara, told police that one of her husband's last phone calls was to a hotel executive asking him to deliver $10,000 to the Horseshoe, a Vegas casino.

"If that's a ransom demand, I don't know," she said.

But she did know. No one asks for money to pay the ransom in anticipation of a kidnapping. Not how it works. The ten grand was for something else and Bramlet was out there somewhere in the desert.

She told police that, as far as she could tell, her husband had not been exceptionally fearful of anything in recent days. He had received no threats that she knew of.

"I'm praying, thinking positive. I have not lost hope. He has never carried a gun," she rambled. "He just never thought about anything that way."

Some were eager to eliminate foul play from the speculation. Bob Scaffidi, controller of Karl's Silver Club, said he'd seen Bramlet recently and the guy was depressed, very upset, like he'd just about had it and needed to take a time out." Or worse. "He's had setbacks lately. I hope he decided to take a slight vacation."

Police in Nevada and Illinois wondered if there was a connection between Bramlet's disappearance and the hit on Henry "Mickey" Cogwell, at Cogwell's home only hours later. Cogwell was the head of Local 304 of the Hotel and Restaurant Employees and Bartenders Union, and he was shot to death in his home. There wasn't automatically a connection, although it was weird they happened the same day. Cogwell, along with being a union chief, was also a member of the Black P Stone Nation, a federation of fifty-five Chicago street gangs. It could've been anything.

They found Bramlet's nude, battered, and decomposed body three weeks after he was abducted, late on a Thursday, March 17, discovered by a group of hikers in the high desert west of Mount Potosi, about thirty miles west of Vegas. He was under a pile of rocks, a shallow grave, shot six times, including once in each ear.

The case was solved when one of the three men who attacked Bramlet, Eugene Vaughn, blabbed about his participation to a girlfriend, who told her friend who turned out to be a secret police informant and boom, case closed.

The other two killers were a father-and-son team, Tom and Gramby Hanley, who pleaded guilty to the murder and received life without parole. Vaughn cooperated with the prosecution and received a lighter sentence.

Another, even larger example of the Mob taking out a union leader is Allen Melnick Dorfman, Chicago insurance man, who was appointed to "consult with" the Teamsters' union fund. Those funds then flowed directly into Las Vegas. It bought the central Vegas strip, making a brief stop for laundering in the Union Bank, of which Dorfman was president.

Dorfman was a marine during World War II and came home with a Purple Heart. He was a four-grand-a-year physical education teacher at the University of Illinois' Navy Pier branch in 1949 when his stepfather, Paul "Red" Dorfman, cut a deal with Jimmy Hoffa that turned Allen into the Teamsters' insurance man. Red could cut deals because he was the president of the Chicago Waste Handlers' Union and in that capacity knew all the guys. Allen was his mom's son from a previous marriage and had been adopted by Red.

Hoffa wanted to expand his power. Red Dorfman agreed to introduce Hoffa to top Outfit guys like Tony Accardo in exchange for Hoffa throwing his kid some insurance work. Hoffa and Allen Dorfman rose to power, more or less side by side.

For Dorfman, the payoff came when Hoffa combined the pension and welfare funds to create a giant fund that could be more conveniently siphoned for Nevada real estate. Officially, Dorfman was a consultant with the Teamsters pension fund.

His advice almost always amounted to: You should give a major loan to this Las Vegas speculative real-estate venture.

Dorfman developed a high profile, and managed a perpetual tan that was in the major leagues with mine and George Hamilton's. He was known for his style, and his golf game, which was exceptional.

He was first indicted in 1964 with Jimmy Hoffa for jury tampering in Tennessee. Hoffa was convicted, Dorfman acquitted.

On July 28, 1967, Dorfman and a friend, Perry Franks, were pulling out of Dorfman's Deerfield driveway in Franks's Cadillac when two hooded gunmen jumped out from behind a bush with shotguns. Franks hit the gas in reverse and the gunmen fired, ripping out the Caddy's right front fender. As Franks fishtailed into the street and shifted to forward, two more shotgun blasts hit the side of the car and one hit the rear.

In 1971, Dorfman was convicted by the feds of taking a $55,000 kickback in New York to arrange a loan, earned him seven months in the pen.

In 1974, he was indicted for fraud in connection with another loan. This time his codefendants were Tony "The Ant" Spilotro, whose hotheadedness was in the process of ruining Vegas, and Joey "The Clown" Lombardo. The men were acquitted when the key witness Daniel Seifert became unavailable, on account of being gunned down by four men outside Seifert's office building.

By the 1980s, Dorfman was notorious for his double life, functioning both as a wealthy businessman who gave large sums to charities and had friends in high places, while simultaneously a confidant and asset of top Outfit guys. His philanthropy was a gentle nudge to the world to look the other way when Dorfman was conducting business. The Little City Foundation, which benefited the mentally handicapped, named Dorfman their "Man of the Year" in 1977. The award ceremony dinner was attended by Mayor Michael Bilandic and other local bigwigs.

As for his business dealings, they were as complex as they were crooked. He was said, at his peak, to control fourteen companies, ranging from the 300-employee Amalgamated Insurance Agency Services in Chicago to an apartment complex in Vegas. He and his wife spent a lot of time in a million-dollar home in Miami.

In 1982, Dorfman was indicted for racketeering, part of the overall sweep of RICO charges designed to wipe out much of the Chicago Outfit, as well as the Five Families of New York. Not only were the hoods concerned that Dorfman was going to flip, but they blamed him for their problems, as it was his office that had been bugged by the FBI, and recordings made there that provided the evidence for the indictments.

According to the feds, those recordings demonstrated that the Teamsters "had a lock on Vegas" and had been skimming millions from casinos. He became known as "the Mafia's Banker."

Dorfman was convicted of his charges, which specifically stemmed from his attempt with others to bribe a U.S. senator in Nevada. Three days before he was scheduled to be sentenced, the sixty-year-old was in the parking lot of the Purple Hotel in suburban Chicago when he was shot six times and killed.

Patrick Healy, executive director of the Chicago Crime Commission, had a nonchalant reaction to the murder: "I am surprised he lasted this long," Healy said.

Dorfman didn't get to become a government witness, if that was what he was going to do. His lawyer during his racketeering trial, Harvey Silets, and his prosecutor, U.S. Attorney Dan K. Webb, both denied that Dorfman was cooperating. Despite those denials, there were signs that Dorfman was turning. Only a few days before Dorfman was killed, U.S. District Court Judge Joel Flaum ruled that Dorfman's insurance company and other assets should be returned to him. A deal, it seemed, had been made.

Webb refused to say Dorfman was contemplating flipping, but he did acknowledge how valuable a witness Dorfman would have been for the government had he chosen to flip.

"Dorfman was probably aware of more information on more mobsters than maybe any other single individual around the country," Webb said.

Yeah, Dorfman was gone—but the recordings remained and were used to convict Outfit bigs Joey "Doves" Aiuppa, Jackie Cerone, Angelo "The Hook" LaPietra, and Joey "The Clown" Lombardo.

Dorfman was with his associate Irwin S. Weiner when he was hit. The men had just parked at the north end of the hotel parking lot, nose pointed toward Lincoln Avenue, and were walking toward the hotel restaurant single file. When they were fifty feet from the hotel, they were accosted from behind by men with guns out and level at their hip.

"This is a stickup," one of the men said, although it's hard to understand why as the speaker immediately began to shoot with a .22 pistol. Weiner ducked behind a car, but the men weren't interested in him. Seven bullets in a tight grouping hit Dorfman in the back of his head. Eight spent cartridges were found at the scene.

Weiner told police that the shooters were unmasked when they approached but pulled ski masks on after the shooting. They fled on foot down Lincoln Avenue. Other eyewitnesses saw the men get into a Dodge Monaco, driver already in place, with multiple antennas sticking up out of the hood.

CHAPTER 9
Out West

Las Vegas (Spanish for "The Meadows") began as a settlement, a cluster of homes around a rest stop on the new railroad that linked Salt Lake City and L.A. To service the trains, fresh water was piped in, making it an oasis for those who enjoy a dry heat.

In 1931, Nevada became the only state without gambling laws. A year earlier, construction had begun on the Boulder Dam, with so many construction workers that Vegas's population grew from 5,000 to 25,000.

The first gambling license in Las Vegas went to a joint called the Northern Club on Fremont Street, which became the first paved road in Las Vegas. The Las Vegas Club and the Hotel Apache followed.

They were nothing like modern casinos. Many of the first gambling places were hastily constructed, with horseshoes nailed to the wall over the screen door. Those early places did have one thing in common with the later hotels: showgirls. The construction workers building the dam were just a little more than 100 percent male, and, as they say, tits sell.

The birth of the modern casino came in 1945. That was when Meyer Lansky and Benjamin "Bugsy" Siegel arrived in Vegas. Lansky and Siegel were partners in crime as youths in Brooklyn. Now they had a grown-up plan: They would build a tremendous casino in the middle of the Mojave Desert, in a remote outpost called Las Vegas.

"Here we'll have fun," Lansky said, braving the one-hundred-degree heat, and looking out over the alkali flats spotted with creosote bushes and samphire. "We will build a house of gambling and we will call it the Flamingo."

That was what he said in public. In private, this scheme was Siegel's. Lansky thought Las Vegas was "in terrible shape" and so hot that "the wires in the car would melt." But he trusted Ben and invested generously in Siegel's dream.

The plan was not entirely outrageous. The El Rancho and the Last Frontier were already there, cowboy joints, a little dusty and rough for the Beverly Hills crowd that Siegel liked to hang with. The Flamingo would be a *luxury* hotel-casino.

Why Flamingo? Lansky later explained, "We thought up the name one day when we were at Hialeah Race Track in Florida. There's a pretty little lake there and in the evening you can watch the flocks of pink flamingoes rise in the sky. There's a local legend that flamingoes are a sign of good luck and anyone who shoots the birds will have seven years of misfortune. So, because of the good luck connection, Bugsy had the idea of naming our Las Vegas project."

Critics told Lansky he was nuts. There was nothing to do in Las Vegas. Lansky just smiled. Of course, that was the whole point. If gambling was the only game in town, that is what visitors would do. There was money around, gas was cheap, and it was a four-hour drive from L.A. if you stepped on it. That was all that mattered.

Today, Vegas is a major-league town, the bigs, with an NFL franchise, major league baseball on its way, and a starry strip that goes for miles, an industry in itself, and it all began with a visit by Bugs and Meyer, planting a flag in the sand at the corner of Fremont and Second Streets.

On September 13, 1945, Moe Sedway, on behalf of the bosses, purchased a thirty-acre plot, the only structure on which was a long-closed motel. To build the Flamingo, Lansky hired Phoenix-contractor Del Webb, who was pals with J. Edgar Hoover, and would go on to own the New York Yankees. The budget: a million dollars. Webb's instructions: build the greatest casino in the world. Webb put in a huge, illuminated pillar in front of the casino, a shiny phallus so large and bright that travelers picked it up—and its carnal message—on the horizon from many miles away.

Lansky was not Siegel's only investor. Billy Wilkerson put up cash, and even took charge of some engineering elements, as he was not just a major publisher, of *The Hollywood Reporter*, but an early architect of the section of Sunset Boulevard that would become known as the Sunset Strip.

Gus Greenbaum was in. The Berman brothers. Moe Sedway invested. After an initial publicity campaign at the beginning of the project, Lansky returned to Florida and Siegel went through the rest of his painful Flamingo experience with unfriendly partners crowding him, and his reasonable friend Lansky thousands of miles away.

And there was little that was reasonable in the way Siegel constructed the Flamingo. He wanted every element to be exotic and rare. Construction became complicated. The war in the Pacific had only been over for a few weeks, and getting supplies to build anything was problematic. Luckily for Webb, his clients knew a little something about the black market. The supplies—rare wood, fine marble—were expensive but they were acquired. Thanks to Siegel's connections, some of the materials came from Hollywood, out of warehouses used to build movie sets. In Italy, Mafia ships were loaded up with marble and exotic lumber, shipped across the sea and trucked westward into the desert. Labor was an issue as well. To keep a construction crew in the heat for that long Lansky had to pay wages (fifty dollars a day) usually reserved for brain surgeons.

Some major installations had to be done twice. The first boiler room was too small. Building a bigger one ran an extra hundred grand. Air-conditioning, a relatively new concept out-side of movie theaters, was installed but didn't work. Original materials were sometimes prohibitively flammable and needed to be replaced. The budget ballooned from one million to seven. Investors were steamed—to say the least.

Those investors insisted that the casino should open even if not ready. So, the Grand Opening was scheduled for the day after Christmas, 1946. There would be a gala floor show em-ceed by show-biz vets Jimmy Durante and George Jessel. Xavier Cugat's band would play.

But the project remained hopelessly snakebit. A vicious rain-storm hit L.A. on December 26 and discouraged potential cus-tomers from making the drive. It was hoped that the gala would be "star-studded," but as it turned out the biggest name to show up was Paramount actor Sonny Tufts.

The casino remained open while construction continued into the spring of 1947. And even the gambling did not go as planned. For reasons that remain unclear, winners outnumbered losers to the tune of $750,000 over the first few months. In-vestors said that, with the vig firmly in place, this kind of a loss was mathematically impossible. Suspicion was that Siegel was putting the profits plus some in his pocket. Lansky knew the importance of running gambling enterprises honestly. Siegel, it was assumed, lacked that kind of wisdom. Billy Wilkerson took out a $600,000 loan to keep the Flamingo going, but he wasn't happy about it, and he knew who to blame.

In the meantime, Siegel was no more emotionally mature than he had been when shooting competing bootleggers for the fun of it. He needed to borrow money, lots of it, and it might've been wise to stay civilized, but he couldn't do it. He beat up a customer at the Colonial Inn in early 1947 because the guy called him Bugsy.

"The name is Ben," Siegel said before busting the guy's ribs.

Soon thereafter, he tried to get Wilkerson to sell him his one-third stake in the project so he could resell it for a profit, or something, but when Wilkerson didn't roll over, Siegel threatened him: "I don't think any place you live will be healthy for you." He said it in front of lawyers, and Wilkerson began to think of Ben Siegel in a "him or me" kind of way.

The Flamingo reopened March 1, 1947, with the Andrews Sisters topping the bill. Siegel had less than four months to live.

I never got to meet Bugsy Siegel. At 10:45 p.m. on June 20, 1947, the shortest night of the year, Ben Siegel, now forty-one years old, was reading a newspaper on a chintz sofa in the living room of the Beverly Hills rented home of his thirty-year-old girlfriend, Virginia Hill—a pink Moorish mansion on North Linden Drive.

Hill, a "Southern socialite" known to be rough around the edges, was in Paris. As the summer solstice approached, Hill told friends she was summering in Europe on holiday, but in reality she'd left the country a week earlier because Siegel beat her up. Siegel was sitting on a sofa reading the L.A. *Times*. Behind him was a window facing the street. The drapes were open. Siegel's head was illuminated by a table lamp.

According to Chick Hill, Virginia's brother, Siegel was troubled by an odor in the house.

"What's that smell? I smell flowers," Siegel reportedly said. Nobody else could smell anything.

Chick and Jerri Mason, Virginia's secretary, went upstairs, where Chick told her that he had a weird feeling: "When someone smells flowers and there are no flowers, it means they are about to die," Chick said.

With that, the quiet moment was disrupted by gunfire. Nine steel-jacketed slugs came through the downstairs window. Four of the shots struck Siegel, two in the head and two in the body, and Siegel was killed instantly. One of his eyes was blown out and found fifteen feet away on the tiled floor of the dining room. One of the shots that missed struck a painting of a wine-drinking nude, and another shattered a statue of Bacchus that had been resting on a grand piano.

With Siegel at the time of the shooting was Allen Smiley, a

Flamingo investor. He, too, had been sitting on the sofa but dove to the floor when the shooting began. His jacket had a bullet hole, but Smiley was unharmed.

Las Vegas went up one resort hotel/casino at a time, each with its own drama, each being bigger and fancier than the one before. In the 1960s, with Castro in control of Cuba, Las Vegas grew in leaps and bounds, with ownership of the casinos divvied up between the Mob families.

Ten years after the "pool party" at Cal-Neva, I was again in Nevada, and my vague assignment was to "stay at the Trop for a few weeks." I reported to Nick Tanno, who managed the Tropicana, but there really wasn't anything for me to do. It made me antsy after a while.

I called Mr. Costello.

"What's up, Kid?" He sounded weak. I could hear the age in his voice. I didn't like to think about facing the world without him.

"I'm bored," I said.

"Why don't you open a nightclub in the hotel? Look around, and pick out a place," he said.

The place I picked out was Tiffany's restaurant in the Trop. I had myself named "Executive Host" and turned it into a disco-dancing club open eighteen hours a week—Thursday, Friday, and Saturday nights from midnight to six.

I was excellent at publicity. I got it into all the papers throughout Nevada and California. We got a nice crowd. Many celebs. Then, *the* celeb walked in. It was Elvis and his manager, Colonel Parker. We treated them like kings.

I contacted the PBX—that's Private Branch Exchange, a panel of switchboard operators that connects outside calls—and told them to inform all the Vegas cab drivers that Elvis was at Tiffany's. The place quickly filled up and there was a line outside.

* * *

Since the club was only open part-time, I split the rest of the time between Vegas and L.A., meeting Mickey Cohen and the L.A. guys.

I promised to tell you how my relationship with Mickey Cohen grew complicated. This is what happened. It was the mid-seventies, while I was running Tiffany's.

There was a club I used to hang out at called Jubilation on Harmon Avenue, run by Paul Anka. I kept a table there every night. Everyone was going there. I had my own booth and a booth in reserve in case I needed it. At that time, I was paying everyone off in cash.

I met a woman there, had no idea who she was. This woman— we'll call her Jennifer, not her real name—came to Vegas with her girlfriends, looking for adventure. One night, she and I got drunk and hooked up like anybody else. A few months later, she came to me with a solemn expression on her face.

"I'm pregnant and you're the father," she said.

"I don't even know your name," I said.

"I'm Jennifer Cohen. You know my dad."

The blood drained from my face.

"Mickey Cohen?"

"That's him."

Me, being a gentleman, I contacted Mickey Cohen and told him I needed to have a sit-down with him. I was scared shitless. I was convinced that he was going to take my head off.

Mickey and I met in the coffee shop of the Sands Hotel. The place was a moneymaker. After the second show, the coffee shop was the only place you could go and eat. All of the high rollers held court there, at least on the weekends.

I sat down in this booth and there was Mickey Cohen, scowling. Just the way his face normally looked. There were some of his guys in the booth also.

"Mickey, I got to talk to you."

"You're among friends, Kid, talk."

"I need to talk to you privately."

He looked at me for a moment and we moved to a private table.

"What do you need to tell me?" he said as he sat. Impatient.

"Your daughter Jennifer is pregnant."

"What the fuck are you telling me for?"

I didn't say anything.

Then he got it. "It's you?"

I said, "Yeah."

"Okay. If you plan to have this kid, I want you to make me a promise."

"Anything you want, Mickey."

"If it's a boy, you got to raise him Jewish."

"No problem."

"And the other thing I want you to do is don't marry her."

"What?"

"I don't care if she wants to marry you or not, don't marry her. She's a spoiled brat. Her mother destroyed this girl."

Again, I said, "No problem." I was starting to think he was going to let me live. I could feel my shoulders relax and lower a bit.

When the child was born, he was a boy, and Jennifer insisted on naming him Gianni Russo.

"But I already have a son named Gianni Russo," I said.

She didn't care, and Gianni Russo became his name.

But that's not quite the end of that story. Spin forward thirteen years and we're having a bar mitzvah for the boy. Everybody's there. Sinatra. Steve Wynn. They're all there out of respect. Mickey Cohen has a grandson! I'm there with a yarmulka on. And that was when the unintentional comedy began. Turns out, there is no way you can translate "Gianni Russo" into Hebrew.

So, the rabbi is going through the ceremony, Hebrew, Hebrew, Hebrew, Gianni Russo, Hebrew. Everyone laughed. Well, Mickey Cohen turned around and stared down all who found that *amusing.* The next time the name came up in the Rabbi's

ceremony, there was silence. The name came up about twenty more times and no one dared let out a peep.

It was around that time, early 1970s, they opened a place on Rodeo Drive called The Candy Store and Sinatra, Dean Martin, Sammy Davis, and Gene Shacove used to hang out. Shacove was the L.A. hairdresser to the stars. In fact, they made the movie *Shampoo* about him starring Warren Beatty.

The Candy Store had a fun setup. During the day the place was a regular candy store. But at nine p.m. it would reopen as a nightclub. When you walked in there were still girls behind the candy counter, but they were different girls—hostesses. You flashed a card (I got mine through my friend Lucille Ball) and they took you behind the candy counter and through a door into an elaborate nightclub.

I spent a lot of time hanging out at the Beverly Wilshire Hotel and it was there that I met the diminutive but legendary Harry "Swifty" Morgan, aka Lemon Drop Kid, who ripped off Al Capone and got away with it, mostly because Scarface had a begrudging admiration for a dwarf with balls. Morgan was old by the time I met him. Sinatra was taking care of him, paying bills and giving him passes to his shows. He lived for free at the Wilshire until he died.

It was around the time I was hanging around Sidney Korshak's Le Bistro that I was introduced to the Beverly Hills Bank, which at that time was mobbed up. And that was how I started with the double escrow.

I had one of the biggest deposits in an L.A. bank. I was double-escrowing properties. We were flipping them when they were still in escrow. I could make two, three hundred thousand dollars in a day. That was illegal. So, I was always looking over my shoulder in L.A. just in case a G-man was on my tail. After all, I was living a lavish lifestyle.

During the time I was flipping properties in a rapidly growing

Los Angeles, I lived in The Wilshire on Wilshire Boulevard, between Westholme and Thayer Avenue. That wasn't just any building. It was a large architectural masterpiece, by Richard Magee. It had a limestone-and-copper exterior. Out front there was a grand fountain and a circular motor court entrance. There were many other celebrities living there.

That building was (and is) considered one of the finest condominium buildings in L.A. It has twenty-seven stories, ninety-seven units, and some of the finest service around. There are floor-to-ceiling windows, and private elevator entrances.

Eventually, because of my sketchy business practices, I had to move out, and I mean sneak out, because it was under FBI surveillance. The doorman told me the white van parked outside had feds inside wearing headphones. I don't know if they were there for me, there were many possible targets in the building—Dominic "Donnie Shacks" Montemarano (who dated actress Elizabeth Hurley) comes to mind—but I didn't like it and moved. I had a company go in without me and remove my stuff.

CHAPTER 10
Me and the Greatest Movie Ever Made

I was cruising Beverly Hills in my beautiful black-and-gold Bentley, with double sunroofs. I hired drivers and rode in the back. One of my first drivers was a kid out of Rhode Island, Frank Vallone. I used to call him Primo—as in Primo Carnera. He was six-four, so I sent him to my limo builder in Chicago to be measured. I had to take the passenger seat out and put in an extra-wide driver's seat. I always sat behind where the passenger's seat would have been, and the extra space I used for the bar, phone, and TV set.

After a decade and a half of being known as just "The Kid," my ego needed a boost so I decided to do whatever I had to do to get *name recognition*. I felt like, name-wise, I had some lost time to make up for. Fame was what I craved. I needed to be in—fanfare, please—the exciting world of show business.

I never saw a movie when I was little because I was sick, but as soon as I got out and had some money I went to the cinema every chance I got. I'd go to the 3,500-seat Paramount in Times Square, air-conditioned and open all night, and lose myself in the fantasy world.

I began fantasizing about being an actor at thirteen, and it never stopped. Years later, when I read Mario Puzo's book *The Godfather* and heard it was being made into a movie, and they were casting unknowns, I got the fever.

I was a twenty-eight-year-old Vegas businessman from New York and understood the world in which *The Godfather* took place. I was clearly right for the movie.

I correctly assumed that every Italian guy in Hollywood was thinking the same thing, guys with names, so I was going to have to go some to be noticed.

I would make my own movie, an audition reel, that would wow the producers. I assembled a nonunion film crew. I bought a can of discount 16mm film from Allen Film in Las Vegas. I had dealt with them before. I had a show on Vegas TV at the time, I was the host of *Thursday Night at the Movies*, with my two stores at the time as the sponsors. I rented equipment and produced a professional quality thirty-seven-minute screen test.

On it, I auditioned for Sonny, Michael, and Carlo—that is, godfather Vito Corelone's two sons and son-in-law. In the first scene I played Michael, Vito's son who'd just returned from World War II and wasn't involved with family business. In the scene, Michael sits at Vito's bedside after the attempt on Vito's life. Michael says, "I'm with you now. I'm with you." Next, I played son-in-law Carlo Rizzi, getting the shit kicked out of him by Sonny. In the third scene, I played Sonny, trying to convince his father to go into the drug biz.

Someone told me once that my audition reel would have cost $86,000 to make in a Hollywood studio. Only cost me fifteen. When the film was developed and I looked at it, I was disappointed. My performances were fine but there was something wrong with the film stock. It was very old film, and the result was a washed out look, fade-o-color, almost a sepia tone.

Still, I thought, it was good enough.

Now I had to get the reel into the hands of Paramount producer Al Ruddy, who was best known at the time for producing the TV series *Hogan's Heroes*. Through a friend of mine, Pookie Newman, former secretary for Twentieth Century-Fox producer Darryl F. Zanuck, I met Bettye McCartt and her husband. I was dating Pookie and she and Bettye were best friends. The

McCartts were among my first Vegas friends, and I stayed with them for a while, before I had my own digs in order. I met them through Clint Eastwood, who at the time was making spaghetti westerns. They were house-sitting for Clint, and I stayed in their guest room for a while and cooked for them. They were sorry to see me go.

Bettye was now Al Ruddy's assistant.

"Bettye, I need to get my audition reel to Ruddy in a memorable way," I said.

Bettye thought for a second, then gave me an inside tip: "Ruddy's hot for Asian women and British cars," she said.

"Asian?" I said.

"Yes. Preferably Chinese."

That was all the info I needed. I already had the British car—and I knew where to find the Asian woman. A friend of mine, Rob Lee, producer of the *Folies Bergere*, had the most beautiful showgirls in Vegas.

I hired a beautiful driver from Rob Lee's cast. Her show-biz name was Chyna, and she could drive. I had a sexy chauffeur outfit made for her, the wet look, made out of what looked like leather, but shiny. She wore a micro skirt, dangerous stillettos, and had perfect posture.

Bettye got us permission to drive the Bentley onto the lot. Chyna's instructions were to give the reel to Mr. Ruddy in person. Later she described for me in detail what happened.

Chyna drove very slowly into Paramount, past the lots and offices. She could see the movement in the office blinds as execs were peeking out to see what was going on with the fancy car and the unbelievably sexy driver.

She got into Al Ruddy's office and handed my package to Ruddy himself, saying, "Mr. Gianni Russo would appreciate your consideration for the roles of Sonny, Michael, or Carlo in your upcoming production."

Then she left, got back in the Bentley, and returned to me to report.

What I didn't know was that director Francis Ford Coppola and Bobby Evans, head of Paramount production, were having an argument. Evans wanted the film in rich Technicolor. Coppola wanted black and white, because he thought it was grittier, and suitable for a period piece that takes place just after World War II when films still tended to be in black and white.

The old-time movie moguls were largely gone by the early 1970s, but I knew some of the new guys. One was Charles Bluhdorn, who was the CEO of Gulf+Western, which owned Paramount Pictures. (I learned from my connections in Milan that Bluhdorn had connections there as well. I don't know how much money Bluhdorn was making for them, but I do know that, at first anyway, the last thing those guys in Milan wanted was for Paramount Pictures to make a movie called *The Godfather.*)

Bluhdorn knew how to make money but didn't know that much about making movies, so he let his creative people—Evans and Peter Bart, for example—make the creative decisions. When it came time to decide what type of film to use for *The Godfather,* Bluhdorn was on Evans's side. Moviegoers in the 1970s expected color. They thought of black and white as lesser.

So, my sizzle reel, my screen test, got a lot of attention. It was passed from studio executive to studio executive, not because I was a great actor but because my audition had the "look" that Coppola wanted for *The Godfather.* The movie was eventually made in full color, but the photography was such that the movie retained a lot of Coppola's desired dark-and-moody feel.

About a week later I got a letter saying, "Not at this time." I'd failed the audition. Oh well, back to the drawing board. I wasn't planning on giving up.

None of this was going on in a vacuum. At that time Joe Colombo, who'd taken over what was left of the Profaci family and renamed it after himself, was on a campaign to get Italian Americans treated more nicely.

His organization was called the Italian American Anti-Defamation League. He put it around that he was worried about the reputations of all Italian Americans, but truth was he formed the group to help his son, who'd been busted by the feds for extortion. Colombo complained that all Italian Americans were being treated like gangsters, and it wasn't fair.

As I was making my screen-test film for whatever part I could get, Colombo, who I'd known for years because of my association with Frank Costello, was using Mario Puzo's book, *The Godfather*, as an example of how the entertainment industry urged the public to think about Italian Americans in a certain way.

Of course, there were those, even within Colombo's own family, who recognized that Colombo's war was hypocritical. He really was a Mob boss, and his son really did warrant federal investigation.

One important critic of the Anti-Defamation League was Carlo Gambino, who not only disliked grandstanding of any kind, but felt that attacking law enforcement was always bad for business. Colombo had his troops picketing the FBI offices in Manhattan, carrying signs that said:

Forever
Bothering
Italians

Colombo saw plans to film *The Godfather* as another example of anti-Italian prejudice, one he planned on stopping. Some wannabes stole director Francis Ford Coppola's car in Little Italy. They returned it after a few hours, but the message was sent: To shoot the movie in their neighborhood, he was going to need to get permission.

That wasn't the only incident. Somebody planted a bomb in the middle of the night and blew the gates off the main en-

trance to Paramount's Hollywood studios on Melrose. That terrified the bigwigs at that studio. They knew they were going to
have to make concessions to get their picture made.

Colombo hired attorney Barry Slotnick to represent Colombo's Italian American Anti-Defamation League. Slotnick
had a nose for notoriety. He was not only unafraid of any client,
but he also picked and chose the men he represented with one
eye toward his own name in headlines. Slotnick got away with it
because he was a very good lawyer. He was a New Yorker
through and through: undergraduate studies at CCNY, law
school at NYU, paid his dues and learned the ropes defending
weenie-waggers and hypes in New York night court, and rather
quickly graduated to his own pricey private practice.

He defended Bernie Goetz, the subway vigilante, and he argued on behalf of Joe Colombo before the U.S. Supreme Court.
(In later years he repped Steve Wynn, my buddy the casino
owner, and Manuel Noriega, whose exploits we will discuss,
and John Gotti. He gave the Don his Teflon.)

Slotnick was repping Colombo when I flew into LaGuardia,
cabbed into Manhattan, and met with the two of them. I had
this figured out, an everybody-wins scenario. But they weren't
going to give me a lot of time, so I pitched rapidly. I said that
they should work with Puzo, work with Paramount.

"Negotiate," I said, and I could see I had their attention.
"You get them to take out the things you don't like, a word
here, a scene there. Then you work with the unions, release to
the tabloids the locations in the Italian neighborhoods where
they plan to film, where your Fair Play for Italian Americans
pickets might be disruptive to production. We could make a
lot of money if we play this right."

"We?" Colombo and Slotnick replied in unison.

"Yeah, you don't think I'm doing this for nothing, do you?"

They laughed—thank God.

"All right, Kid. Whatcha got?" Colombo said.

I said, "Here's what you do. They are desperate that you guys
are going to shut their movie down, and they've already sunk

a lot of cash into it. What you do is you negotiate. Take this, this, and this out of the script and we'll give you the green light, but . . . the all-important but . . . we get the proceeds from the opening at all the theaters in the world."

And that was what happened. The word "Mafia" doesn't appear in the script—they said "syndicate" instead. There's no mention of being made. No *omertà*. It's a story about a family.

The other caveat was that I got to be in the movie.

Colombo signed to get opening night—which turned out to be the longest opening night in the history of motion pictures. It's still the only picture that played for twenty-four hours straight at every theater at which it played on its opening day—and we made a bundle.

And I played Carlo.

Colombo told Bobby Evans, "Either the Kid gets the part or you'll be shooting your fucking movie on the Moon."

Evans's autobiography was called *The Kid Stays in the Picture*. I always wondered if I was that Kid.

Paramount announced that I had been cast in the film on April 28, 1971, along with John Cazale (Fredo), Richard Conte (Barzini), and Al Lettieri (Sollozzo). Brando's casting had already been announced, but James Caan, who would play Sonny, and Al Pacino (Michael) weren't hired yet.

Being cast in the movie completely changed my life. I had wanted name recognition and boy did I get it. I'm still getting it. I got my SAG card in twenty-four hours and went to work. I had a conversation with Puzo, who not only wrote the book but would cowrite the movie screenplay with Coppola.

I asked him how he came up with the character of Vito Corleone.

He said, "He is a composite. One part of him is Joseph Profaci, because he had the olive oil. Part of him is Carlo Gambino, the old-fashioned demeanor with an old-fashioned Sicilian sense of style. Another part is your guy Frank Costello, the part that had the politicians in his pocket." He smiled.

So, it was the three of them, and he made them into one character.

For me, there was one remaining obstacle: Frank Sinatra. Frank was desperate for the picture to be scrubbed because he knew there was a character in the script, Johnny Fontane, that was based on him and made him look weak.

He called me and asked me "as a friend" to quit the movie.

I asked him if he "as a friend" would have turned down his Oscar-winning role in *From Here to Eternity* if I'd asked him.

He hung up on me.

I wasn't the only connected fellow to be cast in the picture. Al Lettieri (Sollozzo) was Tommy "Ryan" Eboli's brother-in-law, and Luca Brasi was played by Colombo bodyguard Lenny Montana, who'd had a long and successful career as a pro wrestler.

Those were the big roles. There were extras with street cred as well. In my wedding scene, many of the 750 friends and family came from the ranks, including all the mugs at Don Barzini's table who were actual Colombo soldiers.

As for Joseph Colombo, he never had an opportunity to collect on *The Godfather*. On June 27, 1971, around the time we were just about wrapping up production on the movie, I get a call from my friend Tommy Bilotti, who I've known since forever from Little Italy, who was with the Gambinos.

As a kid Tommy ran errands for Johnny D'Alessio, a Gambino capo who ran Staten Island gambling. As a young man he was bodyguard for Alexander "The Ox" DeBrizzi. His first big bust came when he was twenty-nine, for fencing stolen property.

Bilotti was fearsome and earned a reputation as being creatively sadistic and quick to resort to violence. He had a short fuse and could go from calm to furious in the blink of an eye. A federal agent once described him as a "pit bull with shoes on."

I can't tell you when I met Tommy Bilotti. He was a neighborhood kid, running around. As soon as I showed up at age twelve on Mulberry Street, there was Tommy Bilotti, and we were always friends.

Today, Tommy Bilotti is known best for the way he died, dead in the street outside Sparks Steak House, dead in the street along with Gambino boss "Big Paul" Castellano, Carlo Gambino's cousin and brother-in-law, the man hand-picked by Don Carlo to succeed him. (John Gotti had other ideas.)

Because I'd led the life I'd led, I didn't know many soldiers, or capos for that matter. Mr. Costello told me to deal with top echelon only, so as a rule I didn't know guys like Tommy Bilotti, guys who were working their way up. It's proof he was a good friend of mine. If it was just business, I probably would never have been in the same room with him.

One thing we had in common is he wanted to run a nightclub, and at a very young age he moved to Staten Island and ran a club called Crocitto's on Sand Lane, South Beach, known for its hot music on weekends and dancing. Tommy was a mover and a shaker. He married one of the Crocitto girls and took over the club from her father.

And Bilotti did work his way up. His power grew along with his boss's, until by the end he was underboss of the Gambino family. Tommy always stayed close to Big Paul. When Castellano bought a mansion in Todt Hill on Staten Island, Bilotti moved as well to a house nearby. Castellano promoted Bilotti to capo in 1981, and for the first time Bilotti had his own crew. Only months after that, Bilotti was promoted again. When Castellano became the father of the Gambino family, he appointed Bilotti to be his underboss, a move that pissed off Gambino captains who felt more worthy of the position.

Frank DeCicco made plans to meet with Castellano and Bilotti at Sparks (Forty-Sixth Street and Third Avenue in Manhattan) on December 16, 1982, and then informed Gotti and his pal Sammy "The Bull" Gravano of the where and when. So, when Bilotti drove the luxury car up to the steak house, and he and the boss got out, gunmen (allegedly John Carneglia, Dominick Pizzonia, and Tony Rampino) were on the spot and firing. Gotti and Gravano were parked at the end of the block where they could watch the action.

Now Gotti and Gravano weren't the sharpest tacks, but one aspect of the Sparks hit was brilliant. The United Nations was in session and the block was crawling with foreign dignitaries. So, the gunmen wore Russian hats and trench coats. Blended right in.

Castellano and Bilotti died in close proximity, so it is appropriate that their remains are close as well. Both are interred in Moravian Cemetery in New Dorp, Staten Island, Bilotti in a grave, Castellano in a crypt, approximately fifty yards apart.

But I'm getting ahead of myself.

During production on *The Godfather*, Tommy Bilotti called me. It was the night before Colombo's second big "Italian Unity" rally at Columbus Circle.

"Gianni, you going to that rally tomorrow?" he asked me.

I said, "Sure."

"You can't go."

"You crazy? I have to go. I'm on the dais." It was true, there was a chair on the stage with my name on it. Colombo liked my solution to *The Godfather* problem so much, he'd given me a seat of honor.

"I don't care if you got Joe Colombo sitting on your lap. You can't go."

"How come?"

"The old man says you can't go." That meant Gambino.

Well, that was different. I said to myself, oh God, how the hell am I going to get out of this? I thought and thought and eventually picked up the phone and called Barry Slotnick.

I said, "Barry, you got to apologize to Joe for me. I got food poisoning. The only seat I'm going to take today is on the toilet."

He said, "OK, I'll let him know."

So, I didn't go. I snuck out the back door of my building, just in case someone was watching for me in the front, and I went to Mulberry Street. I remember it was a beautiful summer day. And I heard the news on the radio that Colombo had been shot.

The first rally at Columbus Circle in 1970 had been a huge success, but a year later it was a disaster. I wasn't the only one told not to go. Not by a long shot.

The hit on Colombo was done up in a nice neat bow: A beautiful black woman aggressively walked up to Colombo as he was approaching the stage to address the Pride Day gathering. Colombo might have been a hypocrite, but he was a man, and he reacted positively to the woman's approach. Hey, Mama. While he was otherwise distracted, a black guy with photographer credentials hanging around his neck, dressed like a pimp, shot Colombo multiple times in the head. A young member of the boss's security team then shot the black gunman to death and fled. (This play, shooting the guy who did the shooting, was called the double-bang. Like Oswald whacks JFK, Ruby whacks Oswald, *bang, bang.* It insulates the plot's sponsor from the actual hit.)

Colombo was tossed on a stretcher, clinging to life, and rushed to the hospital where he was declared brain-dead and put on life support.

The black shooter was identified as twenty-four-year-old Jerome A. Johnson. Johnson's killer was never identified. The press credentials Johnson wore were counterfeit. He was just a cheap criminal, seven arrests on his record: rape, assault, burglary, drugs. Now he was the rally's sole fatality. No one cared who killed him. Cops threw up their hands. Feds threw up their hands.

Word on the street was that Joey Gallo, whose crew was at war with the Colombos, arranged the hit to make amends with Carlos Gambino. Colombo stole the headlines, but many other New York area hoods were whacked that day. It was a purge, one of those days when Carlo Gambino, the dear man who'd given me a transistor radio when I was a kid in the hospital, was making sure he was and would remain Boss of Bosses.

About forty-eight hours after the shooting of Joe Colombo, I started to get visits and phone calls. The feds wanted to know why I wasn't at the rally. The Colombo family, with Carmine "Junior" Persico in charge while Colombo was in the hospital, wanted to know why I didn't show. I stuck with my story. I ate a bad clam.

In TV footage of the rally, which was now a crime scene, you could see an empty chair on the stage with my name on it. With Colombo incapacitated, Joseph Yacovelli became acting boss of the Colombos, but Carmine Persico was the actual guy calling the shots. And the Italian American Anti-Defamation League quickly faded into oblivion.

The relationship between me and one of my fellow *Godfather* cast members was not always a smooth one, mostly because James Caan could be a jerk. He thought he was funny, but someone could've gotten hurt—and that someone was me.

The incident that led to bad blood happened during the second week of filming, sometime in the summer of 1971, not long after Colombo was shot. Cast members were having drinks at Jilly Rizzo's joint, a west-side tavern known for being Frank Sinatra's favorite.

Caan, ever the smug prankster, told me that Junior Persico was in the back room with his daughter, that I should go back and pay my respects. So, I went back to see Junior, and sure enough there he was with a beautiful twenty-year-old brunette.

I said, "Your daughter is gorgeous. What a beautiful girl."

Carmine's face dropped.

It wasn't his daughter. It was his *goomada*, and Caan had purposefully lied to me. Some of the boys at Carmine's table followed me into the men's room to teach me a lesson, but I was rescued.

Tommy Bilotti, my friend since Day One, was there that night with Vincent "Boozy" DeCicco. Boozy and Tommy rescued me, first from the guys who were going to beat me, and then from Junior.

"Honest mistake, honest mistake. The woman is beautiful," Boozy said.

I told Bilotti what happened.

"I'll kill him right here and now," Bilotti said.

"No," I said, "we still have a movie to make." I added, "You could scare him if you want to."

They took him for a ride, got him shitting his pants, and then told him he should be more respectful to me, who was a friend of many powerful people.

Caan survived the incident, but when it came time for Sonny Corleone to beat the crap out of Carlo in the movie, Caan didn't pull his punches, or his kicks.

Despite that one faux pas in Jilly's, Persico and the film people got along. Junior allowed Coppola access to genuine locations that lent the film supreme authenticity.

Persico told Caan he couldn't hang around the Colombos anymore. Caan was dressed down by Junior: "Jimmy, you want to be a wise guy? Do you? Look, you almost got this kid killed, and I like him. You want to be a gangster? Well, you ain't with us no more. You're with them. You want to find out how to make your movie, ask them."

He pointed at Boozy DeCicco, who was an officer with the Gambinos. So, James Caan was tossed from the Colombos to the Gambinos in a way that made Caan feel less than a hotshot movie star.

To wrap up, Boozy's son, Frankie Boy DeCicco, who lived on Forest Hill Road on Staten Island, worked arm in arm with John Gotti. In fact, Frankie Boy arranged the meeting that drew Big Paul and Tommy to Sparks on that fateful night. So, he betrayed his father's friend, in favor of hanging on to John Gotti's coattails. It didn't do him much good, however.

After Big Paul and Tommy were whacked without Commission approval, commissioners Anthony Corallo (Lucchese) and Vincent the Chin (Genovese) put out contracts on everyone and anyone associated with Big Paul's demise, but with an emphasis on Gotti and DeCicco.

Red Hook psycho-killer Anthony "Gaspipe" Casso and his pal, Lucchese soldier Vittorio "Vic" Amuso, were given the contract.

On an early Sunday afternoon, April 13, 1986, fifty-two-year-old Frank DeCicco and a companion from the Lucchese family, sixty-nine-year-old Frank Bellino, drove in a gray 1985 Buick to a meeting in the Bath Beach section of Brooklyn, which is South Bensonhurst. It was raining so the men ran quickly from the car into the Veterans and Friends, Inc. social club on Eighty-Sixth Street. They forgot something in the car and went back out. Frankie Boy made the mistake of throwing John Gotti's coat over his shoulders as he ran to the car.

While the men were in the club, Casso planted a bomb under the car, approximately under the driver's seat. Gaspipe mistook DeCicco for Gotti and as soon as DeCicco got to the car, Gaspipe blew him across the street.

DeCicco was killed and Bellino was critically injured. The bomb was so powerful that windows up and down the block were blown out by the blast.

While making *The Godfather*, and while doing publicity after its release, I never chummied up to Jimmy Caan—but I did hang out a lot with Marlon Brando. At first, Brando didn't like the idea of a nonactor being in the film, but eventually came to enjoy giving me acting lessons. So, I learned a bit of "the method." He told me to remember scary things in my life when I had to emote fear. So, when Michael tells Carlo he's being moved to Vegas, and Carlo knows he's gonna get hit, I was thinking about the terror of being carried into the polio ward.

Coppola was always looking for reality even in the back-

grounds of scenes, which is why my sister Joanne and her husband and kids are among the Italians hanging out on the
street during the scene where I get a beating.

Here's how that went down: The day before we shot that
scene, we carefully choreographed it. The cameramen were
barking orders, stop there, focus, stop there, focus, so they
knew how to keep the entire scene in focus the next day when
it's shot.

Come the actual shooting, I knew right away I was in trouble
because Caan switched it up. For one thing, he came at me
with a billy club, which he threw and conked me on the head,
opening a cut.

I went down behind the car. We paused and they checked
on me. I was bleeding. They wanted to know if I needed to stop
and I said, no, no, let's keep going. It's my first picture. I don't
want to look like a wimp. Sure, let's keep shooting.

I'm not sure younger viewers quite get it when they watch
that scene today. That garbage can cover that Caan belted me
with was made of steel. Even though I was padded, the steel
chipped my elbow.

I remember crawling out, knowing that he's got to kick me
over so I can roll into the fire hydrant. He kicked me so hard
that he lifted me up. I realized I was being assaulted on camera. That kick broke two ribs.

For those of you who have never had a broken rib, let me
tell you, you can't breathe without it hurting. One sneeze and
you practically faint. And there's nothing you can do to make
it heal quicker. You can't put a cast on a rib.

Watch that scene today and the brutality is apparent. There
is also a key mistake that was never fixed. One of Sonny's first
punches clearly misses me by six inches (yet I sell it like a pro).
They should've used a different angle. I once asked Coppola,
"Francis, why don't you fix that?" There were cameras of that
punch from a dozen angles. It could easily have been switched
to fix the mistake, but . . .

He said, "I can't. Once you win an Oscar, the Academy of

Motion Pictures forbids you to edit it. It's like you can't put a smile on the Mona Lisa's face. You can't touch it."

So, to this day, that punch misses, and I sell it like it broke my jaw. It might be the only error in the whole movie, which is as perfect as they come.

Much of *The Godfather* was shot on Staten Island. Since I was familiar with New York's smallest borough because my grandparents lived there, Al Ruddy took me along when he scouted for locations.

The house they used for the wedding scene was on Longfellow Road, around the corner from Big Paul Castellano's mansion in Grymes Hill—although the interiors were shot in a Long Island studio. Fun fact: the band that played at the movie wedding, the Nino Morelli Band, also played at one of my real-life weddings.

Most of the cast was staying at the Park Lane Hotel on Fifty-Ninth Street. I was living a few blocks away. Brando was staying at the Elysee Hotel on Fifty-Fourth between Madison and Park Avenues. That was where they had the Monkey Bar where he liked to drink. We all had the same call for makeup and hair, so I'd pick Brando up and give him a ride in the Bentley to Staten Island.

One morning Brando and I are having coffee in the back of the car, cruising wide Park Avenue. It didn't matter what time of day it was, Brando warmed up his coffee with liquor. We had the Bentley's service tables down.

We stopped at one red light, two red lights, three . . .

Alongside pulls another car, and there's James Caan's and Robert Duvall's asses hanging out the window. They were having a mooning contest—who could moon in front of the most people.

Brando won the contest, as he mooned between takes during the wedding scene where the Corleone family is having their picture taken. Those poor kids. The sight of Brando's huge hairy ass might've scarred them for life.

Brando didn't care that much about the car, but Chyna was still driving for me, still wearing the same sexy uniform. The wet look. So, that's how I lost her as my driver. We finished filming is August 1971, Brando took Chyna to Tahiti, and we never saw her again.

The New York premier of the movie was at the Times Square Paramount, the same palace theater where I'd first learned about the movies after I got out of the hospital. Returning to the scene of my lonely childhood saddened me, despite the excitement of the occasion. I was sad because I hadn't spoken to Mr. Costello in weeks and knew him to be in failing health. I didn't stay for the picture. I went to the after-party, but only briefly. I was done with *The Godfather*, or so I thought.

I didn't know that the movie was going to be the key to my future fortunes. I'd made $17,000 for playing Carlo, which just about made up for my audition reel. All I wanted to do was get back to Vegas and continue my life.

But it didn't work out that way. There was publicity to do, and with it came the rapid realization that I'd *never* be done with *The Godfather*.

A month before the movie came out, I did my first publicity interview in L.A. I talked about *The Godfather* the requisite amount and switched the topic to me and my many ideas. I'd written a book called *Four Times Seven*. I wanted to buy the rights to *Catcher in the Rye* and make it as a movie. I was an idea guy.

In March 1972, right around *The Godfather*'s premiere, New York *Daily News* columnist Sidney Fields ran a feature about me. He talked to John and Bettye McCartt. Bettye, you remember, was Al Ruddy's assistant, the friend who gave me the tip about Ruddy's fetishes.

Bettye was a good source for Fields. She told him about Chyna and the Bentley. Fields loved it. The article coursed my rags to riches story, beating polio, sleeping in a closet, filling a stove with kerosene each night for heat.

When Fields interviewed me for the column, I didn't specify exactly when and where my fortunes changed, but I told him, "I incorporated myself because I run a couple of dozen corporations. My board of directors has an insurance company president, the director of a big hospital, and an ex-governor of Nevada."

I had to tell a story about how I made money without mentioning the obvious boost I received from Mr. Costello. I told him that while attending high school I made pizzas nine to five and sold greeting cards as my side hustle. I became a building laborer to "please my dad," who was an executive in the musicians union. I kept it up. I decided to invest, so I put my savings into army surplus and stocks, started an investment firm in Florida, a jewelry firm in L.A., and a travel agency in Vegas. I was a millionaire at twenty-one.

I told about fifteen lies in a row, making it sound like I took the money I'd earned as a bricklayer, eight bucks an hour, and parlayed that into a fortune. Discerning readers knew there was a piece of the story missing.

"My corporations own a wig store, a recording company, discotheques, and I produced a twenty-six-episode TV series called *Welcome to My Lifestyle*. Episodes feature Jimmy Durante and Sammy Davis, Jr."

"How did you get the part in the movie?" Fields asked.

I chalked it up to persistence.

There was another feature about me by *Daily News* columnist Peter Coutros that same week. I'd been drawing attention from Manhattan pedestrians by riding around in a white stretch limo, twenty-five feet from license plate to license plate.

"It's the longest running thing on Broadway," I joked.

That car was usually used by Sinatra but he let me use it when he was out of town. It had originally been a Continental town car but underwent major reconstruction, lengthened to make room for a bar, phone, and a TV.

The column said the limo fit right in with my opulent lifestyle. Coutros wrote I looked like I was wearing the great bulk of my fortune around my neck, wrists, and waist. The guy said I had "half of Fort Knox" on my body.

Anyway, when I climbed out of the fantastic car, I was at Lincoln Center, Avery Fisher Hall, walking a red carpet for the opening of the screen adaptation of F. Scott Fitzgerald's unfinished Hollywood epic, *The Last Tycoon*.

The Godfather became a phenomenon, and why not? There was need to do publicity above and beyond the usual three-to-five-day tours for most films. We chatted *The Godfather* to cold-blooded deejays and plastic talk-show hosts for months.

I remember Al Ruddy and I did some publicity together. We were on the Casper Citron late-night radio talk show on WQXR in New York.

Sometimes my name came up in features written about James Caan, an actor who was "never more convincing" than when he beat me and left me in the gutter. That inspired one reader to write in: "What kind of talent was needed to beat up Gianni Russo? Any stunt man could have done as well."

I got a kick out of that—literally.

During the fall of 1972 I dated Liza Minnelli, which got us both mentioned in Charles McHarry's "On the Town" column in the *Daily News*. He wrote: "Liza Minnelli, linked seriously with Desi Arnaz, Jr., has been enjoying the attentions of another escort of late. He's young actor Gianni Russo, seen as the wife-beating son-in-law in *The Godfather*."

I knew even then that I was stuck with that career synopsis. No matter what I did, win a Nobel Peace Prize, and the lead in my obituary will be I'm Carlo. But I haven't let it discourage me. I have had a strong acting career after *The Godfather*.

After playing Carlo, I was a desired commodity. Before 1972 was through, I appeared in *Goodnight, My Love,* a private dick murder mystery with Richard Boone of *Have Gun, Will Travel.* The movie also featured Barbara Bain, of *Mission: Impossible,* Victor Buono, who played King Tut on *Batman,* and Michael Dunn, the little person best known as Dr. Loveless on the TV show *Wild, Wild West.*

In 1973, I was on *The Merv Griffin Show.* Merv was a singer and popular talk-show host, who will probably be best remembered as the inventor of the game shows *Jeopardy!* and *Wheel of Fortune.* It was "All-Italian" night on Merv's talk show. I appeared on the couch with Ernest Borgnine, Anna Maria Alberghetti, Alex Cord, and Peter Barbutti.

I was booked to appear on Merv again, this time in a "tough guys" episode with Robert Conrad, James Caan, and real-life hood Fat Vinnie Teresa of the Boston Patriarca family. That episode nearly went off the rails when Vinnie recognized me from years back, saying, "Kid, is that you?" I stupidly made a joke, being with "tough guys" I wanted to be a tough guy, saying I could make half a mil with one phone call to a guy who was looking for Fat Vinnie. The network stopped taping and U.S. Marshals showed up and I yelled it was just a joke. After a delay, the show resumed and my joke didn't make it on the air.

In 1975, I was in *Lepke,* playing "The Mad Hatter," Albert Anastasia. It was fun because Anastasia was no one to mess with. The movie was about Murder, Inc., the real-life *sette* of pro guns who, not affiliated with any family, perform hits of all sorts at the behest of the Commission, working out of the back room of a candy store called Midnight Rose, in the Brownville section of Brooklyn. Midnight Rose sold more than candy and kept a staff of girls upstairs.

Between movies, Frank Sinatra was giving me singing lessons. I couldn't copy his voice, but I learned from his style, the little casual things Frank did that redefined *cool.* I had an Italian lounge sound and was good enough to get jobs. During the summer of 1975, I headlined at Brooklyn's Copa; I sang Italian classics like "Inamorata," "Volare," and, of course, "Love Theme from *The Godfather.*"

One night during that gig, Tommy Bilotti came to my show. He was living dangerously. He had his girlfriend sitting ringside, while he sat with his wife farther back on the left side of the room.

Before the show, he explained the layout and asked me to play up to his *goomada* during my show.

"Make her feel special, she's sitting alone. She don't think I know you," Tommy said.

So, I did. I picked out the girlfriend and I sang a few songs just to her. Crowd loved it. I finished my show, and I was not in my dressing room for more than two seconds when here comes Tommy Bilotti charging like a bull.

"What the fuck were you doing? I saw the way you were looking at my girl!" he screamed, genuinely angry.

"You told me to!" I protested.

"Yeah, well, not that much," he said.

Luckily for me, just at that moment, Paul Castellano walked in to congratulate me, and said, "Tommy, are you nuts? Calm down."

In July 1976, I was again on Merv, this time with celebs of varying ethnicities. I remember Rich Little and the Lennon Sisters. After that I was a regular. Later in the summer I appeared with stand-up comedian David Steinberg, William Holden, and Loretta Lynn. I plugged my upcoming gig at Dangerfield's, singing a few tunes.

My gig at Dangerfield's was reviewed by Harry Stathos, who said that, even though I was getting singing lessons from Ol' Blue Eyes, I sounded more like Dean Martin, maybe with a little Tony Bennett thrown in. Hell, I'll take it.

On a December Merv, I appeared with Barbara Eden and Richard Dawson. I was on a bunch of times in 1974 as well. All in all, I did Merv's show twenty-three times.

Anyway, if you want to know all the details on my show-biz career, you can check my IMDb page online. I've had a wonderful career, in film and on the stage. I am particularly proud of it, too. I owe my business success to Frank Costello, I recognize that. But making it in show biz, that was all me.

On February 18, 1973, Frank Costello died, and I felt like an orphan. His funeral was at the Frank E. Campbell Funeral Chapel on Madison Avenue in Manhattan, and his tomb is in St. Michael's Cemetery in East Elmhurst, Queens.

There was a small fuss about the size of his funeral convoy, about the size of the flower arrangements around his coffin, and finally, the size of his tomb, which is larger than many Manhattan apartments. A caretaker at St. Michael's Cemetery was a blabbermouth, told a reporter that the plot alone cost Mrs. Costello $4,880.

"She paid in cash," the caretaker said.

On that five-grand plot they built an elegant marble mausoleum. The contractor who built the structure later said he had no idea that its occupant was famous.

"I didn't recognize the name," the guy said, a smart contractor. He said that he'd taken the job from an elderly man named Amilcare Festa, who turned out to be a trusted neighbor of Frank Costello's mother. He was paid in cash, a series of packets, each containing fifty hundred-dollar bills.

Unfortunately, that wasn't the last time Mr. Costello's tomb would make the papers, all because of an idiot named Carmine Galante, a man who'd vowed to kill Costello but lost the opportunity to a lengthy prison sentence.

CHAPTER 11

My Rise and Fall in Las Vegas, Nevada

In Vegas, I came up with a scheme that made me very rich. And I couldn't have done it without Moe Dalitz, who I first met during my Tour of Bosses and who, while giving me a walking tour, explained to me how casinos worked.

He told me there were two count rooms in the casino. The money went into one count room, the skim came off, and then to a second count room for the "official" tally. Inside the first count room there was a closet door. On it was painted "The Morgue."

"Is that where you put the dead customers?" I asked—sort of joking. I envisioned degenerate gamblers with tags on their toes.

"No, that is where we keep the deadbeat markers," Dalitz said.

"Markers" is casino-speak for IOUs. They weren't collectible because the guys who owed the money only had to cross the Nevada state line to be home free. The casinos weren't allowed to collect out of state.

"But I would bet most of those guys don't know the law," I said. And, I thought, even if they did know the law, they would be men with money and reputations, thus vulnerable to a little good old-fashioned blackmail.

I pitched the idea to Moe Dalitz, then okayed it with the casino bosses, and optioned a half-million dollars' worth of markers for three months, after which I owed the casinos twenty-five cents on each dollar owed.

I then put my traveling shoes on and began to pay visits to those who'd borrowed money from the casinos and then skipped town. As it turned out, locating the debtors was often more difficult than collecting.

I specialized in doctors and lawyers who didn't want their patients, clients, and their communities to know they were degenerates, guys who apparently couldn't count to twenty-one without taking off their shoes and exposing themselves.

I'd call up the doctor or the dentist and make an appointment, pretending to be a new patient. When I got there, and I was alone with the doctor, I would explain the actual reason for my visit. They always paid.

One time I went to see a gynecologist.

"I think you're in the wrong place," he said.

"No, I'm not," I replied. Then I took out the marker and showed him. "Look familiar?"

In six months, I had three million dollars, so I put it on the street to grow. I set up a shylock operation. In Cleveland, I worked with Corky Civella. I'd say, "Here's a million dollars. Put it out there and have your guys collect."

There were far more markers than I could single-handedly pursue, so I put together a staff. They collected and brought me envelopes. I made $30 million collecting debts. Moe Dalitz got a piece. I traveled from boss to boss paying tribute, thanking them for allowing me to collect Nevada debts on their turf.

Everybody won, except for grown men who welched on their bets and should've known better. I ran the marker business for four years and then let someone else do it. I found the job soul sucking, squeezing money out of guys who'd sometimes wrecked their lives, destroyed their families, because they couldn't get away from the blackjack table until they'd blown the college fund and the mortgage.

I was now a big-time earner and officially unafilliated. It was at this point in my life when I faced the most pressure to stop freelancing and become a company man—that is, to get straightened out with one of the families.

I didn't want to offend anyone, of course, but I never saw the advantage in getting a button. Maybe it made sense for some guys, made it so they couldn't be whacked without a Commission vote, gave them a network in which to thrive. But I had been taught the ropes by a Boss, and my contact with mobsters was *never* at street level. It wasn't even at capo level. I flew above the level of security. I worked almost above the family system and was far more mobile than I would have been had I been made. I decided to keep it that way.

After the marker money, I didn't need to work anymore, but I liked making money and had been taught to think big. Soon I had a new dream—to build a $54 million hotel-casino on an empty lot on Koval Lane between Flamingo Road and Harmon Avenue. I was going to call it the Renaissance.

For a long time, I was optimistic. The rose-colored glasses were never more dazzling than on November 22, 1978, the fifteenth anniversary of the JFK assassination, when the board of county commissioners granted me a use permit to build and operate a 650-room, twenty-three-story structure.

To further finance the Renaissance project, I borrowed $30 million from the Teamsters' pension fund—on a napkin. Reporters talked to me. I told them I planned to have twenty-one blackjack tables, four craps tables, a Big Six Wheel, baccarat, keno, and 750 slot machines. The casino, I said, would be 18,000 square feet.

No one knew anything about me, other than I played a

gangster in a movie. They didn't know where my money came from.

I had no criminal record, and the government wasn't looking at me. I converted a large chunk of my marker money as a construction loan through a bank in Italy. I continued to buy real estate.

On April Fool's Day, I threw a big party in a tent at the future site of the Renaissance. Many stars showed up: Siegfried & Roy, Bobby Vinton, Lola Falana, Liberace, Steve Wynn, Wayne Newton, et. al. My daughter Gia and I christened the site by breaking a magnum of Dom Pérignon on a bulldozer. The slogan for the party was "Can You Dig It?" All the swag had that on it. At midnight I pulled a rope and the side curtains to the tent fell to the ground. Everyone walked outside and there were fireworks with the future casino's name spelled across the sky. The sun was coming up by the time the last guests left. But that was it as far as optimism went for the project. In several quick steps I learned I was making a mistake.

I took out a ninety-nine-year lease on the twenty-three-acre lot. I did it for a couple of reasons. I figured I wasn't going to live another ninety-nine years and, plus, I arranged that I didn't have to pay taxes on it until I began developing the property. It was leased. So, I put three or four hundred thousand dollars into Las Vegas Paving and they went in and did all the excavation and prepped the footing for the foundation.

It was now 1980. I was going to make the first draw of the $30 million I'd borrowed when fate intervened.

It started with an article in the paper about me and was cinched by the government's plan to kick the Mob boys out of Vegas and replace them with their own people.

The figurehead for this massive government conspiracy was an eccentric, reclusive, germophobic, aviator/movie and media mogul/oil broker named Howard Hughes. No one saw him ever. There was a rumor that he'd died and his continued life was a hoax. But that wasn't true. Hughes was alive but a whack job who'd only be in the same room with Mormons because he thought them clean.

The newspaper article that got me thinking I'd made a mistake was written by Ned Day, an investigative reporter for the *Las Vegas Review-Journal.* The article was the result of an FBI wiretap. The article was called "Mob Spurns Vegas Godfather."

Day thought it was a riot that I'd "convincingly" played mobbed-up guys in the movies and on TV, and now my name was popping up in transcriptions of FBI wiretaps. His tone was snarky. He called me "impeccably tanned" like it was a character flaw or something.

He quoted sparingly from the actual transcripts, but went heavy on how those transcripts characterized me, which allowed him to use his skills to give me the needle. The tapes, he said, cast me perfectly, as a guy who loved to go to the discos and dance. Again, not a character flaw.

He wrote that I was a hanger-on, surrounded by other hangers-on—"a coterie of sycophants, star-sniffers, and dim-witted bimbos"—with a quixotic dream to build a Las Vegas casino-hotel at the corner of Harmon Avenue and Koval Lane, where there was now just a vacant lot.

He said that I couldn't get through a sentence without hinting at my sinister yet uber-powerful connections "back East." (That might have been true.) He concluded that I was a "two-bit hustler, long on con, but short on cash."

Day got down to brass tacks: the transcripts. They were of a conversation in Kansas City with the Civella brothers, Joe Agosto—head of the Tropicana Hotel's Folies Bergere—and underboss Carl DeLuna. Day called Nick Civella the "Godfather."

NICK CIVELLA (addressing his brother Carl): I read that article about you and him, Cork.

CORKY CIVELLA: He called the other day, said he's coming in Tuesday with a friend.

JOE AGOSTO: Yeah, I know this John [sic] Russo. He doesn't

have a good reputation in Vegas. I want you to know about it. His location is bad. Off the Strip. Not enough rooms to make serious money.

NICK CIVELLA: All right. I'll see what this Russo, when he comes, we'll see, uh, what he's got. And then if he's got anything that sounds good, like it's got any . . .

JOE AGOSTO: But if Russo doesn't have any money.

NICK CIVELLA: Yeah.

CARL DeLUNA: He doesn't have any money.

JOE AGOSTO: He has little money, you said.

CARL DeLUNA: No, he's good for investors.

JOE AGOSTO: Only a fool would invest $30 million in that project.

I liked the article because it made me see how this was going to shake down. The writing was on the wall.

Now here comes the payoff. My hesitation saved my ass. Jimmy Carter was the president at the time and interest on loans for construction projects was 19 percent. My accounting firm, Ernst & Young, said that I would have to maintain a 91 percent occupancy rate at my planned hotel to keep my head above water—that is, just to service my debt.

Lucky for me, I was getting a lot of bad vibes about the thing, not just from Ned Day, and I pulled the plug. It was a good thing, too, because of that wiretap. They were waiting for me to take the draw. If I'd made it, I would have been looking at a long, long prison sentence. I might just now be getting out of jail.

Three nights after I pulled the plug, there was a massive fire at the construction site, all the records, everything was burned. Another tremendous stroke of luck. The site is still vacant— and available.

In future years I would never again be this ambitious in Las Vegas. Remembering how much fun I had running Tiffany's at

the Trop, I decided my next project would be a nightclub—
and I'll get to that soon.

As for Ned Day, his job was needling wiseguys in the morning paper, so he made enemies. A few weeks after he mocked
the Kansas City conversation, his 1983 tan Volvo was torched in
the parking lot to his apartment building on Paradise Road.

Day joked that it was probably a mobster who destroyed his
car, but it might've been a "self-styled media critic."

Ned Day only had a little more than a year to live. During
the summer of 1987 he went on vacation to Honolulu Beach in
Hawaii and died of an apparent heart attack while swimming
in Hanauma Bay.

A long time ago, I did a smart thing. I began keeping a journal of everything I did, and everyone I knew. The first entries
are about Howard Hughes, who was for reasons then unclear
occupying a lot of rooms at the Desert Inn.

Maybe there are people out there now who've never heard
of Howard Hughes. But in his day, the middle of the twentieth
century, he was one of the most famous people on the planet,
newsworthy on multiple fronts.

Hughes was simultaneously an oil tycoon, a fearless test
pilot, a Hollywood mogul, and a defense contractor. His fortune was made by his dad, who invented the rotary drill bit
used to drill for oil. Then the dad set up a system whereby
prospectors couldn't drill for oil on land they owned unless
they used a Hughes drill bit. Instead of having an oil well of his
own, he took points off of every oil well in America.

Hughes was born in Houston in 1905 and showed an early
aptitude for engineering. He studied at Caltech but his mom
died when he was seventeen and his dad died when he was
nineteen so he quit school and took over the formidable family business, the Hughes Tool Company in Houston.

When he was twenty-one, he moved to Hollywood and, money
bulging from his pockets, made self-indulgent films, still silent

at that time, that went over budget and strained the limits of good taste, as perceived during the Roaring Twenties.

That said, he made some really good pictures, like *Two Arabian Nights*, winner of the 1929 Academy Award for Best Directing of a Comedy Picture; and *Hell's Angels*, a World War I dogfight picture that began production as a silent and ended three years later as a talkie.

In 1932, Hughes produced the classic gangster picture *Scarface*, which caused all kinds of agita with the censors because it was so brutal. By the 1940s, his pictures seemed more like vehicles to push his latest girlfriend, all of whom had humongous tits. He was a Hollywood mogul between 1948 and 1953, the five years that he ran RKO Pictures, with studios on Melrose right next to Paramount.

Even as he was making movies in Hollywood, he tirelessly pursued his most passionate interest, aviation. In 1932 he founded the Hughes Aircraft Company in Culver City, California. He was the president of the company and its chief test pilot.

On September 12, 1935, he took the latest plane he'd designed for its first flight and set the speed record, flying at 352 mph. On January 19, 1937, in that same plane, he set a new record for transcontinental flight, going coast-to-coast in seven hours and twenty-eight minutes. The following year he flew around the world in ninety-one hours, fourteen minutes, another aviation record. Soon thereafter he went into his mad money and bought a controlling interest in TWA.

After the Japanese bombed Pearl Harbor in 1941, Hughes turned his attention to designing military aircraft, which first established him as a defense contractor, taking millions of dollars of government money to build the Hughes XF-11 and the H-4 Hercules. Neither plane was used to any advantage in the war effort, however. Up until 1946, Hughes's career as a test pilot had seemed charmed, never causing him more than a scratch. But in 1946, World War II now over, he was flying an

XF-11 when he crashed, suffering near-fatal injuries, including head trauma. That was when he began to act oddly.

Hughes turned his attention to the Hercules, which as of 1947 had still never flown. It was the largest plane ever built, designed to carry 750 passengers. Hughes flew the plane, nick-named the *Spruce Goose*, only while empty, only once, and only for one mile, during which it never achieved much altitude.

As a plane designer hired by the Pentagon, he was a miser-able failure, only technically fulfilling the terms of his contract. It would stand to reason that the U.S. defense department would cut him loose, right?

Instead, they gave him a contract to design helicopters for the Vietnam War. It was all a front. They paid him millions again and that money went directly into buying up hotels in Las Vegas, beginning in 1967 with the Desert Inn.

To make the situation even weirder, Hughes had gone into seclusion in 1950, and was rarely—make that never—seen in public. He might not have been dead, as was rumored, but I feel safe in saying he was a crazy son of a bitch.

He was never much of an aircraft designer to begin with, and now he was in a state where designing helicopters for a jungle war was beyond his capabilities. What was happening? He and his people began staying at the Desert Inn. His people were suddenly everywhere, hundreds of them. It was the start of Op-eration Replacement. Hughes was being used by the govern-ment to infiltrate Las Vegas, installing CIA assets in places where Sicilian mobsters had once been.

At some point, Meyer Lansky called Dalitz and said, "Tell them to get out of the hotel. They are not gambling."

Dalitz tried kicking Hughes out.

"You're taking up too much space and I need those rooms for players in the casino," Dalitz said.

Hughes said no. I'm staying. My people are staying. I'm going to buy the place and you won't be able to tell me what to do anymore. He gave Moe Dalitz six million dollars in cash and a seven-million-dollar loan.

In addition to hotels, Hughes bought great swaths of land outside Vegas, for a large, planned community called Summerlin.

The U.S. government had for years wanted to get the Mob out of Vegas. In Howard Hughes they saw a way to get its big foot in the door. They not only wanted to kick the gangsters out, they wanted to change the culture.

Many people cheat on their taxes to one degree or another, but the problem was nowhere more systemic than in Las Vegas where *everyone*, from the moguls to the waitresses, only admitted to making a fraction of what they actually made.

I know this for a fact. Cocktail waitresses who were making two hundred dollars a night would tell the IRS they made forty. What you earned in Vegas stayed in Vegas.

The government tried the old-fashioned way of cracking down. They held investigations and forced wiseguys to take the Fifth a couple hundred times, but it got them nowhere. So, they went at it a different way.

They put government operatives on the wait staffs of the casinos, to root out and rat on tax cheats. Female federal intelligence agents were getting jobs as cocktail waitresses, talking to the other waitresses and getting the dope on what was really going on.

They used Howard Hughes and "his people" like a money-laundering machine. One by one, Hughes's people replaced those in place. Eventually wiseguys were being shown the door by a Mormon saying: "Have a nice day."

The government's attempted takeover of Vegas was well timed. The Old Guard in the American Mafia was getting very old—"dying off" was how a CIA memo put it—and the new guys were hotheads who were easier to manipulate.

When Howard Hughes bought the Sands, he built a five-hundred-room circular tower to serve as the hotel. With Hughes in charge, the Rat Pack were no longer as welcome. Hughes was jealous of Sinatra's relationship with Ava Gardner.

Hughes placed a limit on the amount Sinatra could bet and Frank went ballistic. Frank was used to unlimited credit, and half expected his IOUs to be torn up because of all the business he brought into town. People came by the thousands to Vegas to see Sinatra. Why should he ever get a check?

Frank, berserk, drove a golf cart through the window of a Sands coffee shop, which scared the shit out of Carl Cohen, the Sands' casino manager, who was having breakfast inside. Gathering himself, Cohen beat the shit out of Sinatra, who wasn't very big, and knocked out two of his teeth.

During that transition period, Moe Dalitz and Meyer Lansky (aka the Old Guard) were aware of what was going on. They told all employees who knew about the first count room to never, ever mention the first count room. Because the Hughes people were learning casino operation one job at a time, the skim continued to be picked up on Monday morning and transported east.

One thing the corporate thinkers took care of after the takeover was the rule that markers could only be redeemed inside Nevada. The rule was changed so that any marker issued in a Vegas casino was a "corporate loan" and subject to collection anywhere. That put a hard stop to my collection business.

Plus, cameras were being installed everywhere.

I knew it was time to get out.

During the takeover, Hughes's right-hand man was federal asset Bob Maheu, a lawyer from Maine who earned his degree at Georgetown, joined the Hughes Corporation in 1955, and became the primary liaison between Hughes and the rest of the business world, a fact made more peculiar when Maheu claimed that he'd never actually seen Howard Hughes in person, and always had to relay messages through a Mormon.

Maheu was also a CIA guy. There's a law that says the CIA is not allowed to operate on U.S. soil, that's the FBI's job, but those guys didn't follow the rules. The CIA had its tentacles everywhere. When Maheu first got to Vegas he needed to learn what everyone did, so he was—for awhile—really friendly with me and all of our people.

At some point he figured out that the casinos of Las Vegas were divided up among the Mob families. The Riviera was Detroit. The Desert Inn and the Stardust were Chicago. The Dunes was New England. Caesars belonged to the Jewish faction.

Maheu was well chosen for his role. Since the early 1960s he'd been the liaison between the CIA and the Mob. It was Maheu who originally contacted Johnny Roselli regarding a hit on Fidel Castro in 1960. Through Roselli, Maheu met and befriended Sam Giancana, Santo Trafficante, and Meyer Lansky—the three men who lost the most when Castro closed the Havana casinos.

Maheu functioned as intermediary between CIA security director Sheffield Edwards and Sam Giancana to discuss efforts to terminate Fidel Castro. Also involved with the plots against Castro were General Charles Cabell, brother of the Dallas mayor, and Johnny Roselli. The plots that came out of this anti-Castro braintrust all seemed a little squirrely, poison pills hidden in a cold cream jar, exploding cigars, etc. When the whole plot turned and the target switched from Havana to Dallas, such nonsense was forgotten and the old reliable bullet-through-the-brain technique was used.

There was also only one degree of separation between Maheu and Lee Harvey Oswald, as Maheu worked closely with Guy Bannister, who in 1963 dangled a "pro-Castro" Oswald on street corners in New Orleans as bait in hopes of catching Communists.

But what was the real story behind Hughes and why no one ever saw him? Truth was, the government figured it would be easier to use Hughes as a cardboard cutout for their activities in Las Vegas if Hughes was incapacitated, so they strung him out on heroin. He was a junkie, with all the money in the world for his next fix. He stopped cutting his hair and nails. He was a basket case by the time they removed him from the hotel. They flew him out at night, took him back to Texas to die.

Having cleared my head after my Renaissance delirium, I decided to open a nightclub. Moe Dalitz helped me to choose a location. Steve Wynn gave me his old bar with a black onyx overlay when he remodeled the Golden Nugget, and I opened Gianni Russo's State Street, 2570 State Street.

In a town where everyone was trying to build bigger and more mind-boggling, I went for cozy and intimate. The club was open from six p.m. to six a.m. and offered fine dining with entertainment. It was plush and luxurious inside, but outside, on purpose, it looked like a dump. The outside was done up with dumpsters to make it look like a back alley. Patrons had to knock, and were checked out through a peephole before being allowed in. We didn't have a password, but there was a speakeasy feel.

"What the hell is this?" everyone said. Then they came inside, door opened by a doorman in tux, and their mouths dropped open. Opening night in 1981 was fantastic. Frank Sinatra, Dean Martin, Sammy Davis, Jr.—Thursday, Friday, and Saturday, for no money.

It was during this time that Frank was giving me singing lessons and one night at the State Street I got up and sang a set. Frank was there, the proud teacher. Rickles was there and—after heckling me mercilessly—booked me to warm-up for him for the next two years.

One of my employees at the club became famous. Steve Schirripa, who was a student at UNLV and later, of course, played Bobby "Bacala" Baccalieri on *The Sopranos*, was one of my bouncers. He also went on to be my friend ever since.

I had all my phone operators calling the cab companies. Every time someone got in a cab that weekend, they were reminded that the Big Three from the Rat Pack were performing at State Street. The club was an immediate success.

The stars kept coming: Paul Anka, Louis Prima, Engelbert Humperdinck, Wayne Newton. Rickles would show up and call everyone a hockey puck. I made sure there were always celebrities in the place, so when Mr. and Mrs. Kansas City came in, they could go home and tell their friends they saw Frank and Dean at Gianni Russo's State Street.

I was particularly generous with cabbies who worked the airport.

"Looking for something to do tonight? You might want to eat at the State Street," the hack would say, "I heard Sammy's gonna do an impromptu show tonight."

And they came. Boy, did they ever. Most of them left alive.

But not all.

Chapter 12
Table Reading with Pablo Escobar

I made the newspapers twice in 1988. The first came in January, when the Nevada Gaming Commission gave me my gambling license, allowing me to install fifteen slot machines. That doesn't seem like such a newsworthy thing, but the issue was how much of my mobby reputation came from the Mob and how much came from roles I had played in movies.

I went into Joe Colombo–mode and told the press that all Italian Americans must face rumors and innuendoes about their Mob involvement, me more so because I'd portrayed a gangster in many movies. I said I had no contact with any real members of organized crime families.

The second time I was in the papers was just before Halloween 1988 because I'd killed a man in my club. He needed killing, there could be no doubt about that, but I still had a hassle on my hands, no fault of my own.

The guy I killed was a Cuban named Lorenzo Morales, a well-dressed thirty-year-old customer. I knew he was somebody because his tab was being picked up by one of the big casinos, and I'd comped him with a $1,200 bottle of Cristal champagne. A few minutes later, Morales smashed the bottle and used it to cut up his date's face. She was Lois Manners, a cocktail waitress at the Stardust that Morales had just met.

I ran over there to stop him, and he came after me, cutting me under the chin, causing a wound that later needed eighty-four stitches.

At that time, I packed two pocket guns, gold-plated, .25 caliber. I liked them because they fit in the pockets of my vest, but they didn't make a very big hole. I pulled one of my guns and shot Morales in the forehead, a wound that stopped him in his tracks but failed to knock him down. I shot him four more times, once in the head and three times in the chest. That did the trick, and he fell dead.

"I'm going to need a bigger gun," I said, blood pouring from the nasty cut under my chin.

Fun fact: I was stitched up by Dr. Elias Ghanem, who was Elvis Presley's personal physician nicknamed Dr. Feelgood.

Only hours after the shooting, and me getting stitched up, the district attorney cleared me of all criminal involvement, which was nice of him, but the real problem was the guy I killed. I was ready to head home when I learned I was in trouble. A Las Vegas police captain wanted to know if I was acquainted with Morales.

"Never saw him before, why?"

"We did a check on him. He's in town doing cocaine business."

"Never touch the stuff."

"Yeah, yeah, but you should know who he's in town doing cocaine business for."

"Who?"

"He flew in a few days ago from Colombia. He works for Pablo Escobar."

The guy I killed was connected, and not with the Mafia, but a third-world drug gang called the Marielitos, who were working under the auspices of the Medellín cartel overlord Pablo Escobar, the so-called "King of Cocaine."

Some of you older folks might remember the days when "boat people" from Cuba were arriving on the shores of Florida, fleeing the Castro regime. Around 1980, Castro, just to be mean, emptied a few of his prisons and put these guys on boats and rafts at Mariel Harbor in Cuba and pointed them toward Miami. Some made it and some didn't, but those who did, predicably enough formed a gang called the Marielitos. They sold cocaine, which they got from Escobar.

Escobar was a bad, bad man. Surprisingly, his parents were legit. Dad was a farmer, Mom a schoolteacher, but he must've thought they were suckers to work so hard and went into a life of crime when he was a teenager.

He had a talent for forgery and earned a decent living as a young man creating fake diplomas, mostly for doctors who weren't really doctors. Although he was already thinking big and had started a smuggling operation, his first bust was for stealing a car.

But that was the end of the small-time stuff. In the mid-1970s he went into drug smuggling and became the U.S.'s largest supplier of nose candy. He was said to have made upward of a half billion—that's billion—dollars *a week* and was one of the richest men in the world.

He was very different from other billionaires. He had no bank account, no investments. It was all in cash, and he needed warehouses to store it all. I read that he lost millions of dollars a year because it was eaten by rats. But the cash flowed in so fast that the rats could eat all they wanted, and Escobar didn't care.

He had his own zoo with two hundred animals, many imported from the jungles of Africa. It wasn't unusual for planes to land on his private airstrip carrying bails of cocaine and a hippopotamus.

My fears grew worse. After getting stitched up, and talking to the D.A. and the police chief, I returned home—I was living next to Moe Dalitz at the Las Vegas Country Club—and found that I'd had visitors.

I would have said that, as I had a state-of-the-art security system, breaking into my place was impossible, but I would have
been wrong. I quickly surmised that my visitors were practitioners of a strange religion and they'd set up a whole threatening presentation, with a four-foot circle of blood, a photo of
my daughter (not a portrait but a surveillance photo taken
only hours earlier with a long lens), dead chickens—whose
blood had been used to make the circle—and salamanders
with needles through their heads.

I had no idea what I was looking at, so I sought expert advice. I called an anthropology professor I knew at the University of Nevada at Las Vegas (UNLV). She came and looked at
the thing.

"What is it?" I asked.

"Not good," she said. "Santeria."

"I've heard of that. Voodoo or something, right?"

"Well, it is known by several names. It's made up of African
beliefs mixed with a sort of bastardized Christianity. The official name is Regla de Ocha."

"What's that mean?"

"The Rule of the Orisha," she said, acting as if that made it
crystal clear. She saw my eyes glaze over and said, "Rule of the
Head Guardian. Another name is La Regla Lucumi, which means
'the way of the saints.' The practices of Santeria are never discussed outside of the group, but over the years there have
been a few blabbermouths, which is why I know about it. In
Brazil, they are known as Candomble Jeje-Nago. Their enemies call it Macumba, which means 'evil witchcraft.'"

"Where in Africa?"

"The original beliefs came from the Yoruba and Bantu people in southern Nigeria, Senegal, and Guinea Coast. Somewhere along the line those beliefs mixed with Catholicism.
Slaves brought the religion with them when they were forcibly
moved to other parts of the world. Here in North America
many slaves were baptized as Catholics and their native prac-

tices were suppressed, so Santeria formed over the generations."

"They praying to the same saints as me?" I asked.

"Sort of. The names of old religious entities have been
changed to Christian saint names, but have retained their earlier godlike roles. The African god of thunder and lightning,
Shangs, is now St. Barbara. Elegba, god of roads and gateways,
they now call St. Anthony."

"I'm alive because of St. Anthony," I said.

She continued, "You can find Santeria anywhere where there
used to be African slaves. These days it is most common in the
Carribbean, especially in Cuba. That's how it became secret.
Since Castro, and his ban on religion, practitioners of Santeria
have gone underground. Here in the U.S., Santeria is prac-
ticed in many big cities—Miami, New York, L.A."

"Same God as me?"

"Again, sort of. They call God Olorun, which literally means
'Owner of Heaven.' Olorun is aided in the running of the
world by the Orisha, lesser guardians. Worshippers feed the
Orisha through sacrifices."

"Jesus," I said. I didn't like any of this. "What do they sacrifice?"

"Usually chickens. But sheep and goats, too. The blood is
collected and offered to the guardians. There is a lot of varia-
tion from group to group because none of this was ever written
down. They have no equivalent to our Bible. It is an oral tradition and is passed down from generation to generation."

I gestured at my new display. "What's this mean?"

"It is Colombian. You have friends in Colombia?"

"No."

"It's a message from a man named Morales's brother, that
mean something to you?"

"Uh-huh." I could feel the blood draining from my head.

"He is vowing to avenge his brother's death. What they're
going to do," she said, "is kill your pets, kill your kids, and kill

you last. Sorry, but that's what it means. Maybe you should call the police."

"Don't worry about me. I know what to do," I said.

But I didn't. It would take me some time to formulate a plan.

Santeria was next to unknown in America at that moment, but only a few months later, it acquired an evil reputation when Santeria practitioners were among a gang of drug runners who murdered a dozen men in Matamoros, Mexico, just on the other side of the Texas border. It was unknown if any of the dead men had been sacrificed and reports included disclaimers that the bodies were not evidence that Santeria either condoned or encouraged human sacrifice. It was evidence, rather, that those who took on drug runners in Mexico got whacked.

There was only one thing to do. I had to get to Escobar and explain myself or else they were going to kill my kids. When the professor from UNLV left, I thanked her profusely. Alone, my first phone call was to Manuel Noriega.

Yes, that Manuel Noriega, a man as big and feared as a third-world leader could be. Noriega came from ultra-humble beginnings, born into a poor Colombian family. He went to one of the top high schools in Panama and won a free ride to the Chorrillos Military School in Lima. After graduation he returned to Panama and was commissioned an officer in the National Guard. He made his big move when he was a top operative in a military coup that toppled Arnulfo Arias and thrust into power his coconspirator Omar Torrijos. Predictably, there was a counter-coup attempt to oust Torrijos, and Noriega helped stifle it. Torrijos was president and Noriega was Chief of Military Intelligence, a position that Noriega used to move drugs. Lots and lots of drugs. Despite this, early in his career, he worked hand in hand with the CIA, working to tamp down anti-American sentiments in the third world, so that Castro's takeover of Cuba and subsequent allegiance with Communism didn't create the same "domino effect" that Americans had feared in southeast Asia.

Noriega also had a nasty reputation as Panama's top intelligence officer, using the brutal tools at his disposal for suppressing all threats to his business and power. Torrijos died in a plane crash in 1981 and Noriega used the vacuum to strengthen and consolidate his power. Now he was General Noriega. His reputation for brutality and ruthlessness made American intelligence eager for his removal, the same spy network that had for years been using information that Noriega supplied.

Uncle Sam's urgency to get him out leaped when one of Noriega's vocal critics, a guy named Hugo Spadafora, was found beheaded. Since the real reasons were secret, the American press was told that it had to do with Noriega's support for the Contras of Nicaraugua who were fighting for control in El Salvador.

When the U.S. authorities learned that Noriega had sold restricted American technology, and was using U.S. institutions to launder money, they leaned on him, and he quickly realized the jig was up.

When Noriega ran for president, the people voted and the votes were being counted when Noriega, not liking the preliminary results, announced the election a fraud, stolen, declared himself leader of Panama, then made himself scarce.

It was around that time I called him. Noriega was wanted and laying low in the Dominican Republic. I knew him from years back when I was a courier, and he was doing major business deals. I couldn't tell you how many hundreds of millions of dollars he moved through the Panama banks. Some of it was for Pablo Escobar. Noriega wasn't just a globally huge cocaine dealer, he helped Pablo Escobar get rid of his money.

I remember it was a Sunday. Noriega wasn't at the number I had, but the person I spoke to said he'd deliver the message and perhaps Noriega would call me back.

While I waited, I called John Gotti. I knew he dealt with

product from down there. Maybe he could help. Shows how desperate I was.

There had been a lot of water under the bridge since Gotti got kicked out of the Ravenite for disrespecting me back when we were kids—but he still didn't like me. He was the same immature jerk he'd been as a teen, his prime skill being his ability to maintain Top Bully status. He pushed people around. It was all he could do.

"John, I gotta talk to you."

"Come see me," he said. And so we would be in the Ravenite together again, this time with him in complete control.

That Monday I flew to LaGuardia Airport and went straight to Little Italy. I had the driver let me off a few blocks from my destination and walked to the Ravenite.

"What?" said a hulk of a guy standing just outside the door.

"Gianni Russo, here to talk to Mr. Gotti."

The door opened.

"He's in the back room," the doorman said.

I remember thinking that the Ravenite, which was a dump, looked like a clubhouse made by fourteen-year-old boys: stuff tacked to the walls, mismatched furniture, garbage everywhere. The place needed a good scrub. After leaving my sparkly and glamorous world in Vegas, the Ravenite looked like a janitor's closet.

Gotti gave me that smile. He was Boss. Nobody was kicking him out of the Ravenite anymore. I only got in because he said it was OK. He was loving the fact that I was coming to him. Savoring it.

First words out of his mouth: "So now you're a killer."

"How'd you hear about it?" I asked.

"It was on fucking *Entertainment Tonight*," he said with a throaty laugh. The shooting in my club didn't make the crime news, it made the celebrity news.

"I'm not a killer, John," I said. "The guy stabbed a customer of mine. Then he did this to me," I said, gesturing at my still bandaged face. "My guys didn't take care of it, so I did.'

I told him the guy I hit had connections in Latin America and Santeria creeps were making voodoo charms in my house.

"I need to get to Bogota and talk to Escobar," I said.

He looked at me for a second like I had two heads. Then he laughed, tears in his eyes. I didn't see what was so funny. He began to nod vigorously.

"Well, you got a problem now," he said. I amused him.

"I need to go there. Otherwise, they're gonna kill my kids."

His eyes widened. "OK. Sounds good," he said, eyes still twinkling. "I'll tell you what, I'll buy the ticket."

I didn't need his ticket, but I supposed it would be a mistake to refuse it.

"Thanks," I said.

"But only one way," he said.

"How come?"

"Because you ain't coming back!" And then he laughed again.

And he did buy the ticket! If he called Escobar to let him know I was coming, I don't know to this day. My plans to meet Escobar were made with the help of Noriega, who eventually called me back.

I explained I'd killed one of Pablo Escobar's guys a couple of nights before.

"Who did you kill?" Noriega asked.

"Lorenzo Morales."

"How'd you kill him?" Noriega asked. "That guy's rough."

"I shot him between the eyes."

"All right. I talk to him." He meant Escobar.

Noriega later got back to me. The meet was set up. He gave me the name of a church outside of Bogota where I was supposed to go.

So, I went to see Escobar, to tell him my side of the story, and pray that he wouldn't whack me on the spot just for fun.

The flight to Bogota lasted ten hours but seemed like days. Bogota has the same kind of urban sprawl as New York or L.A., and you can drive for an hour and a half and not leave the city.

So, I was pleasantly surprised when it was only a ten-minute cab ride from the airport across the Bogota savanna to the church.

Inside the church it was very dark and cool. At first, I thought the place was abandoned. Then my eyes adjusted to the dark and I could see one guy kneeling by the altar. Above it was a religious icon unlike any I've ever seen before or since. It was a Blessed Mother, and it looked like she was standing on a globe of the Earth, and there were flames and people reaching out of it to her. Very spooky. It was an icon designed for a man who needed to be dragged up out of hell.

As I walked toward the altar, I could hear creaking in the pews. One by one, men with rifles sat up straight. That was scary shit, but the weirdest thing about that moment was that I could smell burning flesh.

There was Escobar, who was praying while holding his left hand over a lit candle, burning his fingertips. I don't know if he was doing it to hurt himself on purpose, pay penance for some sin he felt guilty about, or if he was trying to get rid of his fingerprints.

It was like one of those dreams where you're trying to walk down an aisle and your feet feel stuck. It seemed forever till I got to the front, but I made it. I could see Escobar's left fingertips were scorched and badly blistered.

"You Gianni Russo?" Escobar asked.

"I am," I said.

At that moment, boom, out went the lights.

When I woke up, my head was killing me. Somebody had bopped me on the head from behind with the butt of a gun. I was in a prison that Escobar had built in a basement. A small, barred window near the ceiling provided the only light. There were body bags all around me.

Once my guards saw I was conscious, they took off all my clothes and tied me to an iron chair with no bottom, so my privates hung down. These guys had a field day swinging a stick

that had a rubber ball chained to its tip. They thwacked that ball against my sensitive area until I threw up. I passed out. I begged to die.

When the torture stopped, I looked up and there was Escobar and in his hand was a book called *The Making of The Godfather*.

He said, "Why didn't you tell me you were Carlo? I love that movie." Then he barked an order to his men: "Clean him up and take him up to the house."

The house. What a house, built like an Italian hacienda. Escobar apparently wanted to be Italian. In fact, he named the estate Hacienda Nápoles. It had a statue of a dinosaur out front and a bullfighting ring in the back.

One wing was a hall where Escobar kept his collection of classic cars. And the previously mentioned zoo where ostriches, giraffes, camels, and zebras were caged—along with the hippopotami, of which there were upward of forty. Most but not all of the hippos were imported. Several had been born there.

Escobar was a typical Mob boss. He mixed intimidation— "You wouldn't want to be thrown to the hippos, would you?"— and philanthropy. He gave away so much money to Colombian charities that the peasants who had very little called him Robin Hood. He financed major projects designed to improve the Colombian quality of life, hospitals, affordable housing, and even a new soccer stadium.

Of course, there is no way to count the number of men he killed. He used to talk about the "silver or lead" option. If someone was in his way he would either be bribed or killed. The latter was cheaper.

Thousands were whacked. Collateral damage didn't concern him. He didn't care how many innocents he killed to take out his target. He once had his men plant a bomb on a plane, killing over a hundred people, one of them being a rat that Escobar wanted erased.

So, I had great balls of fire, and not in a good way, plus

my head had an egg-sized lump and throbbed. I was still scared shitless, and I was having dinner with Escobar in his dining room. His men were all around, but they weren't sitting with us.

"Why did you come here?" he asked me.

I told him how Lorenzo Morales died. "I did my homework. You have a daughter Gina and I have a daughter Gia. When I learned that Morales was a Santeria, I knew they would kill my kids, so I came to you."

He stared at me for a minute. Then he got up and walked to the other end of the table. I thought he was going to cut my head off. But instead, he gave me a hug.

He spoke softly. "There are few men like us. I will handle this. But before you go, you got to do me a favor."

I said, "Anything you want."

I was thinking, cut the grass, wash the windows, anything you want me to do.

"I want you to do the closing scene in *The Godfather*."

"Which scene?"

"Your closing scene. The scene where Michael comes to confront you. Come with me."

We went back to his end of the table and I was told to sit in his chair.

He walked over to the foyer, so he could come in the way Michael Corleone did in the movie.

I said, "Do you want me to write the lines down for you?"

"No, no, no, I know the lines."

He did the entire scene with me, line for line. I'm guessing my acting was great, and I didn't need any of Marlon Brando's method. I was actually scared shitless. When the scene was over, he gave me an airline ticket and—just as Michael had done to Carlo—he walked me out to a car.

I felt a little better when Escobar opened the back door so I'd ride in the back seat. As soon as my ass hit the leather, everyone in the car said, "Hello, Carlo." And then they laughed.

"Don't worry," Escobar said cheerfully. "I'll straighten every-thing out."

I was lucky to be alive, that was certain. I thought there could be an advantage for me, here, and while I was in Escobar's good graces I suggested we do business together. It's a move others might not have made, considering the circumstances, but I was used to dealing with these major guys. I'd been meet-ing and dealing with bosses since I was a kid. I told Escobar that I already moved things for Noriega. Escobar said great. He loved the idea. Him and Carlo from *The Godfather*, a team. It made him happy. It made me a mint.

He slammed the car door. Me and my throbbing gonads were driven to the airport. I thought my adventure was over, but no. When I landed in Miami, my plane was boarded by Drug Enforcement Administration (DEA) agents who dragged me off in handcuffs. I told them I was headed to Vegas, and they said I'd be making a stop in Washington first.

I was put on a small jet and flown to D.C. When they realized I was Carlo from *The Godfather*, they took off the cuffs. In D.C. we took a car to DEA headquarters on K Street. Turned out, they'd had their eyes on me ever since my meeting with Gotti in the Ravenite.

When I flew to Bogota to meet with Escobar they thought I was a new cog in Escobar's cocaine operation. They had sur-veillance photos of me taken outside the Ravenite, at JFK air-port, and at the airport in Bogota.

"Whatcha up to, Gianni?" they asked.

So, I told them the truth, only leaving the very last bit out. I shot a guy in my Vegas club, the guy worked for Escobar, so I went down there to ask that they not kill my family. The story satisfied them.

Noriega's days of freedom dwindled down to a few. He was hiding out in the Vatican's diplomatic mission in Panama City when they nabbed him. By that time, the U.S. army had invaded

Panama, an invasion during which a marine was killed. U.S. forces weren't allowed in the Vatican mission, so they launched a psych op on him. They drove Noriega out in the open by blasting heavy-metal music outside day and night until Noriega decided surrender was better than having to listen to another Black Sabbath album.

He was flown to the U.S., charged with various racketeering charges, drugs, money laundering, and he was tried in a court-room packed with press. The world took delight in some of the weird facts that came out at that trial. Noriega always wore red underwear to ward off the evil eye. That kind of thing.

It was a risky maneuver for the U.S., which had to suppress the fact that during Noriega's rise to power and for years after-ward, he and the CIA were allies—not to mention business partners—in the fight against Communism.

It all goes to show, you never know which way the wind is going to blow. Noriega was America's friend and then its arch-enemy. Same with the Taliban in Afghanistan. They were our al-lies when they fought the Russians and our enemies after 9/11. The enemy of my enemy is my friend—but never forever.

Escobar wasn't the only madman to treat me differently after hearing I was Carlo. Saddam Hussein—you remember him—summoned me once to his hotel room (this is before the Gulf War and his status as America's enemy). He had my scene cued up on his VCR so that he could play the movie while I was in the room.

How did I get in a hotel room with Saddam Hussein? you might ask.

My jobs continued to resemble the very first errands I'd run for Mr. Costello as a kid, only on a grander and grander scale, until eventually I was an international courier. In that role, I knew a guy named Adnan Khashoggi, who was the world's number-one arms dealer.

At the peak of Khashoggi's power he brokered arms deals between the Kingdom of Saudi Arabia—the only country in

the world owned and ruled by a family, the Sauds—and an American firm, Lockheed.

He'd gotten a head start as a kid because his dad was the king of Saudi Arabia's personal physician. By the time he was attending college (in California) he was already brokering major deals, arranging, for example, to sell three million dollars' worth of trucks to Egypt, for which he picked up a cool $150,000. That'll buy a few textbooks.

By 1963, he was supplying U.S. covert operatives with weapons for an operation in Yemen. One of his first business friends in America was Richard Nixon, whose successful 1968 election campaign was financed in part by Khashoggi. He once gave Nixon's daughter a $60,000 watch. As an adult, his mission on behalf of his country was to convert Saudi oil, of which there was much, into a defense system (and offensive capabilities, of course) worthy of one of the world's richest countries.

He brokered a deal in which Great Britain firms Marconi and Westland Helicopters supplied military aircraft and weapons to the Saudis in exchange for oil. Here in the U.S., Khashoggi's deals were always described as "shadowy."

He was arrested in Switzerland, did some luxurious jail time, then got in trouble in the Philippines for laundering money for Ferdinand Marcos. By 1980, Khashoggi was building his dream yacht, the *Nabila*, named after his daughter, which at the time would be the world's largest private yacht at 281 feet. It had a sundeck covered with bulletproof glass, chamois leather–lined cabins, with hand-carved onyx in the bathrooms. There were 150 telephones aboard, and a satellite communication system used to arrange arms sales and global commodities trades.

But the boat was not designed for business as much as for seduction. World leaders, kings, presidents, prime ministers would come aboard, be given whatever they desired—girls, food, or cash—and by the time they got off, so to speak, they were putty in Khashoggi's hands.

If you want to get a good look at that super-boat, it's fea-

tured in the 1983 James Bond picture *Never Say Never Again*, posing as the yacht of SPECTRE supervillain Maximillian Largo.

Khashoggi made headlines in the 1980s with another familiar name, when he sold that fantastic yacht to Donald Trump for $29 million. Trump renamed it the *Trump Princess*. By the time I dealt with Khashoggi, he was known to many Americans because his name came up during the Reagan administration's Iran-Contra scandal, in which Reagan's man, Oliver North, arranged for the release of hostages in exchange for selling weapons to Iran.

I got close with Khashoggi. In fact, I hosted his fiftieth birthday party at Gianni Russo's State Street. He was very popular with the casinos of Vegas because he'd drop millions. (Khashoggi once managed an eight-million-pound debt at the London Ritz Hotel.)

All the clubs wanted to host his party, but Khashoggi said, "I'm having it with Gianni Russo."

The other casinos wanted to be in on it, too, so they gave me money. I ended up making three or four hundred thousand dollars on this party. I got very creative. I rented a couple of semi-trucks and parked them outside my club. We emptied the club out, removed all of the furniture. We started on a Sunday night. I had pure white sand brought in, palm trees, and I got every showgirl I could get in Vegas, who were many. It was funny. They all knew Adnan and were eager to work the party because he tipped with hundred-dollar bills, often more than one. Anyway, by the time we finished, we'd created a Middle Eastern party. Arabian nights. Everybody was sitting on the floor on big pillows. And Khashoggi loved it.

Saddam Hussein was at the party. When U.S. troops were hunting him down, nobody ever talked about the days when he came to Vegas and was treated like a king because he dropped so much loot at the tables.

* * *

Getting back to my Bentley, once I began moving commodities from power source to power source, the Bentley became an important player in my operation. I built a twenty-foot container for the car, and I shipped it everywhere I went. As it was my car and my container, I could put whatever I wanted in it, and send it anywhere. I flew places. The car went by cargo ship. When I wasn't traveling, I stored the container in Long Beach, California.

I had the container completely customized to survive rough seas. We put clamps down and welded them to the floor. We attached four-inch moving straps and wrapped those around the wheels, so no matter how rocky the ride, the car couldn't move. Just in case that didn't work, we padded the entire inside of the container. We put racks in the front that would come down over the entire hood, and that gave us extra storage space.

We would place the car so that its rear was hard up against the end of the container, which meant there was space at the other end. That space would usually be filled with crates of other commodities. I have to admit, there were plenty of times when I did not know what was in the container with my Bentley. I didn't want to know. (And if I did know, I didn't want to admit I knew.) All I needed to know was who would receive the stuff. Once people found out about the system, they used it with confidence. I'd be given suitcases. Sometimes packages arrived from Saks Fifth Avenue, and they'd go straight into the container. The system worked great.

Customs didn't want to have anything to do with the container. Nobody once opened it up and looked inside. We also didn't have to worry about problems at the docks. Tough Tony Anastasio was my confirmation sponsor. We were taken care of on the waterfront.

There had been a lot of bosses on the piers, but Anthony Anastasio was the toughest. He first set foot in Brooklyn in

1924, age eighteen, when he, like his older brother Albert Anastasia, jumped ship at Red Hook. He wasn't just tough, either. He was shrewd and made a lot of important friends because of his position in the longshoremen's union.

If you were a loudmouth activist on the docks during Tough Tony's time, you'd have your legs broken. Not only were you unable to work for months, but your twin casts up to the hip were advertisements telling others to keep their mouths shut.

There were guys during the Tough Tony era foolish enough to "represent labor" on the piers. Twenty-eight-year-old longshoreman Pietro Panto was one of those guys, and to no one's surprise, he didn't live long.

At Panto's final speech in 1939, delivered in Italian, he told a gathering of 1,250 longshoremen in South Brooklyn's Star Hall that it was time for a change, time for dockworkers to stand up for their rights. Anastasia had spies in the crowd. They reported back that Panto was planning an ILA revolt. And that was all she wrote. Panto was whacked.

In 1948, a Red Hook lawyer named Jim Longhi wanted to end the days of longshoremen being afraid to talk aloud about the abuses they suffered at the hands of thugs. He arranged for Paul O'Dwyer, the former D.A. and now NYC mayor's kid brother, to come to Red Hook and address the longshoremen, give them a pep talk and tell them that the gangsters who ran things on the waterfront were on the run.

O'Dwyer gave his speech: "This is a new day, men! The day of the gangster telling you that you can't speak is finished. This is Emancipation Day for the Italian longshoremen of Red Hook, and you are not bound by these thugs anymore. Freedom of speech has come to the waterfront, when a man may speak without fear."

One fellow, a tough-looking guy, raised his hand and said, "You mean anybody can get up there and speak?"

O'Dwyer nodded enthusiastically and invited the man to

come up and speak his mind. The man moved to the front and took O'Dwyer's microphone.

"My name is Anthony Anastasio," the man said. You never saw a crowd disperse so quickly. That was it for the free-speech movement. When the time came to next approve their contract with their union, the ILA deal passed in a landslide.

That's the guy who stood up for me at my confirmation.

Packages left with me always arrived at the correct location on time. Business was great. I customized the bumperettes on my Bentley so that they could hold seventy-five pounds of 99.9 percent pure. The statute of limitations on that is thirty years, so I'm good.

I had to be careful when moving big money. I couldn't walk into a bank because someone would say, "Hey, there's Carlo from *The Godfather!*" Not only was I a celebrity, but I was often seen in the right places with the right people. I was at the Cannes Film Festival. I was at Wimbledon. The car, of course, drew attention wherever I shipped it, but no one suspected it was the key to a massive smuggling campaign. I made no attempt to be inconspicuous. The car had Las Vegas plates on it, which always got a reaction. My vanity plates read GR7.

Every year in April, Frank Sinatra and I would go to the Red Cross Ball, which was held by my old friend Princess Grace in Monte Carlo, Monaco. About two and a half weeks before the ball, I would ship the car over.

My guys would bring the Bentley down to Long Beach where it and its sealed container were loaded onto a cargo ship. The customs guys would come. I gave them cash. They checked a box on their clipboard.

Speaking of flying, a quick word about how different things were before 9/11. I could go to the airport five minutes before a plane left, put cash on the counter, sign my name "Mary Poppins," and get on the flight. No security, no screening, nothing. Pay your money, get on the plane.

That was for everybody. Things were even easier for me. In Chicago, if I flew on one particular airline, I could show up minutes before takeoff and if the plane was full, they'd kick somebody off. The reason for that was, we were doing a lot of business with the Vatican, and the Vatican owned the controlling stock of this airline. Much more about *that* chapter in my life in chapter 14.

CHAPTER 13
Watching the Spilotros Die

Anthony "Tony the Ant" Spilotro was born in Chicago in 1938, at a time when Al Capone was imprisoned for tax evasion, and "Greasy Thumb" Gudzik was counting Capone's money in a Kedzie Avenue restaurant.

Spilotro never knew a life other than gangster life. He and most of his brothers went into the rackets. He dropped out of school as soon as he could and did some juvie for shoplifting.

He got his button at twenty-one, by which time he'd made his bones several times over. Apparently, he *liked* killing—and it was his reckless bloodlust that did so much damage. He became a trusted Outfit soldier and was sent by Sam Giancana to Vegas to "protect the skim."

As anyone who's seen the movie *Casino* knows, Spilotro (played by Joe Pesci) was not a man well in control of himself. Spilotro replaced Marshall Caifano, another guy known for his brutality. The Outfit had Frank "Lefty" Rosenthal (Robert DeNiro in *Casino*) running the Stardust on the Vegas strip and Spilotro was supposed to make sure the money that was supposed to head east headed east.

The idea was to do this without attracting unnecessary attention, but Spilotro wasn't great at keeping a low profile. He and I didn't get along from the start because he didn't know about

my Chicago connections. Like John Gotti back East, Spilotro didn't understand how I got my juice and was suspicious, and whenever they were suspicious they were hostile, attacking anything they didn't understand. Gotti was once slapped for disrespecting me. For Spilotro, things would go much worse.

While trying to do his job in Nevada, Spilotro was under investigation in Chicago for the 1963 mutilation murder of a real-estate broker and Mob bill collector who did the wrong thing. Eventually Cook County busted him. He worked a deal where he could commute from the Illinois court to his office in Las Vegas while on trial for murder.

Spilotro seemed relaxed and confident throughout the trial and sure enough the jury acquitted him after about a nanosecond of deliberation. At first, Spilotro had a codefendant, Sam "Mad Dog" DeStefano, a Windy City goon, but Mad Dog didn't make it to the trial.

DeStefano had lived for twenty-plus years in the unassuming Galewood community. One quiet Saturday morning in the spring of 1973, the sixty-three-year-old DeStefano left his house by the garage door and walked into a twelve-gauge shotgun blast to the face.

For two and a half hours Mad Dog's remains lay in full view of passersby, but there weren't that many passersby. It was almost noon when a neighbor saw the gory mess. The neighbor yelled and caught the attention of a telephone repairman who was working in a nearby alley. The repairman called the cops.

Those who were expecting a large Mafia to-do for DeStefano's funeral were disappointed. It was a small affair, a ten-car caravan from the Queen of Heaven Chapel to the Mount Carmel Cemetery in Hillside, Illinois. There were as many feds there with binoculars as there were mourners.

In 1974, Spilotro completely lost control. There were more murders in Vegas that year than in the previous quarter-century combined, and it was all him. That year, Spilotro was arrested and charged with stealing from the Teamsters' Pension Fund.

He got off when a key witness died, you guessed it, from a shotgun blast to the face.

Spilotro's sloppiness led to the feds having to do something, and once they started to scrutinize the money pipeline it became harder to efficiently skim the day's take.

Spilotro pushed in ways that made him annoying and a drain on profits. He opened a gift shop in the Circus Circus casino-hotel, which was in direct competition with the hotel's own gift shop.

Another thing Spilotro did during his reign of terror was shoot up my beautiful stucco house on La Paloma Drive. It was a Sunday afternoon, which at my house meant "Sunday Sauce," during which I'd cook for a table full of A-listers. The guests were at a long table in the dining room. Behind the dining room was a den where my daughter and her kids were.

Mid-meal, two cars pulled up out front and sprayed the house with bullets. In the dining room, guests hit the deck and screamed. In the family area, my kids were sitting stiffly in their chairs, eyes wide with terror.

There was plenty of damage, but no one was hit.

I wouldn't have minded keeping it quiet, but again my fame made that impossible. Somebody shot up Carlo from *The Godfather*'s house, they reported on *Entertainment Tonight*.

Luckily, during construction, I'd geared my architecture toward defense. I built on an artificial hill, with twelve steps—four and a landing, four and a landing, and four and a landing—to get to my front door. The reason was, in case somebody wanted to shoot through the windows from outside, all they were going to hit was the ceiling. The walls were reinforced with rebar concrete eight inches thick.

Spilotro was frustrated with me because he couldn't figure out what I was doing. I had all this respect, and all of these doors opened for me, and yet I wasn't made. In fact, I didn't

trust most mobsters, which is why they didn't know what I was up to.

Truth is, I had never met Spilotro before he came to Vegas. I had heard of him, and I knew he was coming. I knew Tony Accardo well, as for years I'd seen him once a month, dropping off and picking up. Plus, I worked with Nick Nitti, and he knew all those guys. Later on, Accardo was known for his cooking, and if we had something to talk about, I would go to his house on a Sunday. His summer kitchen was two stories below his house.

After my house was shot up, I further fortified it against attack, taking down one dining room wall and replacing it with bulletproof materials.

I couldn't go to Chicago right away because I had to deal with Las Vegas authorities who were investigating the shooting. I told them again and again that I had no clue who fired those shots, and after a couple of days they believed me, or gave up trying to make me talk, and that was about the end of their investigation.

When that was over, I went to Chicago to talk to Accardo. Obviously, it wasn't just me that Tony Spilotro had pissed off with his erratic behavior. Accardo seemed to know why I'd asked to see him.

"What's he done now?" Accardo said wearily. No name necessary.

I told him about my house.

"At your home?" Accardo said. "I'll reel him in."

Some time passed, it was now mid-June 1986, and word on the street was that Tony Spilotro, forty-eight years old, and his brother Mike, forty-one, had been called back to Chicago for a sit-down with Mr. Accardo.

When I heard that news, I was hoping the Ant would be relieved of his Vegas duties and given a new assignment where Accardo could keep an eye on him. I couldn't have been more wrong.

I understood why Tony was being summoned—but why Michael? Everyone liked Michael. He never pissed off anyone. Plus, he was connected but never made. He was a member of his brother's crew, but never used as muscle. He drove for Tony, when Frank Cullotta wasn't available. He ran errands, and I'd heard that Tony gave him his own Sports Book to run. But none of that should have pissed off anyone in Chicago. What did Accardo want with him?

I didn't worry about it too much. I had a feeling that Vegas wasn't going to have Tony the Ant to kick around anymore, and it was OK with me. Then I got a phone call that changed my way of thinking. It was a Wednesday, June 14. I picked up the phone.

It was Johnny Roselli.

"Hey, Kid. The Boss needs to see you," Roselli said.

"He say why?"

"Nope, he said now."

"All right, on my way."

I could feel my heart pounding. The fact that Accardo hadn't personally called me was not suspicious. He never used the phone.

I called Roselli back from the Vegas airport to tell him when I'd arrive at O'Hare. Well, if Tony Spilotro was going to be dressed down by the Boss, I guessed I was in for some discipline as well, although I didn't know what I'd done to deserve it.

When my plane landed in Chicago, I hoped to see Johnny Roselli waiting for me with a smile on his face. But, no. I was met at O'Hare by two sourpuss Outfit guys I'd never seen before. Both got their suits at the Big'n'Tall store.

I tried to make small talk with them, but they weren't in the mood. They wouldn't tell me where we were going or what was going to happen when we got there. This was troubling. Plus, their moods didn't improve. They remained downright glum.

I thought I might get whacked right there in the airport,

then I took a deep breath and calmed myself down. They led me to a black Lincoln Continental in Parking Lot B.

"You want me to sit in front?" I was worried that this was a setup to imitate my final scene in *The Godfather.*

"No, sir. You in back," they said. Well, that was good. Again, as I got in back, I took a deep breath and tried to calm myself down.

"What's your names?"

One was Paulie, the other Vinnie. At first, I couldn't tell which was which. They were in their forties and looked like bone-breakers. I tried to convince myself that they were my security detail. Before we'd even made it out of the airport, the driver said, "We're a little early. You want to get something to eat?"

"I could eat," I said.

We got out of the airport and almost immediately pulled into an Italian restaurant. The joint was busy, and everyone seemed to know Paulie and Vinnie. The food was excellent. I ate well. My escorts opened up a little, talking about women, food, and gambling. We lingered over coffee, but I still wasn't relaxed. Paulie and Vinnie were checking their watches every twenty seconds. Clearly, we were on someone's schedule—probably Accardo's, I figured.

During lunch, I determined which of my hosts was which. After glancing at his watch one last time, Paulie got up and went to a pay phone. When he came back, he said, "Okay."

We got up, returned to the car, and were once again on the road—this time no longer early. I tried to keep track of which way we were headed. We headed south for a time, but not long. I saw a sign that read WELCOME TO BENSENVILLE, which was a middle-class neighborhood with freshly painted houses, manicured lawns, and clean streets.

We pulled into the smooth blacktop driveway of a ranch-style house with white aluminum siding. There were other cars parked in the driveway and on the street out front, a dirty green Plymouth on the street, a freshly washed black Cadillac next to us in the driveway.

"Okay, we're here," Vinnie said.

"Where's here?" I asked, still acting like I had no concerns about what was about to happen.

"Michael's getting made today. We couldn't tell you till now," Vinnie said, but he said it a little quick, and it didn't immediately register.

"Michael?" I asked.

"Spilotro. Tony's here, too, gonna stand up for his brother."

I bought this. At first. Accardo killing two birds with one stone—so to speak. Anthony was going to get dressed down for his behavior in Las Vegas, and his affable brother was getting his button. By the end of the day, I figured, Anthony would be back in the fold, probably demoted, and Michael would be straightened out. I still hadn't figured out my role. Witness?

It was only seconds later that my thinking returned to reality. It was the cross-purposes that bothered me. There was no way that Accardo would reward one brother and punish another at the same time. I started to feel the tickle of fear once again at the back of my neck.

Paulie got out of the car and opened my door for me. As I got out, he and Vinnie flanked me. That wasn't a good sign. They were concerned I might bolt. Now that tickle at my neck was a bead of sweat running into my collar.

I looked around. I was in suburbia, walking up a smooth concrete pathway through a lawn that looked like it came off a golf course, past multiple colorful flower beds that looked professionally tended. It seemed like ten minutes before we made it the sixty feet or so to the neatly maintained house's front door.

Paulie knocked.

I felt a little better when my old friend Johnny Roselli answered the door. He had a big grin on his face, which made me feel marginally better. Trouble was, I'd seen that grin before and sometimes it spread across Roselli's face when he was doing some pretty ghastly stuff.

Still, I considered him a friend. Not so much the guy standing

behind him who now caught my eye. It was Frank Cullotta, who was Tony the Ant's right-hand man—even crazier than his boss.

Cullotta was thirty-one years old at the time and Tony's friend since childhood, a member of the Hole in the Wall Gang burglary ring in Vegas. Cullotta was born in Chicago, son of an independent criminal. His dad died when he was eight at the tail end of a lengthy police chase. Cullotta needed to earn after his dad's death and became a shoeshine. He and Tony Spilotro first met when they were little and battling over shoeshine turf. When the boys realized that their fathers had known one another, they themselves teamed up, and Spilotro considered Cullotta his close friend right up until the moment he realized Cullotta had betrayed him.

I had my own friend/enemy relationship with Cullotta. He'd done me favors, and he'd tried to kill me. That happened one morning, at a time when Spilotro was really pissed off at me. What had I done? I wouldn't let him in my club. He considered himself the Hot Shit of Vegas and I had my bouncer keep him out. He was beyond furious. Spilotro was so out of control, I couldn't have him in my club. He'd be putting a bullet into a roulette wheel or something. But I put myself at risk when I treated him like a criminal, which he was.

And that was my excuse.

I'd go to the door with my entourage and say, "Sorry, Tony, you're in the Black Book. I'll lose my license if Nevada catches you in here."

Spilotro, however, didn't care if he was in the Black Book, he wanted in. One morning, about three a.m., Spilotro showed up determined to get in. He never reminded me more of John Gotti, unclear as to what to do when bullying didn't work.

My parking lot attendant was Gino LoPinto, who's famous now as a club owner, and I was grooming him at the time. LoPinto was also a UNLV student, where he'd gotten in on a baseball

scholarship. I gave him the valet parking concession and that's where he started to learn the ropes.

When Spilotro showed up, LoPinto would send me the first warning signal, call me on his cell phone, "Spilotro's out here." To further piss Tony off, we'd let him wait in line outside to get in and wouldn't send him away until he got to the door. With the door shut in his face, he'd be pounding and yelling, but he didn't enter.

My club stayed open all night, closed at six a.m., at which time I would take my crew out to eat. There were all kinds of overnight pizza joints. And there was one place we liked in the Maryland Square shopping center, which was built in 1968, the first big shopping plaza in Vegas, off Maryland Parkway. Wonder World was there, a sprawling discount department store about the size of Rhode Island.

We were coming out of the pizza joint, and heading toward my Bentley, which was in the parking lot. I had it parked off by itself because I didn't want anyone to bump into it. Every time some careless driver dinged my Bentley it cost me thousands of dollars. At that time in the morning, the lot was pretty empty and the Bentley was sitting by itself.

My driver at that time was a guy named Ralphie. I'd made a deal with the State of Nevada to use recently released inmates as my support staff, and Ralphie was one of those. Not only were these guys looking to go legit, but they loved me for giving them the opportunity.

I created a culinary school for white-collar crime guys—a rehabilitation program, I called it—so I had ex-cons working in my kitchen, which was open twenty-four hours a day. There was a cheap motel right next to my club, and that was where they stayed. They'd get out of the joint and have a job, a signed work permit, and a roof over their heads waiting for them.

There were other clubs in town where getting the dishwasher to show up was a problem, but not for me. These guys

were intensely loyal for the favor I was giving them, and I was always fully staffed.

Ralphie had been with me for almost ten years. Ralphie told me many times that he was so grateful for what I'd done for him that he'd be willing to take a bullet for me. And that, sadly as it turned out, was what happened that horrible morning.

My crew and I were walking back to the Bentley after eating and I saw a car drifting toward us, slowly. The pizza parlor was behind us and Wonder World was in front. I made eye contact with the driver of the approaching car—and I could see it was Cullotta. While I'm looking at him, he pulls a gun, sticks it out the driver's side window, and starts firing at me.

Ralphie threw me to the ground, took four bullets to the chest, and died in my arms.

The police came, of course. They took me downtown and talked to me for days.

I told them I didn't see who was shooting. They said I had to have seen because they checked, and the sun was already up. I said I was being thrown to the ground during the shooting and didn't see anything except up-close blacktop.

For days it went on, and I never said it was Frank Cullotta.

About four days after my final grilling by the cops, Cullotta slipped a note under my door.

It read *I owe you one.*

Now, in the suburbs of Chicago, I would get an opportunity to cash in that chip. I thought about Spilotro and Cullotta being childhood friends, and how they had both fired a gun at me. Those of you who've seen the Scorsese picture *Casino* know that the Ant only had one real friend in Vegas, and that was Lefty Rosenthal, played by DeNiro. Spilotro got his buddy's wife hooked on coke and she OD'd in 1982. She was played by Sharon Stone in the movie. Frank Cullotta was a technical advisor on the movie. Frank Vincent played his character.

"One day I'm going to be the Boss of the Outfit," Spilotro

told Cullotta back when the boys were still shining shoes. Spilotro said he knew how to get to the top: "You got to earn a shitload of money and be able to kill without conscience." By the time he was a young man, he'd developed both of those skills.

Cullotta at that time said he didn't want anything to do with Outfit guys. He chose to remain freelance and brought home extra cash by breaking and entering businesses in the middle of the night, and mugging men as they exited banks. His independence wore off, however, and by 1978 when Joey "The Clown" Lombardo told Cullotta he was going to Vegas to help Tony the Ant protect the casino-skim in Vegas, he said yes, sir, anything you want, sir. He did have one question, though: "Why me?"

"Spilotro's got trust issues, to put it mildly. You're the only guy he trusts."

Since Cullotta was a breaking-and-entering (B&E) man, he brought his burglary crew with him to Vegas and the Hole in the Wall Gang started up again, this time in Vegas.

They didn't just break into places at random. They gathered intelligence first. By the time they picked the lock, they knew there was going to be a large cache of cash or jewels on the other side. Cullotta's gang was state of the art, experts at getting around surveillance and alarm systems.

As it turned out, Cullotta was nuts to a degree that even impressed Tony Spilotro. The most famous story was that Cullotta once tried to get a confession out of a Mob associate he suspected of being an informer by putting his head in a vise grip. As Spilotro stood by and cheered, Cullotta turned the crank. The poor bastard finally confessed but Cullotta was enjoying the torture so much he kept turning the crank until the guy's eyeballs popped out of his head, his skull cracked like an egg, and he died.

After they disposed of the guy's mortal remains, popped-out eyeballs and all, Tony the Ant, Cullotta, and other members of

their crew went out to dinner at a fine Italian restaurant. At dinner, Spilotro raised a glass to the man they'd just snuffed.

"Here's looking at you, you rat fuck," he said.

Spilotro took tribute from the Hole in the Wall Gang swag but never went along on their Las Vegas heists. He did, however, buy a jewelry store, so he'd have a place to sell the hot ice. Spilotro, in fact, had demanded tribute from all independent criminals on the Strip, and was in this manner siphoning money that, by the Outfit's way of thinking, should have been going to them.

Back at the nice house south of O'Hare Airport, it was Cullotta who gestured for us to enter. Paulie and Vinnie exchanged greetings with Roselli and Cullotta in a low mumble, which I didn't like.

"We're in the basement," Cullotta said.

I didn't like the sound of that much, either.

I got to the top of the stairs, which were narrow, wooden, warped, and wobbly. They made noise when you stepped. For Vinnie and Paulie the sound was louder, almost a crack. But we got down there. It smelled bad. At first everything was too dark for me to make it out, and no one was in a hurry to turn on the light.

As my eyes dilated, I could see two male figures off to my right. They were tied to chairs and gagged, still alive but covered in blood. They appeared unconscious, but I could hear them whimpering.

At first, because of all the blood, I couldn't tell who they were. I stared and stared, and in a flash realized that these were the Spilotro brothers, Anthony and Michael. There were three other guys off to my right, big men. From the waist up they wore only blood-spattered white T-shirts, and each held a baseball bat in his hamlike fist. (Baseball bats were Tony "Joe Batters" Accardo's signature.)

There were plastic sheets draping the walls and covering the

floor to catch the blood spray. My brain tried to make sense of this. Other than their skulls, maybe, I don't think there were any unbroken bones in their bodies. Their bones were displaced, some compound fractures, and the Spilotros looked malformed.

I knew why Anthony was being beaten. I was among those who'd griped about his behavior. But why Michael? I realized that the "Michael-is-getting-made-today" story was so much bullshit, just a lure.

And why was Frank Cullotta, who was supposed to be Anthony Spilotro's best friend, standing there, alive and well, and acting like this scenario was just another day at the office?

And, of course, my mind scrambled over my most urgent thought: Was I next?

As if he could read my mind, Cullotta walked up me and placed a hand on my trembling shoulder.

"Relax, Kid, you're okay," he said. And he winked at me. I realized I was cashing in that chip I'd earned when I didn't give him up for shooting at me and killing Ralphie, my driver.

I tried to speak. My lips moved silently for a moment, and then I heard myself say, "What? What?"

I'm no tough guy. Never pretended to be. My dealings with gangsters had always been at a very high level. I hadn't been "on the streets" since the days when I sold pens. So, this scene may have been "normal" to guys who are used to "doing gangster things," but it wasn't to me, and I was sickened.

Then I realized why Cullotta was there. It was the Mafia way. When a guy's time is up, his best friend is given the assignment to take him out. The killer then must prove he serves the organization over his friend.

In this case, I learned Cullotta was tasked with luring Anthony and Michael to the scene of their demise, and he told the brothers Michael was being made. Tony figured he was going to be demoted and his brother was being promoted, and Cullotta let him believe that.

You couldn't really blame Cullotta. If he had refused to lure his friend to his death, he would have been in a third chair in that basement having his ribs broken one at a time with a Louisville Slugger.

Cullotta even went to O'Hare and picked up Tony, with a fake smile. And Tony probably never suspected a thing. He probably still felt like his connections were too strong. Although his standing with the Outfit had been slipping for more than a decade. His mentor, the guy who groomed him and taught him how to do street crimes, was Sam Giancana, who had been bumped off eleven years earlier. Spilotro might've thought he had friends in Chicago, but not really.

I looked around the gruesome scene. My pupils were fully dilated by this time, and I could see in greater detail. I looked at Frank Cullotta. His eyes were cold and dead.

My mind slipped back in time. I ran through everything I knew about these guys. Tony Spilotro was not just a pain in the ass doing his best to wreck Vegas, he was also a stone killer with a reported twenty-five notches on his gun. Vegas police had for years shadowed Spilotro and his friends, including Cullotta.

I thought back to 1979 when a Vegas conman named Sherwin "Jerry" Lisner was indicted. Lisner's lawyer was recorded telling a restaurant owner that Lisner was going to testify against Spilotro and Cullotta.

When Spilotro heard that, he said to Cullotta, "Well, you know you got to whack him now, don't you?"

Cullotta did the deed, on October 11, 1979, but it didn't go smoothly. Cullotta broke into Lisner's home and shot him in the head with a .22 handgun. The bullet didn't kill Lisner, who ran around the house bleeding. Cullotta next tried to strangle Lisner with a power cord from a water cooler but the cord snapped. Cullotta had incapacitated Lisner enough to reload his gun. He shot Lisner in the head repeatedly until he was dead and then dragged him out back and dumped his body in the backyard swimming pool.

By 1982, Cullotta knew that he needed to do something, or he'd be the next to be hit. That summer he finalized an agreement with the feds, confessing to and subsequently being indicted for three hundred crimes committed in Nevada, including four murders. Cullotta was convicted, sentenced to eight years, but only served two. After that, he entered the witness protection program in Texas and then Mississippi. But the Outfit must've known where he was. When it came time to lure Spilotro to his death, Cullotta was given the job.

Back in that horrible basement, Cullotta still had his hand on my shoulder.

"Why am I here?" I managed to ask.

"Direct orders from the Big Man," Cullotta said. That meant Accardo.

It occurred to me that it was my complaint about Tony the Ant shooting up my house that caused the brothers to be brought in for the final punishment. Again, Cullotta seemed to read my mind.

"It's for all the bullshit Spilotro's done in Vegas," Cullotta said, referring to Tony. "He was told over and over. Back off. Take your orders. Protect the skim. But he wouldn't listen. He thought Vegas was his own personal playground."

"Frank, what about Michael?" I asked.

"The only way we could get Anthony here," Cullotta said. "He's dying to keep him from avenging the death of his brother."

"And me," I said. "Why have me here to see . . . this?"

"No idea," Cullotta replied. "Maybe ask the man the next time you see him."

At that moment, conversation stopped and the beatings continued. The men with the bats were professionals and precise with their blows. They followed what became a predictable pattern: shoulders, chest, legs. Everywhere but the head. The head would be saved for last. The sounds the victims made were pitiful and horrible. Michael was now motionless but moaning.

Anthony, however, was still struggling against his ropes, despite the beating he'd received and was receiving.

I looked at Anthony and I could see that he was looking back at me. His gaze was fixed on mine and for reasons I can't explain, I couldn't look away. I got the impression that he saw me as a potential ally, that I was the one who could raise my hand and stop the abuse. He had it all wrong, of course.

I said, "Frank, could you take off Anthony's gag for a second?"

I had to know why Anthony was beseeching me with his eyes. If I didn't find out, I knew it would bother me for the rest of my life. Cullotta shrugged his shoulders in a "why not?" way.

"Nino, take the gag off the Ant."

Nino did as he was told.

Anthony's lips started to move but no sound came out. I moved closer without asking permission to do so, but nobody said anything. I could smell Anthony, a combination of shit, sweat, and blood.

"Yeah, Anthony, what is it?" I asked.

"Gianni," he gasped. "Tell them to stop beating Michael. He ain't done nothing. Please."

I could feel my whole body shaking. It was an impossible request. I snuck a quick glance at Michael, and he wasn't moving, maybe already dead. I felt a twang of sympathy. I couldn't believe I felt sorry for him.

"Gianni," he started in again. "Tell my mother. Tell her, okay? Tell her we went away. Tell her . . ."

But Cullotta reached out to pull me away from Anthony.

"That's enough, Gianni," he said.

I became a spectator again. Turned out Michael was still alive and the beatings went on for another hour—which seemed so much longer, destined to be repeated over and over in my traumatized brain.

The thing that got to me after a while was the smell.

The beatings continued until the brothers stopped whimpering.

"Enough," Cullotta said, holding up a steady hand.

The men in the bloodstained wifebeaters put down their bloodstained bats.

Cullotta reached into his waistband and pulled out a .45 semiautomatic pistol. Both brothers' heads had slumped forward, only the ropes preventing them from spilling onto the floor.

The business end of the .45 was less than an inch from Anthony's head. Cullotta put a hand to block some of the blood he expected to splash back at him. He pulled the trigger. I jumped at the sound.

I saw the results. As it turned out, Cullotta did not have to worry about splashback. The blood all went behind Anthony, and with little energy, mostly falling to the floor in a pool behind the Ant's chair.

Cullotta then shot Michael in the same way, and it was over. Someone, either Paulie or Vinnie, handed Cullotta a clean towel and he used it to wipe off the gun. He dropped the gun into a plastic bag, which the other goon held open.

"That's that," Cullotta said to me, and headed up the stairs. I didn't move right away. "Come on, Gianni, unless you want to help cut them up."

I was put in a car and taken back to O'Hare. I don't remember much about the ride.

Soon thereafter, a farmer in a cornfield thought he'd discovered evidence of poaching. He dug up the new grave, expecting to find the remains of a deer. He found what was left of the Spilotros.

Cullotta's miserable life was spared because of his job luring Tony the Ant. It was not the first time he'd betrayed Spilotro. He'd already flipped on the Ant when authorities were busting up the Hole in the Wall Gang.

The Spilotro family tried to have a funeral for the brothers in a Catholic Church but were turned down. The Church was worried about potential scandal. Anthony's funeral ceremony

was a fifteen-minute quickie in a Chicago funeral home, then straight to the cemetery where Spilotro was buried close to Sam Giancana.

I was through with Vegas. I announced I was leaving my club on State Street while on stage in the club on New Year's Eve, 1989. It was time. The club had lasted seven years, an eternity in Las Vegas. It had been a great run.

During the early 1990s, I worked on my show-biz career. One picture I was in was *The Freshman*, about a naïve kid, played by Matthew Broderick, who encounters "The Godfather."

The picture would only work if they could get Brando to play the part, which was the last thing he wanted to do, until they offered him ten million dollars at which time he asked when he should be there.

While we were making *The Freshman*, there was a nerve-racking coincidence. John Gotti got in touch with me and wanted me to arrange a meeting between him and Brando. Then Brando asked me to arrange a meeting with Gotti. So, I had to do it. The meeting took place at the Ravenite during *Monday Night Football*, when the feds were most likely to be watching TV and not us.

Brando dressed like Don Corleone but didn't stuff his cheeks with cotton. Brando and Gotti sat at a Formica table and laughed for hours as I watched from afar. Brando was doing sleight-of-hand magic tricks and Gotti was eating it up. Both Gotti and Brando were thankful for the favor I'd done them, which couldn't be a bad thing.

Kissing Las Vegas goodbye, best of times, worst of times, my wife and I moved to L.A., where I had built a three-story English tutor off Mulholland Drive, a windy road that runs across the tops of the Hollywood Hills, forming a sort of border between the L.A. basin and the Valley. It was a very exclusive neighborhood. My neighbors included Tom Selleck, George Clooney, and Jack Nicholson.

In L.A., I was yet again the target of an insane hood who wanted to control me even though he could barely control himself.

His name was Joe Denti. He was a New York thug who moved out to Beverly Hills and started having dinners on Sundays. And he kept sending me invitations to come, which I ignored.

One day, I was in Café Roma on Cannon Drive in Beverly Hills and one of Denti's goons came up to me and asked why I wasn't answering Mr. Denti's invitations.

"Please tell Mr. Denti that I'm not coming because I can't. I was told not to go," I said.

"Why?" the goon asked.

"Because Mr. Denti's house is wired, and that van that's always parked out front, that's FBI," I said.

Mr. Denti didn't like that answer. He had a hard-on for me and I knew he was going to come after me. It didn't take long.

A few days later, I was having dinner with my wife and grandmother in Nicky Blair's Restaurant on Sunset Boulevard next to Le Dome. Blair was a Hollywood old-timer, who'd appeared in seventy-five movies (*Viva Las Vegas, Ocean's Eleven, The Manchurian Candidate, Diamonds are Forever*, etc.), often playing a restauranteur or maître d', over a forty-year run. Two of Denti's goons came in and headed straight for me. One said, and I quote, "You're coming with us, fuck face."

In front of my wife and grandmother!

As he said it, he drew back his coat to show me he was packing. What he didn't realize was I was packing, too, and it wasn't the pocket gun I'd used on Lorenzo Morales. This was a Smith & Wesson .38. I didn't even bother to pull the damn thing. I stuck my hand in my pocket, pointed the gun, and pulled the trigger twice. I shot one of the goons in the knee and the other in the shin.

Between you and me, I have ruined more suits by shooting through my pants. When goons put their arms between my arms, I quickly shoved my hands in my pockets. They thought they had the upper hand, but I had my hand on my gun.)

I went outside, told my driver to go inside and pay my check and to take the ladies to the Polo Lounge, which my grandmother liked, and I called the Beverly Hills Police Department and told them what happened: I was about to be kidnapped, so I shot the guys. I was cleared and I never heard from Denti again.

California likes its criminals to have a touch of sophistication. Denti had none. He was a dese-and-dose New York hood, a shylock, and he thought he was going to move to L.A. and rule the world.

Not long after the shootings, Denti died while screwing two broads at the same time on a Sunday night—so that eradicated the problem.

CHAPTER 14
The Vatican Wash 'n' Dry

My Vatican career came earlier than some of the adventures I've already discussed, but I wanted to tell you about it last.

There was a time when I didn't know the Vatican was corrupt, when I figured the pope and the cardinals were so close to God that they never sinned, never did anything wrong, and existed solely to be a guiding light for Catholics all over the world to get into Heaven. I thought the Vatican was as rich as it was because it took tribute from the offertory baskets at Masses around the world.

As an adult, I learned differently. The Vatican was just another mob, and there was money to be made.

For non-Catholics and others who might need a refresher course, the Vatican is the traditional home of the pope, the undisputed leader of the Roman Catholic religion. It is built inside the city of Rome, although it has since 1929 been recognized as its own nation, on the site of St. Peter's tomb, Peter being one of Jesus's apostles and the first pope.

There is evidence that the Vatican was infiltrated early on by freemasonry, a fraternal secret society that moved back then in mysterious and possibly sinister ways. The Vatican complex is laden with freemason symbolism, most obviously in "Cleopatra's Needle," an obelisk in the Piazza de San Marco. The word

Vatican comes from the Latin for *prophet.* Long before Christianity, the site was home of a Roman temple of the oracle of Apollo, whose prophecies were called *vaticinia.*

Today people think of the Vatican as a purely religious entity, although until the middle of the nineteenth century, its secular role was public knowledge. The pope was the governmental ruler of portions of the Italian peninsula.

Physically, the 109-acre Vatican sits on the west bank of the Tiber River. The piazza of St. Peter's Church sits in the southwest corner. A square containing Belvedere Park and administrative buildings is north of the piazza. To the west of the park are the pope's palaces, and beyond those are the pope's gardens. The western and southern boundaries of Vatican City are marked by the Leonine Walls.

Vatican City dates to the fifth century, when Emperor Constantine the First built the basilica of St. Peter's (on the historically accepted site of St. Peter's tomb), and Pope Symmachus built a palace nearby. There was a schism in the Catholic Church during the fourteenth century, and for a while the pope was exiled to France while an imposter resided in the Vatican.

The amount of gold in the palaces and churches in the Vatican City is amazing, but it is theorized that the complex's greatest wealth is in its art collection, which was assembled in large part by the Renaissance popes (Sixtus IV, Innocent VIII, Alexander VI, Julius II, Leo X, and Clement VII).

There is in the complex an underground area known as the Secret Archives, which contains thirty miles of shelving, packed with documents and manuscripts dating back to the beginnings of the Roman church. The librarian of this storehouse of secrets is always a trusted cardinal. For most of the Vatican's history no one was allowed inside the archives, much less to read any documents. All bishops when promoted to cardinal take a pledge (very *omertà*-like) to "preserve the secrets of the Church."

Beginning in the late twentieth century, Pope John Paul II allowed a few chosen journalists under extremely restricted circumstances to enter the archives and do research. The scope of the secrets the archives hold and the scandals they prevent are just as unknown now as they were five hundred years ago.

The secrets I learned about the Vatican come from *my own personal experiences* there and the people I spoke with. In the years since I began visiting the Vatican regularly for professional reasons, the Church's number-one scandal had been that, even though all Catholic priests take a pledge of celibacy, a frightening percentage of North American priests have been accused of sexually abusing their constituents. Whether the secrets kept in the Vatican are of a sexual nature is unknown.

Okay, here's my part of the deal:

My introduction to the Real Vatican—the for-profit business that sold comfort with its right hand while it laundered Mob money with the left—came during the spring of 1978, when Tony Accardo summoned me to Chicago for a meet.

We sat down in his Chicago mansion—the one with its own bowling alley—and he laid out the operation. I would be partnering with Nick Nitti, who I'd worked with for years. We'd be taking the Vegas skim via our favorite airline, the one owned by the Vatican, on flights in which our other working partner, Captain Ferrara, was flying. Ferrara was very close to Accardo on our end, with the Vatican on the other, and the perfect pilot for the job.

The operation began in a Nevada bank where worn Las Vegas currency was exchanged for crisp uncirculated bills. Those were packed tightly into engineer bags and flown by us to Italy once every two weeks.

Nitti and I were given government courier licenses by Lloyds of London under assumed names. On the Italian end of the trip, we'd give the bags to Archbishop Paul Casimir Marcinkus, who came from Illinois. Marcinkus was friends with Accardo, and as head fiduciary oversaw the Vatican Laundromat.

I don't know how Marcinkus got to be an archbishop. Probably not by praying. He might've been a top guy in the Catholic Church, but he was also a gangster. Marcinkus would put the Mob money to work, invested it wisely, and everybody made money.

Marcinkus was born in 1922 in suburban Chicago, youngest of five kids, in a poor working-class family. He grew into a six-four brute, once a formidable rugby player, and joined the priesthood in a parish in suburban Chicago.

His nickname was "The Gorilla" and he was muscle for the pope. Pope Paul VI liked a big man, and the Gorilla became the pope's boy. The pope gave Marcinkus a job as an advance man, luxury trips scouting out locations for future international tours. And when the pope traveled, he wanted Marcinkus at his side, ready to get between him and any incoming. During one stroll through an airport in the Philippines the Gorilla was called into action when a man with a knife came at the pope. He was intercepted and rendered harmless by Archbishop Marcinkus's efficient counterattack.

In addition to scouting and bodyguarding, Marcinkus was never shy about the fact that he also dealt with money, a lot of money, going this way and that, coming in and going out. His quip was, "What do you expect? You can't run a church on Hail Marys alone."

That always got a laugh.

The pope put him in charge of the Vatican's bank even though he had no experience in finance. He was president of a bank that was known from 1971 to 1989 as the Institute for Religious Works. During his time as president, he developed sketchy associates, most notorious of whom was Michele Sindona, an ex-con and confidence man who died in prison in 1986 when somebody slipped cyanide into his Chock full o' Nuts.

Over the course of fifteen years, $300 million in cash went

from Vegas to the Vatican. They'll wash away your sins and wash your money while they're at it.

I loved the job. It was relaxing. No one was interested in catching us. There was no one who wanted to, no one who could.

Marcinkus's reputation took a hit in 1982 when he was indicted, and people got their first glimpse into what the Gorilla was up to. He was charged with being an accessory in the multibillion-dollar draining of Banco Ambrosiano, a large Italian bank with close ties to the Vatican, suddenly soaked dry by the archbishop—never to be cardinal.

That was the start of a major scandal, worsened by the mysterious death of Banco Ambrosiano's chairman, Roberto Calvi, who was mafioso. His nickname was "God's Banker," and they found him hanging from a London bridge, officially a suicide.

As Calvi was one of those who could have given evidence to connect the Mafia and the Vatican, there was a theory that he'd been offed, and the spectacular nature of his death was a warning to others who couldn't keep their mouths shut.

With the revelations, the Vatican paid out $244 million to creditors who'd lost money in the Ambrosiano collapse. This fact was much publicized. See how wonderful the Vatican is? Only later did it come out that the money had come from the Vatican pension fund.

Initial attempts by the Italian government to arrest Archbishop Marcinkus were easily rebuffed by the Vatican, as they are not part of Italy but an independent state, and therefore not bound by Italian rulings. Marcinkus, the Vatican added, had diplomatic immunity. (An Italian judge ruled in Marcinkus's favor, guaranteeing he'd never stand trial for his crimes.)

Always good for a quote, a reporter put a microphone in front of the Gorilla.

"I may be a lousy banker," Marcinkus said, "but at least I'm not in jail."

It warms the heart.

In his later years, Marcinkus became more open about the things he'd done while Pope John Paul II's main thug. He admitted that during John Paul II's reign, they'd gotten involved in European politics, helping to finance an anti-Communist movement in Poland.

He never did have to go to jail. He was forced to retire in 1990 and moved to a housing complex around a golf course in Arizona. Marcinkus died of lung disease in 2006 at his home in Sun City, Arizona, at the age of eighty-four.

Okay, so that's the guy we were dealing with. When Nitti and I arrived in Italy with the cash, Marcinkus was usually there in person to receive. Other times he'd send a limo with a priest driver and priest bodyguards. We were aware that we were not the only couriers, that there were bags of cash arriving every day, sometimes being delivered by airlines employees, including pilots.

Nitti and I would stay at the Ambasciatori Hotel in Rome, and return home in a relaxed manner, empty-handed.

I moved money and commodities for the Vatican during the reigns of three different popes. I started with Pope Paul VI and continued through John Pauls I and II. I met Pope Paul VI once, and when he passed away during the summer of 1978, Nitti and I flew to his funeral.

I expected that the money-laundering operation would continue, being as it was a well-oiled machine. Instead, there was an awkward pause in the deliveries. I later learned that this was because the new pope, John Paul I, when told about the gangster activity, ordered it to be stopped.

John Paul I only lasted thirty-three days before he was killed for not getting with the program. He was taken out, given a hot shot of an untraceable drug, because he wouldn't play ball. They found the sixty-five-year-old pope dead in his chambers on September 28, 1978. The official cause of death was a heart attack.

Who killed John Paul I? I have no inside dope. We weren't in that circle, and we didn't want to know. A guy named David Yallop wrote a book claiming that Archbishop Marcinkus was part of the conspiracy to assassinate Pope John Paul I. Of course, Marcinkus was the man who received the money that Nick Nitti and I delivered, but as for his alleged role in bumping off the pope, I cannot confirm.

In his way, Yallop let the Vatican off the hook, saying that the business with the Mob and money laundering was the work of a group that had infiltrated the Vatican, not the Vatican at all, but members of a secret Masonic lodge that had wormed its way into both the Church and the Vatican Bank. Whatever.

Here's what I know: Once John Paul I was in his grave and II took over, the deliveries of cash resumed, with Nick Nitti and I dressed to impress, precisely on time, with suitcases in hand.

John Paul II, the Polish Pope, became the pope I was closest to. He's now a saint, known as John Paul the Great. We really got close.

He confided in me that he had a son with the housekeeper in the rectory at his last church in Poland. He asked me to keep in touch with his son, who was a little younger than me. I never disclosed to the kid that I knew who his dad was. I don't know where he is today. I think he went back to Poland. When his father was in Rome, he was there.

I still talk to John Paul II every day. In my apartment (and in all my homes), I have an intricate altar, where I pray. There are artifacts on it that you can't believe. And I pray to St. John Paul II.

After I completed a major drop from the Vatican, John Paul II gave me a gift that I keep in my vault. They are six ink drawings that Michelangelo gave to Pope Julius II in 1508 to get the job to paint the Sistine Chapel. The painting would be completed four years later, much of it painted by the artist while flat on his back atop a scaffold.

There are times in my life when I amazed myself with how

far I'd come. The little terrified boy who lay in hell while thousands died around him now was in London, holding up a paddle with a number on it, bidding on masters by Peter Paul Rubens and William Manners.

But the Michelangelos are the highlight of my collection. I do not know what they are worth. I'm not sure anyone knows what they're worth. I don't want to get into exactly what I have. People will want to buy them from me and they're not for sale. But rest assured, any thieves out there, you can't get to them.

I stuck with the job as courier to the Vatican for a full five years, made tons of money.

For the record, in 2012—long after my Vatican business was done—there was another major papal scandal when almost a half billion Vatican dollars earmarked to go to charitable causes were invested instead in London real estate. The plan was to convert an abandoned department-store warehouse into luxury apartments. When the real-estate deal was botched, the operation was exposed and a dozen defendants, one of them a cardinal, were arrested and tried for embezzlement, abuse of office, money laundering, and fraud.

The cardinal was Angelo Becciu, who when arrested was third in charge at the Vatican. Becciu normally would have been immune to prosecution because of his position, but Pope Francis lifted that immunity and ordered Becciu to stand trial. He was convicted and sentenced to five and a half years in prison.

The story was presented as Pope Francis cleaning house. Would any house cleaning have been done if the cardinal and his staff hadn't been caught with their hands in the cookie jar? I don't know.

While that was going on, a second scandal piled on, this one known as Vati-Leaks, in which a leaked document revealed that gay priests were being blackmailed, and that Pope Francis's predecessor, Pope Benedict, had accepted bribes to procure an audience with him.

Now, the Vatican survived all of that, and maybe today things aren't as corrupt as they were, but I doubt it.

Because of my dealings with the Vatican, I got other international courier jobs with ever-bigger packages to deliver to and from powerful people. Just after New Year's 1979, I received a phone call from a General Mobabba of the Iranian army who I knew through common friends. My ex-wife was a patient of his doctor's daughter, who was in turn married to my friend Teddy Jacobs, with whom I attended the premiere of *The Godfather*.

The general told me he wanted to hire me but couldn't describe the job over the phone. I asked him to at least give me a hint, and he said he'd heard about my work for the Vatican.

"I'm a big admirer of the pope," he added.

Now I knew what he wanted—although the fact that an Iranian general knew about my role in the Vatican money-laundering machine was a little bit disconcerting. Iran was in turmoil. Big changes were coming.

The shah of Iran, a friend of the U.S., was about to be overthrown by the Ayatollah Khomeini, who was America's enemy. It was like Castro in Cuba all over again, and there was a lot of wealth to get out of the country before the shah was forced to flee.

The shah, born in 1919 in Tehran, was Mohammad Reza Pahlavi, the son of the previous shah of Iran. Dad had taken over after World War I, emerging from a field of political chaos, and was popular for much of his reign, as he did wonders for Iran's twentieth-century infrastructure. New roads were constructed. Schools and hospitals were built. Women were emancipated from the restrictions of orthodox Islam.

When World War II came, the Allies occupied Iran to keep it from falling into Axis hands, and the shah was forced to give up his leadership in favor of his son, who agreed to play ball with the West straight down the line. The son was educated in

Switzerland and took over autocratic rule from his dad in 1941 at the age of twenty-two. He was not just a friend of America but was determined to modernize his nation. He also made himself—but not necessarily his nation—unbelievably rich by developing Iranian oil fields.

He'd faced challenges to his reign. In 1953, he was briefly deposed by his premier, Mohammad Mosaddegh, but was re-installed as Iran's leader after intervention by British and U.S. intelligence.

Now, in the late 1970s, there was no saving him. The people of Iran had been told they were being ripped off by the shah, that he was keeping all the oil money for himself and not sharing it with his people.

The most damaging accusation was that he was not a good Muslim. The nation, as Muslim as any on Earth, was told that the shah was allied with the devil (that is, the Western powers), and needed to be gone so that Iran could become a good Islamic nation—and one in which the country's oil wealth would benefit its citizens.

Our mission, should we decide to accept it, would be to get the shah's money out of Iran and into the Vatican, the pope's monetary laundromat. I got Nick Nitti to make the travel arrangements for me. He was my partner during the Vatican runs and one of the few people I completely trusted.

Nitti and I met at McCarran Airport and flew to Mehrabad International Airport, which was an armed camp. We were greeted on the ground by six men in Western-style business suits and driven to downtown Tehran in three military vehicles.

They asked us how much money we could carry out of the country and seemed pleased when we replied in terms of weight rather than value. We carried bags out of the country. What was in them didn't matter to us. They liked that.

We put together the logistics and then Nitti and I flew to Sicily to recruit a crew of men who could carry that weight for

us. A Sicilian Mob boss lent us six of his strongest guys. We also recruited Captain Ferrara, our Vatican pilot, to fly for this mission as well.

The plans were for us to return to Iran the following day, pick up the money, fly it out to Sicily, pay off the local boss for his help, and then fly to Rome to deposit it in the Vatican. That done, Nitti and I would fly back to Chicago.

Anxiety started immediately. Word was that the shah's reign in Iran was to end in hours rather than in days. The tough part was going to be to get his money out of six different Iranian banks without attracting attention from the ayatollah's armed troops, who were seen in increasing numbers in the streets of Tehran.

We split into three teams so each team would only have to get the withdrawal from two banks each. The money itself was waiting for us, as arrangements had been made with bank employees the previous day.

In each case, the van would back up to the bank, and be loaded up with overstuffed duffel bags of cash. That part went okay. With all six banks emptied, vans loaded, we hit the road for the fifteen-minute ride to the airport.

Then things got dicey.

We immediately encountered a caravan of the ayatollah's armed vehicles. They were well armed and armored but lacked speed. We floored it, got it up to ninety miles per hour, and blew past them like they were standing still.

Panic nearly set in as we neared the airport and saw the gate guards we'd bribed weren't there, replaced by well-armed ayatollah goons. So, we couldn't stop. The only chance we had was to drive through the fence. The front van hit the fence full speed and drove on with part of the fence still attached to its snout. The following two vehicles drove through the brand-new gate.

Sensing our trouble, Captain Ferrara was on the tarmac ready to help load the plane. The exchange from the caravan to the

plane took only a few minutes but seemed much longer. Nitti and I climbed on the plane and seconds later we were in the air, heading for Sicily.

At Leonardo Da Vinci International Airport, the cash was unloaded onto a truck. And then we could relax.

Bottom line: by the time the shah was exiled, his money was safe—and I was rich enough to never have to work again. The shah didn't have long to enjoy all that money, however, as he died during the summer of 1980 in Cairo, Egypt.

I did have one last Vatican adventure, and sadly it involved 9/11. On September 11, 2001, I was in Australia on a charity trip with Bill Clinton, the former president. When news came of the attacks in New York and Washington, Clinton was scooped up and flown to an undisclosed location.

I asked if there was a seat for me and they said no. I couldn't fly back to the U.S. as air space there was closed, but I did get permission to helicopter to a military base where I was put on a flight to Italy.

While in Rome, I was allowed to drive one of the pope's official cars. Now, by coincidence, Mr. and Mrs. Bob Newhart and Mr. and Mrs. Don Rickles were vacationing in Rome. I saw them and pulled up to a curb where the foursome was eating at an outside table. I poked my head out to say hi.

Rickles couldn't resist: "Hey look, Gianni Russo stole the pope's car!"

That got the attention of a photojournalist and the headline the next morning was, POPE HAD A LATE NIGHT.

The Vatican took the car back and said I was on my own.

I finally made it back to the U.S. on September 20.

EPILOGUE

I've had a lifetime to consider the events of my youth, a story of a cursed boy who becomes a charmed boy. I understand that it doesn't happen in real life, but it happened to me, so excuse me if I believe there was magic involved.

You can call it anything you like. Being the guy I am, I call it divine intervention.

Isn't it obvious that when Chin raised his gun to shoot Mr. Costello in his apartment house foyer, St. Anthony nudged his arm a little bit, resulting in only a glorified graze wound?

Mr. Costello was needed alive, because he was the one St. Anthony had chosen to save me.

All right, let me tie up a few loose ends.

Here's why I like Barry Slotnick: When Joe Colombo was in the hospital, brain dead after the Rally Day hit, Barry used to go and visit him. Joe didn't know he was there, but Barry went anyway, maybe to make sure Joe was getting the best possible care.

Barry is old and retired now, but his son Stu Slotnick is still my lawyer. We've made a lot of money. When Paramount, with whom I'm a partner in an imported food company, put out a

streaming TV series called *The Offer*, which was supposed to be
about the making of *The Godfather*, they weren't clever enough
to stick to the facts.

I first heard about the series when the guy they hired to play
me, actor Branden Williams, called me on the phone. He'd read
the script and I hadn't, so I should have realized something was
up when he said, "You're not going to hurt me, are you?"

I said, "Hurt you? Why?"

He said, "I heard a lot about you . . ." I should have known
right then and there that something was wrong.

I didn't watch the miniseries when it came out in 2022. But
soon after it premiered, my grandson came to me and said,
"Papi, my friends say you really beat that lady up."

I said, "That's only in the movie."

And he said, "No, no, they said you did it for real. They saw
it on TV."

So, I watched the show. In the eighth episode, "Crossing
That Line," they go into Talia Shire's dressing room and she's
got ice packs on her face. She pulls them down and her face is
all bruised.

They ask her what happened and she tells them that "Gianni
Russo" had beaten her. And, in the show's script, that's why
James Caan beat me for real in the famous scene. It got worse.
In the scene, the assistant director suggests they cut the scene
because it looks like "Gianni" is hurt, to which Al Ruddy says
that "Gianni" is a "punk" and to let Caan beat him up some
more.

Now I'm a lover, not a fighter, so I had no idea what they
were thinking or why they thought I'd let them get away with
it. Anyway, Stu Slotnick sued for "defamation per se." We won,
the settlement was huge, and from now on, all showings of *The
Offer* have a disclaimer that the character "Gianni Russo" presented in the picture shouldn't be confused with the real guy.

"The part of Gianni Russo has been fictionalized," was how
they put it.

The check I got from Paramount for my damages was bigger than the fifty-two years of residuals I'd received for *The Godfather*.

You may wonder, why was Paramount so stupid? How did they think they were going to get away with defaming me, per se or otherwise? The answer, I think, is that they based the miniseries on a story told by Al Ruddy, who was old and not at his sharpest, confusing reality with a script.

Weak. They should've checked their facts, that's all there is to it.

Al Ruddy's decline was slow. He lived until May 2024, when he passed away at the age of ninety-four.

I stayed friends with Frank Sinatra right till the end. At least until his wife Barbara began to cut him off from his friends and family.

Frank's kids called Barbara and asked to see Frank.

Barbara said, "The doctor says no visitors."

Frank asked to see his kids because he knew he was dying, and Barbara said no. She called them to tell them he'd died. I knew Barbara Marx from the early days. She'd been down on everything but the *Titanic*, a tip hustler for friends of ours. Barbara was working for the Detroit mob, as a beautiful chorus girl.

Back then, every showroom had a chorus line. Those girls, when their show was over and it was two and a half hours before the next one, would get dressed and go out and mingle with the high rollers. They would nestle up to some guy, blow on his dice, and palm a few of his chips while he was otherwise distracted.

I think of Frank often, but it's hard to remember Ol' Blue Eyes now without thinking of him weeping over his drink, telling Don Rickles about his role in Marilyn Monroe's murder.

The truth about Marilyn, and the Kennedys, keeps leaking out little by little, but the official story regarding their deaths remains the same. Maybe there are still good reasons why the

government doesn't want the truth to be known, that it could be manipulated at the top level in this fashion. Maybe people don't like to think they've been lied to.

These days I'm still looking for trouble. Until recently, I would dress to the nines, be dripping with jewelry, and hide a sawed-off shotgun under my coat. I'd walk around bad neighborhoods in Manhattan and almost wish someone would mug me, so I could blow them away.

Then I had dinner in my apartment with a very high-ranking member of New York law enforcement and he told me that Venezuela alone had eight gangs in New York City, and that they traveled in packs of five to eight guys.

"I don't care how tough you are, Gianni," he said. "You mess with them and you're going to get hurt."

It would have been the Escobar incident all over again. And that's when I stopped.

The Copacabana moved from its original location off Central Park back in the nineties, but there's still a really nice restaurant at that location. It's called Avra Madison now, and when I go there I sit in Booth 15, which is the same location as at the Copa in the old days. I still use the secret bathroom that Mr. Costello had upstairs.

Costello left me six apartments. I use two and rent out the other four. I make a few bucks and I live here for nothing. I know I could retire. I could have retired many years ago, but why would I want to?

I never got past first grade—if you don't count beauty school—but I've done all right. I've lived a lot of life and I've listened to the right people. People say that I make a lot of smart business decisions, but all I can say is I had the best teachers.

When I first started, I didn't know what I was doing but I was excellent at taking advice. Do this. Do that. I did it, and it

worked out. I remember once I had safety deposit boxes all over Las Vegas stuffed with cash. I said to Frank Costello, "I've got so much money."

He said, "Buy land."

I said, "It's desert."

He said, "Buy."

So, I was buying land for $1,500 an acre. The value of that land went up and up and up. Some of that desert I own is now called Green Valley and they've built hotels on it. I haven't done the math but I've got accountants who tell me that by the time this book is published, my net worth will be surpassing a major milestone—so why should I retire?

For years Meyer Lansky was my advisor. I may not have been to school in a classroom, but when guys like Lansky would talk, I absorbed every word, all of which helped me along the way. I remember he introduced me to penny stock, and I made a bundle. On his advice I bought stock in Lum's, a restaurant chain that sold hot dogs with sauerkraut that was soaked in beer. I invested in the company and soon thereafter the two brothers who ran Lum's, Clifford and Stuart Perlman, bought Caesars Palace; my stock became Caesars World stock and tripled in value.

Please don't think I'm greedy. I remember how much a transistor radio meant to me when I was a sick kid in quarantine. I have a charity now called Yes, You Can. I give scholarships to kids in need.

Here's the end story of some of the powerful men you met in this book:

Chicago boss Tony Accardo was like Costello, a one-woman man. Accardo lived a long life, and died of heart and respiratory failure in Chicago on May 22, 1992 at the age of eighty-six. He was a fantastic manager of men. The Outfit during the time Accardo was Boss ran far more smoothly than the Five Families in New York. It's hard to get that many egotistical

guys—Italian guys!—to work together, but Accardo had the knack.

Accardo mellowed in his later years, but clearly, he had his limits. In 1978, his luxury home was burglarized. The police never got to arrest the suspects as they were found dead with their throats slit.

Nick Civella, who preferred anonymity when I first met him, was thrust into the public eye against his wishes during the 1970s when Kansas City police planned new civic and convention centers on Twelfth Street, which necessitated the complete razing of the city's scummy Mob-operated porn strip.

This forced the boys to relocate. At that same time, the city was turning the old River Market area into an arts and entertainment district called River Quay. It started out as a hippie collection of fashionable shops, nightclubs, and restaurants, but was quickly infiltrated and then taken over by Civella. That started a war not between Civella and the city but between Civella and competing mobsters who claimed rights to the River Market turf. The result was a rash of arsons. Two bars were firebombed. A suspected arsonist was found tortured and mutilated to death in the parking lot of Kansas City International Airport. Kansas City police bugged some of Civella's hangouts in hopes of learning more about the turf war in the River Market area, and instead they found evidence that Civella was skimming Vegas.

In the early 1980s, the FBI launched an investigation into the Civella brothers and their casino connections. The investigation was called Operation Strawman and involved a lot of wiretapping. The feds learned that Joe Agosto, the head of the Tropicana Hotel's Folies Bergere, was sending cash from the casino to Mob bosses in Kansas City, Milwaukee, and Chicago.

In Kansas City, those envelopes were going to Nick Civella. The feds were starting to think that Agosto was more than the owner of the topless revue, but that he was also secretly run-

ning the casino and overseeing a skimming operation—which, of course, was true.

In 1979, Gaming Control forced the sale of the Tropicana to Ramada Inn, Inc. Agosto's downfall was assured by this time, and sure enough he was destined to rat and die of a heart attack in the fed pen.

In 1981, Nick and Corky were indicted, charged with skimming the Trop. In 1983, the brothers were convicted. Nick died soon thereafter in 1983 of cancer, and Corky took over until he, too, went to jail. Corky died in prison in 1994.

It was Corky's son, "Tony Ripe," who went on to be top dog in Kansas City. He collapsed and died while playing golf in 2006.

Colombian drug kingpin Pablo Escobar, with whom I'd read lines from *The Godfather*, made a mistake when he blew up a plane with a hundred people in it to kill a single rat. The authorities stopped being bribable, and were now—for the first time, really—concerned with bringing him down.

In 1991, Escobar sent a message to the police: He was willing to turn himself in and face the music, as long as he got to build his own prison. The balls on this guy! And the authorities said OK!

So, he built the most luxurious jail in the history of incarceration. It was called La Catedral, the only jail ever to have its own nightclub and landscaped grounds, plus telephones and fax machines so business could continue.

And he probably would have forever gotten away with this if he hadn't tortured two men to death in La Catedral. Police came in and took him to a real prison.

It's hard to keep such a powerful man caged, and he escaped from prison in July 1992, which began a massive manhunt involving Colombian police, U.S. officials, and—most dangerously—members of rival cartels eager to take out the competition.

The day after Escobar's forty-fourth birthday, December 1,

1993, his hideout in Medellín was discovered and promptly raided by Colombian police. There was a chase and a gunfight straight out of the movies. Escobar was shot to death.

The Tropicana, site of my first Vegas nightclub, was blown up in October 2024, blown away like sand in the desert—and they're going to use the lot for a major league baseball stadium, for the old Philadelphia/Kansas City/Oakland/Sacramento Athletics, the A's, who are moving yet again, this time to Vegas.

The Trop opened in 1957 and had become hopelessly out of date.

Today, Vegas is all about futuristic architecture: globes and fountains and towers and pyramids, facsimiles and classic facades, all as thin as razorblade-cut garlic, with state-of-the-art bells and whistles.

I have been working very hard, as of late, to repair some of the damage to Marilyn Monroe's legacy. She was one of those unfortunate souls who, given no self-esteem as a youth, went on to absorb limitless fame, a bright, shiny superstar rather than the insecure warm-blooded person she was.

During the spring of 2024, we managed to landmark Marilyn's house, which had been slated for destruction. It had just been purchased by independent film producer Roy Bank and his wife, reportedly paid eight-plus million for it, and they planned to tear it down.

What I would like to do is for the Banks to take the money they were going to spend on razing the house, and contribute it to Marilyn's legacy, to join the committee to build a Marilyn Monroe Museum.

We hope to get the city of Los Angeles to donate the land for the museum. The reason they would do that is we would pay for construction of the museum and the city would get a tourist attraction for nothing.

But we aren't just concerned about the house. We're con-

cerned about history, seeking to have her body exhumed and re-autopsied, so that her death certificate can be changed from suicide to homicide. (That's the motto: From Suicide to Homicide.) I would then have her reburied at the site of her museum, so people can pay their respects while touring her museum.

My legacy? I've got fourteen kids, twenty-three grandkids. That's good for starters. I'm a writer now, a philanthropist. I have made contributions to the recorded and film arts. I'm good with what I've given to civilization.

And so, I bid farewell, for now. Those are the Mafia Secrets I know. It's not so much about dirty laundry or basement ceremonies, but more about how the world works, the shadow governments, and the quietly powerful, independently wealthy groups of men who can snap their fingers and make it happen. I rose from quarantine in Bellevue to the World of Billionaires.

I *am* a made man—only by God.

Mafia Rules

The Mafia, an organization to which I've never belonged, comes with its own strict code of behavior. My life would have been very different if I'd gotten buttoned up as a kid. It wouldn't have made sense for me, so accustomed was I to dealing with the men in charge.

Here, then, are my final secrets revealed: the Rules.

- All members must be 100 percent Italian. As generations of American-born hoods come and go, this rule is harder than ever to follow. In some families, the rule has been amended, with recruits only needing to be 100 percent Italian on their father's side. Many made guys attach themselves to non-Italians, because they'll be friends with whomever they choose, and sometimes ops need technical skills. And these guys are very important. Take Lansky. Not Italian. But you'd consider putting him on the Mob Mt. Rushmore, because he was the architect of the whole thing, talking softly into Lucky Luciano's ear.
- All communications must be oral. Nothing regarding a racket or family strategy is ever to be written down. A written communication can be future evidence in a courtroom. Not everyone has followed this rule, even at

the top. In 2007, a boss named Sal Lo Piccolo was searched by authorities and found to have a list of Mafia rules in his pocket. It was probably his cheat sheet for an upcoming induction.

- Nonmembers are not allowed to introduce themselves to a member. A third party, a person the member already knows and trusts, must make the introduction.
- No women. They can be assets but not members.
- Bosses must be always shown absolute respect, even under the most informal circumstances. All failures to show respect, say behind the boss's back, should be reported immediately to the boss.
- No member shall attack another member without permission of the Commission. Petty squabbles that lead to violence are almost always bad for business.
- Members shall never ask another member his surname. Nicknames, preferably multiple nicknames, are encouraged. If you ask a made man what his last name is, he will assume you are a cop or an informant.
- Because of electronic surveillance, members shall be particularly vague when communicating messages: "Did you see the guy about that thing?" It isn't poor articulation, it is tradecraft.
- The rule against discussing the family business to outsiders is absolute, but there is also a restriction on how much members can say to one another within the family. Everyone is assumed to be on a need-to-know basis.
- When a boss summons a member, he must immediately report to the boss and do as he says. None of this "I gotta drop my kids off at school first" bullshit. Let your kids play in traffic. The Boss needs you.
- Here's the first rule Mr. Costello taught me: Always be on time. In a world without written communication, meets are all-important, and no one wants to wait for the guy who's late. Guys have been whacked for less.

SOURCES

BOOKS

Benson, Michael. *Encyclopedia of the JFK Assassination.* New York: Facts on File, 2002.

——————. *Who's Who in the JFK Assassination: An A-to-Z Encyclopedia.* New York: Citadel Press, 1993.

Burnstein, Scott M. *Motor City Mafia: A Century of Organized Crime in Detroit.* Mount Pleasant, South Carolina: Arcadia Publishing, 2006.

Davis, John H. *Mafia Dynasty: The Rise and Fall of the Gambino Crime Family.* New York: HarperCollins, 1993.

Dimaggio, June as told to Mary Jane Popp. *Marilyn, Joe & Me: June DiMaggio Tells It Like It Was.* New York: Penmarin Books, 2006.

Jordan-Heintz, Sara. *The Incredible Life & Mysterious Death of Dorothy Kilgallen.* Chula Vista, California: Page Turner Press, 2023.

Marschall, John P. *Jews in Nevada: A History.* Las Vegas, Nevada: University of Nevada Press, 2008.

Palamara, Vincent Michael. *Survivor's Guilt: The Secret Service and the Failure to Protect President Kennedy.* Walterville, Oregon: Trine Day, 2013.

Raab, Selwyn. *Five Families: The Rise, Decline, and Resurgence of America's Most Powerful Mafia Empires.* New York: Thomas Dunne Books, 2005.

Russo, Gus. *Supermob: How Sidney Korshak and His Criminal Associates Became America's Hidden Power Brokers.* London: Bloomsbury, 2008.

Scott, Peter Dale. *Deep Politics and the Death of JFK.* Berkeley, California: University of California Press, 1993.

_____. *Dallas '63: The First Deep State Revolt Against the White House.* New York: Open Road, 2015.

Server, Lee. *Handsome Johnny: The Life and Death of Johnny Rosselli.* New York: St. Martin's Press, 2018.

Spoto, Donald. *Marilyn Monroe: The Biography.* New York: Cooper Square Press, 2001.

Yallop, David. *In God's Name: An Investigation Into the Murder of Pope John Paul I.* New York: Basic Books, 2007.

PERIODICALS

Alton Evening Telegraph
Asbury Park Press
Baltimore Sun
Chicago News Journal
Chicago Tribune
Decatur Daily Review
Eugene Register-Guard
Fredericksburg Free Lance-Star
Fresno Bee
Italy Magazine
Jewish Daily Forward
Las Vegas Review-Journal
London *Independent*
London *Daily Telegraph*
Los Angeles Times
Lynchburg Daily Advance
Milwaukee magazine
Milwaukee Journal Sentinel
New York *Daily News*
New York Post
New York Times
Pittsburgh Post-Gazette
Pittsburgh Press
Playboy

Publishers Weekly
Reno Gazette-Journal
Rochester Democrat and Chronicle
Sarasota Herald-Tribune
Spokane Chronicle
Spokane Register-Review
Staten Island Advance
Tampa Bay Times
Time magazine
Toledo Blade
Washington Post

WEBSITES

ABC7Chicago.com
AllThatsInteresting.com
CatholicNews.com
DeadlineDetroit.com
Heavy.com
KCHistory.org
KCLibrary.org
NPR.org
ShepherdExpress.com
TheMobMuseum.org

INDEX